THE
EDITH
FARNSWORTH
HOUSE

Michelangelo Sabatino

THE EDITH FARNSWORTH HOUSE

Foreword
Scott Mehaffey

Essays
**Dietrich Neumann
and Ron Henderson**

Afterword
Hilary Lewis

ᴄᴍ

Architecture, Preservation, Culture

Edith Farnsworth's desk (with portrait with her mother and her translations of Italian poetry) recreated for the exhibition *Edith Farnsworth Reconsidered*, spring 2020.

POOL Eugenio Montale

Across the tremulous sheet of glass
flitted the mirth of flowering belladonna,
and clouds pressed through the branches of the trees;
rippling and faded, the scene
rose from the depths and surfaced.
A pebble soared and dropped,
breaking the tensed sheen:
the soft mirages shivered and displaced.

But there is more than a design
upon a surface once again serene;
to interrupt is vain:
it strives to live but soon it is effaced;
it drowns if you survey, and sinks again:
it forms and dies, and has not had a name.

"Pool," from *Provisional Conclusions: A Selection of the Poetry of
Eugenio Montale* (Chicago: Henry Regnery Co., 1970), translated by Edith Farnsworth.

Putting Edith back into the Farnsworth House

Scott Mehaffey

Purchased at a Sotheby's New York auction in 2003 for $7.5 million dollars, the Farnsworth House, designed by Mies van der Rohe, changed hands from its second owner, Lord Peter Palumbo, to its new conservator, the National Trust for Historic Preservation. Together, the National Trust and Landmarks Illinois, its partner in purchasing the house, have rightly been lauded for keeping one of the world's great modern treasures accessible to the general public.

For its first fifteen years since it became a publicly accessible site in 2004, the house continued to be marketed as an experience of high design by one of the greatest architects of the twentieth century; the visitor experience was it's "All About Mies" (a playful but problematic slogan from a top-selling tee shirt available for years in the visitor center). Despite the fact that Dr. Edith Brooks Farnsworth—a successful nephrologist and, from all accounts, Mies's intellectual match—commissioned the weekend house, she remained relegated to the shadows. Many visitors incorrectly assumed Dr. Farnsworth was a man. This erroneous assumption was corrected with

the official renaming of the Edith Farnsworth House on November 17th 2021, along with a comprehensive reinterpretation of the site. We now remind visitors that the client and patron behind this iconic work of American architecture was a forward-looking and accomplished professional.

Designed as a one-room weekend house on a rural site along the Fox River in Plano just west of Chicago, the minimalist steel-and-glass pavilion continues to provide its visitors with a cinematic view of its natural surroundings. In her unpublished memoirs, excerpts of which are included in this book, Edith Farnsworth recalled her winter 1944–45 visit to the site where her eponymous house would be completed six years later: "We...walked down to the riverbank where we found the most inviting easy-chairs between the swelling roots of two immense black sugar maples whose shade was repeated and extended by the hackberries, the lindens, and the walnut trees grouped about us." One-quarter-inch plate glass allows visitors to be simultaneously *a part of* and *apart from* nature. Like Henry David Thoreau, Edith Farnsworth went to the woods "to live

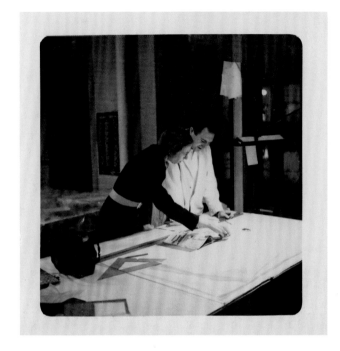

Edith Farnsworth and Myron Goldsmith in conversation about house design in the first Mies van der Rohe Office, 37 S. Wabash Ave, 1950.

deliberately": to retreat, reflect, and refresh. Mies, who spoke with few but carefully selected words, summarized the experience by stating, "If you view nature through the glass walls of the Farnsworth House, it gains a more profound significance than if viewed from the outside. This way, more is said about nature, it becomes part of a larger whole."

Mies's observation somewhat undermines the conventional view of the house—typically envisioned as a formal object on its site, reproduced over the decades so heavily with iconic exterior views—and points to the interior dimension of the house, both in architectural terms and how it was actually lived in.

Between July 2020 and December 2021, the exhibition *Edith Farnsworth Reconsidered* opened to the public. The exhibition (curated by me in collaboration with Professor Nora Wendl and Architect Robert D. Kleinschmidt) reinstalled for the first time the interiors as they would have been seen during the early 1950s when Edith first occupied the house. Our curatorial mission was to show Edith chose to inhabit the space with a careful selection of midcentury modern furniture and an array of objects with personal meaning, including two stone Chinese guardian lions (colloquially known as foo dogs) placed at the far edge of the lower terrace, facing the house.

This exhibition provided an important reorienting of the experience of the house, demonstrating Dr. Farnsworth's agency and own design sensibility.

Peter Palumbo, the home's attentive and cosmopolitan second owner, is remembered for restoring the iconic house in the 1970s and again in the '90s. He also installed a range of modern and contemporary sculpture in the house and throughout the site. With the help of architect Dirk Lohan, Lord Palumbo introduced a combination of Mies- and Lohan-designed furniture. Informative interviews with Palumbo and Lohan are included in this book. During the three decades Peter and his wife Hayat owned and improved Farnsworth, they purchased additional farm acreage, kept horses and vintage aircraft and automobiles, and entertained many notable figures, including some of the twentieth-century's best-known artists, architects, and other creatives.

Until recently, the Palumbos were not recognized for hosting many of the late-twentieth-century's great artists. This recognition increased Farnsworth's cache and positioning in public consciousness—and situated art as an integral part of the Edith Farnsworth House experience. The exhibition *Every Line is a Decision: The Life and*

Edith Farnsworth House living room with traditional furniture, roll-up basswood blinds, and view of lower terrace foo dogs, photographed by Thomas Gorman, early 1960s.

Legacies of Peter Palumbo (March 2022 to December 2023) allowed for a richer history of the Palumbos' careful stewardship of the site to emerge. The exhibition is part of a broader initiative that includes an artist-in-residence program launched in 2015. Additionally, the ever-changing exhibitions program hosted in our stand-alone Gallery (colloquially known as the "Barnsworth," designed and built by IIT College of Architecture Professor Frank Flury and his students), has helped expand our audience and encourage repeat visitation.

Exploring the private lives of now-public houses is not new, but exposing sometimes uncomfortable truths takes both courage and commitment. The National Trust for Historic Preservation's contemporary initiative to "tell the full American story" does justice to the contributions of women, people of color, the LGBTQ+ community, and all Americans in shaping our nation and leading us forward. Together with my colleagues at the National Trust based in Washington, DC, we are working to bring history to life through stories of shared human experience. Our efforts to tell the full history of the site are aimed at leaving a legacy of inclusiveness and transparency for our current visitors and future generations.

2024 marks the twentieth anniversary of opening Farnsworth to the public under the National Trust for Historic Preservation and Landmarks Illinois. Anniversaries are a time for celebration but also for reassessing. Nearly one-quarter into the twenty-first century, there's no denying our essential and cross-cultural responsibilities as stewards of the built and natural environment—and the growing need for architecture that invites nature in. This beautiful and informative new book by Michelangelo Sabatino, with contributions by Dietrich Neumann, Ron Henderson, and Hilary Lewis, reveals a multilayered history of this icon of modern living while adding to the extensive scholarship dedicated to the house since it was designed and built. Since arriving at IIT's College of Architecture a decade ago, Professor Sabatino has been a passionate supporter of our programming and exhibitions. This thorough yet accessible book will ensure that the Edith Farnsworth House will continue to serve as a nexus of history, art, and nature with insightful stories of the past and inspiring lessons for the future.

Scott Mehaffey, MS, FASLA
Executive Director & Curator
Edith Farnsworth House Historic Site
National Trust for Historic Preservation

Representation versus Reality

Michelangelo Sabatino

2

1 (Previous spread) Edith Farnsworth House relative to the Fox River and surrounding farmland, nature preserves, and parks, aerial photography by John Teich Hill, fall 2001.

2 Edith Farnsworth House with midcentury Franco Albini desk and Guglielmo Pecorini chair in view, photographed for first official publications by Bill Hedrich, summer 1951.

Once the Edith Farnsworth House opened to the general public on Saturday, May 1, 2004—thanks to a strategic collaboration between Landmarks Illinois, Friends of the Farnsworth House, and the National Trust for Historic Preservation—access to the iconic modern residence was considerably expanded. However, even for visitors today, it requires determination and resources to travel to Chicago and experience it firsthand.

Such is the case with all so-called "destination architecture," sites and buildings outside the major urban centers that still attract a dedicated, design-oriented visitor base. As with other sites where direct access has either been restricted or is otherwise somewhat of a logistic challenge, the Edith Farnsworth House was popularized and has lived in the public imagination primarily through the medium of photography. Over its lifetime, the Farnsworth House's abundant photographic representations have tended to offer competing views of this remarkable weekend country house. By focusing on the house itself, and to a much lesser extent on its relationship to the surrounding natural setting, many of these photographs tend to take the country out of the country house. One only needs to compare the tree-filled photos taken by Chicago-based firm Hedrich Blessing

in the late Summer of 1951 after the house was completed in early 1951 (with screen and wardrobe added in 1952) to the one taken by New York-based François Dischinger published on the cover of *Sotheby's Preview* (December 2003 issue), to understand the power of photography to modify perceptions. [Figs. 1-7] Dischinger's photo to advertise the imminent sale of the house emphasizes a pristine lawn in the foreground, making it appear as if it were located on a suburban lot in a city instead of a rural site.[1] It is worth recalling that even as photography has continued to shape the understanding of the Farnsworth House from afar, with one known exception (such as the photos taken by André Kertész for *House & Garden* in the February 1952 issue), Edith Farnsworth did not regularly appear in the early published photographs of the house. A handful of photos do exist of her taken by friends and acquaintances but these were not meant for public consumption. [Figs. 8-9] Conversely, Baron Peter Garth Palumbo (1935–), the house's subsequent owner for three decades, was the subject of a series of formal portraits in the house (both of himself and with his wife Hayat) that circulated widely. [Fig. 10] Dr. Farnsworth's fundamental role as originating client and patron was thus overshadowed by both the house's architect,

3

3 Edith Farnsworth House with Peter Palumbo-era desk in view, October 2018.

4 Edith Farnsworth House photographed by George H. Steuer, first published in *Arts & Architecture*, March 1952.

5 View from inside the house looking toward the historic black sugar maple, November 2009.

6 The house and the river, fall 1979.

7 *Sotheby's Preview* (December, 2003) with cover photograph of house and Palumbo-era lawn by François Dischinger.

8 Edith with her dog Miss Amy, the first and only photograph of her inside the house to be published, photographed by André Kertész for *House & Garden*, February 1952.

9 Edith with Miss Amy inside the house against the primavera core, photographed by architect William E. Dunlap, c. 1951.

10 Portrait of Lord Peter and Lady Hayat (née Mrowa) Palumbo sitting on porch, 1993.

5

4

6

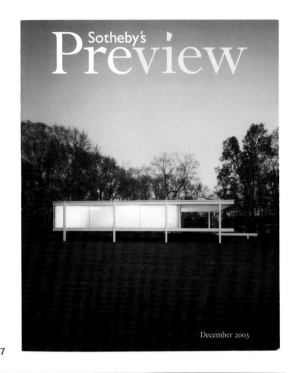

December 2003

7

8

9

10

Representation versus Reality

11

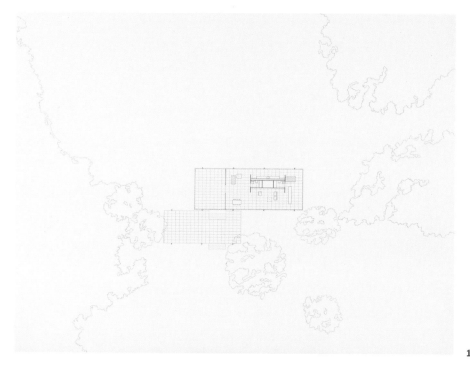

15

12

Ludwig Mies van der Rohe, and its second owner, whose cosmopolitan profile as well as his passion for architecture and art collecting also brought considerable attention to the site. [Fig. 11] By pointing to photography over time and to the role played by mass media, we can better understand the significant gulf between representation and reality as it relates to the Edith Farnsworth House.

Two black-and-white snapshots show Dr. Edith B. Farnsworth (1903–1977) with her attentive silver standard poodle at her side as she gardens in the meadow adjacent to her soon-to-be completed weekend country house, sited on farmland purchased on Dec. 17, 1945 from Col. Robert R. McCormick. [Fig. 12] The house site, along the banks of the Fox River in Plano, Illinois, is located in proximity to the Fox River Drive Bridge, whose iron trusses were eventually dismantled, while the original limestone-clad pillars holding it up were left standing.2 Taken in the Spring of 1950 by her architect friend William E. Dunlap, who was at the time employed by Mies, these two photographs reveal the one-story steel residence

under construction in the distance.3 The meadow on the north side of the house was eventually substituted by a pristine lawn under Palumbo's watch forever changing the atmosphere of this part of the site. As Edith witnessed her house being built, it is unclear to what extent she understood that, even if it was only a weekend retreat off the beaten path, it would significantly transform the image of modern living in America, and beyond. Farnsworth—a nephrologist whose interests in the arts were far reaching and who turned into a consequential patron of modern architecture—commissioned the house to Ludwig Mies van der Rohe (1886–1969) seven years after he arrived to Chicago in 1938. Upon his arrival he began a transformational trajectory as Director of the Department of Architecture at the Armour Institute (subsequently renamed the Illinois Institute of Technology).4 Thanks to his role as architect and educator at IIT, no other architect played such a direct—and indirect role, by way of his students and protégés—in transforming Chicago's postwar skyline.

11 Portrait of Ludwig Mies van der Rohe by Helen Balfour Morrison, c. 1947.

12 Edith gardening in meadow with the house under construction, photographed by William E. Dunlap, late spring 1950.

13 Edith Farnsworth House under construction with unpainted structural steel girders and columns with Mies in the foreground wearing "an enormous black overcoat" (see *Memoirs*, p. 140), winter 1950.

14 Mies observing the installation of core travertine, grain to run parallel with long dimension of house, photographed by architect R. Ogden Hannaford, summer 1950.

15 Final Floor Plan with suggested furniture layout (wardrobe included) and black sugar maple and other trees surrounding house, 1951.

13

14

In Dunlap's two photographs, towering trees appear through the steel skeleton as well as next to the house that was raised approximately five feet above grade in response to the threat of flooding by the Fox River. Another set of closer-up photographs reveals the house's steel structure next to the towering trees. [Figs. 13-14] Eventually, the river spilled over and flooded (or very nearly flooded) the house seven times over the more than seventy years since it was completed.5 The black sugar maple tree that played a significant role, also revealed by the plan, in the way the house was sited and designed is also visible through the steel frame (landscape architect Ron Henderson's brief essay in this book speaks to this important presence on the site). [Fig. 15] The extent to which Edith valued the trees on the site is revealed by a passage in her unpublished memoirs in which she recounts a visit to the MoMA retrospective exhibition about Mies curated by Philip Johnson in 1947:

The art critics and the architects who attended the opening of the Museum exhibit found themselves dwarfed by the immense blow-ups of old photographs which covered the walls: the Barcelona Pavilion, the Tugendhat House with its onyx wall. The little Fox River house was set up on a table and I was distressed that the handmade trees standing around it gave the observer no idea of the great lindens, the maples and the hackberries under which it was to stand. But it was the pivotal point of the exhibit, and I was happy as I boarded the train back to Chicago, reflecting that our project might well become the prototype of new and important elements in American architecture.6

Dunlap's snapshots reveal the degree to which the rural setting, then as now, defines the experience of this weekend country house outside of Chicago, a city whose motto is "Urbs in Horto" and a city that environmental historian William Cronon aptly described as "Nature's Metropolis" in his seminal study.7 Even today, in the field adjacent to the Edith Farnsworth House Visitor Center and Barnsworth Gallery located just off of River Road, one can see a field of hay or massive round bales depending on the time of year. Then as now, the Edith Farnsworth House is a "machine in the garden," and to underplay the role of the garden in its image and day-to-day existence is to overlook a creative tension between the urban and rural that makes this site so unique.8

Although the two photographs taken by Dunlap reveal the main characters of the Edith Farnsworth House story—commissioning client, the building under construction, and its agrarian site—they were never meant for public viewing. Despite these photographs' historical significance, they share little in common with the photographs of a glamorous, urbane, and cutting-edge house created by artists and architectural photographers mostly after Edith Farnsworth sold the house to Peter Palumbo. Unfortunately, many of these photographs, then and today, tend to focus on the building itself while showing less concern for the surrounding natural environment, or its first owner and resident. Repeat visits to Plano can only reinforce an understanding of how the farmland that Edith—and to a lesser extent Mies—visited frequently has gradually been transformed by residential and commercial developments. Since it was completed, especially for those individuals who were unable to actually visit and experience the Farnsworth House until it opened to the general public in the spring of 2004, the forced reliance upon images has increased the house's mystique—and misreadings.

As can be expected of any visual representation, these images—be they works of art or "documentary" photographs—offer personal and oftentimes partial interpretations of reality; they can also ignore the hidden realities of a site as complex as the Edith Farnsworth House. Today,

19

its popularity, at least among artists and architects, is enduring as attests a recent survey of influential designers.**9** Arguably, the house is rivaled in popularity by only two other country houses, the Villa Savoye designed by Le Corbusier for the outskirts of Paris, completed in 1931 and listed as a historic monument in France in 1964, and Frank Lloyd Wright's Fallingwater in Bear Run, Pennsylvania, completed in 1937 and designated a National Historic Landmark in 1976. More recently, in 2019, Fallingwater was ascribed, along with seven other Wright sites, to the UNESCO World Heritage List.**10** Although all three country houses—Savoye, Fallingwater, and Farnsworth—are open to visitors, the photographs of the houses that circulate widely have helped them acquire a life of their own among enthusiasts and professionals who have yet to experience them firsthand. Given that the Farnsworth has considerably less visitors than Fallingwater, for example, its photographs play an even more important role.

While the Edith Farnsworth House lives through its beguiling photographic image that circulates in printed matter of all types, on the Web, and various architectural "knock-offs" around the world, the reality associated with preservation, stewardship, and advocacy of this National Historic Landmark (designated in 2006) is far more complex than mere representation.**11** *The Edith Farnsworth House: Architecture, Preservation, Culture* is the first monographic study to explore the relationship, and tension, between representation and reality over time. The contributions of a series of different protagonists who lived in and owned the house, from when it was first commissioned to the present, are discussed. Architectural historian Dietrich Neumann's essay in this volume places Mies and Edith Farnsworth at the center of a story that begins roughly in the mid-1940s and ends when she sold the house to Baron Palumbo. Select excerpts of Edith's unpublished memoirs, in which she shares her insights and feelings about Mies and the design of the house, are presented here; they reveal how she gradually went from an enthusiastic client to disillusioned owner. This, in part, was also due to the construction of a new bridge that was sited closer to the house than the previous bridge bringing a level of visual and noise "pollution" that forever changed the atmosphere of the site for Edith. Her unpublished memoirs were written after selling her house in Plano and moving to Italy for the last decade of her life.

This book also discusses the contributions of the preservation and stewardship protagonists of this story: Palumbo moved into the house in the early 1970s (even though paper work was started in 1968) and owned it until 2003. Palumbo sold it, following the end of negotiations with the State of Illinois that had initially expressed interest, for roughly $7.5 million at a much-publicized auction held on Friday, December 12, 2003 by Sotheby's.**12** Palumbo, an English property developer turned arts patron

(former Chairman of the Arts Council of Great Britain), had deep ties to Chicago; he served as Chair of the Jury of the Chicago-based Pritzker Prize in Architecture from 2005-2016.**13** He played an important role in extending the life of the Farnsworth House and was joined by Lady Hayat Palumbo once they were married in 1986. Their steadfast commitment to preservation and passionate stewardship of the site involved restoring the house following a series of catastrophic floods, including one in 1996. The Palumbo years also coincided with significant resources being directed to the landscape, with the oversight of Lanning Roper (1912–1983), an American landscape architect who studied and lived in England.**14** In parallel to Roper's transformation of the site from a relatively unkept parcel of land to a designed landscape replete with boathouse, pool, tennis court, and allée of maple trees to lead visitors down to the hill from the entrance gate to the house, the Palumbos also installed a significant number of modern and contemporary artworks across the site. Once Palumbo began to bring family and friends for regular visits, he realized that a weekend house designed for a single woman was great for entertaining but not big enough for overnight stays; so he purchased a late-nineteenth-century Italianate house (formerly owned by the Eldridge family) nearby in Plano. Excerpts of interviews, conducted as part of the research and writing of this book, with Peter and Hayat Palumbo, along with architect Dirk Lohan (1938-), who worked with them over the years on the house and site, are also included in this book.

Since modern architecture was generally understood as breaking with the historical precedent, it has been a challenge to help the general public understand that it too has come to assume a "historic" status. Buildings in the US are eligible for designation once they are fifty years of age. Long-term ownership of a historic modern house like the Farnsworth comes with a series of preservation challenges that the original client and architect could not have imagined, which were left to the Palumbos and Lohan to address.

In 2003, a group consisting of Landmarks Illinois (then referred to as the Landmarks Preservation Council of Illinois), the Friends of the Farnsworth House, and the National Trust for Historic Preservation coalesced to ensure that the house was purchased and saved from the prospect of either remaining in private hands or, more problematically, being removed from the site altogether in favor of another setting. Landmarks Illinois operated the site from 2003 until 2010, and while Landmarks Illinois still holds the easement, from January 1, 2010 onwards, the National Trust for Historic Preservation took the lead in the preservation, stewardship, and advocacy of the Edith Farnsworth House Historic Site.**15** A series of executive directors—ranging from Whitney French (2006–12), the first to officially occupy the position, to Maurice Parrish (2012–18), and most recently Scott Mehaffey, (2018–present)—have contributed in different ways to shaping the site over time, especially in terms of preservation and programming. Significantly, Mehaffey is the first executive director to have trained as a landscape architect. Over the past twenty years since the Edith Farnsworth House opened to the public, it has entered into the arts and culture mainstream.

If the cultural soft power of the toy industry is any indicator of architecture entering the arts and culture mainstream, the fact that in 2011 LEGO Architecture (Landmark and Architect series) released its kit for the Farnsworth House, designed by Chicago-based architect Adam Reed Tucker, would attest to its reach.[16] [Fig. 16] It is worth noting that in the pamphlet accompanying the LEGO bricks of the Farnsworth kit, the focus is almost exclusively on Mies with Dr. Edith Farnsworth receiving only a passing mention. The year after LEGO released its Farnsworth House kit set, it followed up by releasing one for Le Corbusier's iconic Villa Savoye, designed by German architect Michael Hepp.[17]

In recent years, studies about modern twentieth-century houses—ranging from the Villa Savoye to the Jacobs Houses (n. 1 and n. 2) in Wisconsin and the Stahl House in Los Angeles—have shifted away from the architect as the sole focus to include clients and family members; these studies aimed at general and specialized readers.[18] Over the years, numerous individuals have written about Mies's role as architect, while much fewer about Edith Farnsworth. From Franz Schulze (with Edward Windhorst), Paulette Singley, and Alice T. Friedman, and more recently Alex Beam and Nora Wendl, these researchers have focused on the history of a remarkable patron as well as her remarkable architect.[19] Friedman's pioneering book, *Women and the Making of the Modern House: A Social and Architectural History* (1998) is the first study to critically assess Edith's overlooked role within a broader international context of modern residential architecture. A number of monographs have been published with titles almost always referring to the house without Edith Farnsworth's full name.[20] Her first name was officially introduced to the historic site's nomenclature on November 17, 2021.[21] Practicing architects and educators have also repeatedly written about the Farnsworth over the years but have tended to focus almost exclusively upon Mies and his design; in most of these accounts both Edith Farnsworth and the agrarian site spanning just under sixty acres she choose for her weekend house, do not receive much attention.[22]

Depending on the type of photography that is used to tell the story of a building and its inhabitants, personal connections to the domestic space can either be highlighted or obfuscated. Take for example a series of informal photographs taken at the Farnsworth House by local Plano photographer Thomas Gorman in the early 1950s; they reveal, just like those by Dunlap, Edith's preferences in furnishings and the art objects. In particular, a photo Gorman took from outside with the two stone foo dogs Edith installed on the South Terrace reveal that she was anything but an orthodox modernist who was interested in filling her weekend country house with only Mies-designed furniture.[23] [Fig. 17] It is worth noting that a series of plans produced by Mies's office attest to considerations made regarding the placement of furniture. As revealed by the groundbreaking exhibition *Edith Farnsworth Reconsidered* (cocurated by Nora Wendl and Scott Mehaffey with Robert D. Kleinschmidt as advisor and held between July 2020 and December 2021), Edith was very much inclined to purchase a range of midcentury design with what appears to be a particular preference for informal "organic" furniture. Thanks to the *Good Design* exhibition held during the 1950s in conjunction with MoMA at Chicago's monumental Merchandise Mart sited along the Chicago River, and due also

16 Edith Farnsworth House designed by Adam Reed Tucker for LEGO Architecture, in association with the National Trust for Historic Preservation, 2011.

17 Lower terrace with foo dogs, subsequently donated by Dr. Farnsworth to the UChicago Cochrane-Woods Art Center, photographed by Thomas Gorman, late1950s.

16

17

Screened porch with house plants and midcentury furniture (Jens Risom, Bruno Mathsson), likely photographed by Edith Farnsworth, c. mid-1950s.

19 Living room with 1950s furnishings recreated for *Edith Farnsworth Reconsidered*, spring 2020.

20 Living room following flood, fall 2008.

21 Tadao Ando, brush and black ink on white Japanese paper, signed "Farnsworth House, 4/17/2009, Ando."

19

20

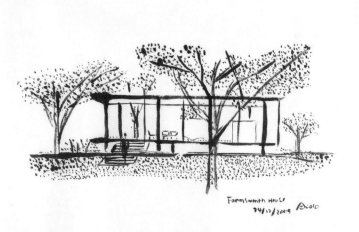

21

to Baldwin Kingrey, a forward-looking design store that promoted midcentury modern design, Edith was able to purchase a range of interesting furniture.**24** Whether Bruno Mathsson's Pernilla Chaise longue (1936), Jens Risom's Low Lounge Chair Model 650 (1941) or Franco Albini's decidedly modernist glass, steel, and lacquered wood desk (first issued in 1928), Edith was discerning with her taste. **[Figs. 18-19-20]** Over the years since her professional relationship with Mies deteriorated, leading to a prolonged lawsuit, Farnsworth was never yielding. **25** Mies's office sued her for outstanding design fees and she countersued. Eventually the Master of Chancery decided in Mies's favor although she only paid a modest settlement. Since she was not a pushover, her male counterparts tended to cast her as "difficult." Note for example, the tensions between Edith and Mies over the choice of curtains and her desire for a free-standing wardrobe.**26** Asked during an interview in the 1950s about his relationship with Edith and whether his client was "difficult," Mies brought the discussion around to the choice of curtains for the house (his preference was for ivory shantung silk):

The professor was asked whether the client was not difficult.
At the beginning, no, but later she was. We got into trouble about the curtains. This is very interesting. I had a great experience with this house. Before you live in a glass house, you do not know how colourful nature is. It changes every day. We had this flooring all the way through, and the wood was very light-coloured. I decided to make raw-silk curtains, in a natural colour. She said, "Not over my dead body." She had had a piece of advice from somebody; she wanted a very strong yellow colour. That material cost us about $7 per 1/2 yard. Our silk curtains cost us $2 per 1/2 yard. That decided her. She did not die, but she was furious.

The professor was asked whether he had ever had any difficulty collecting his fees.
Only with this building. It cost $50,000, and the fee was about $5000 or $6000.

He was asked whether the client liked it now.
I have not the slightest idea. I like it still.**27**

Changing conceptual and technical approaches to photography, video, and film have enriched the representation of Mies's buildings, their clients, and inhabitants over the past decades. Increased access to the sites has also allowed architects and students to sketch the buildings in situ even though this practice seems not to be nearly as popular as reliance upon iPhone photography. **[Fig. 21]** Interpretations of modern and contemporary architecture have increasingly shifted from an emphasis on the aesthetics of space, structure, and material to a focus on the everyday lives of buildings and the people who occupy them over time.**28** A case in point is the collaboration between Mies (shortly after his arrival in America) and Chicago-based photographer William (Bill) Hedrich and others of the Hedrich Blessing firm that signaled a shift from Mies's previous hands-off to a hands-on approach to photographing his projects, especially his personal presence on site for the first set of photos of the Edith Farnsworth House.**29** Bill Hedrich later explained that "Mies was firm in his commitment to what he wanted to see. First of all, every photograph had to be on one point. That means that it's straight on. No perspective. He didn't want perspective shots. [...] Mies was unforgiving in his approach to that. He wanted it his way. You know, it's like, 'It will be this way.' It's Mies all the way. Strong."**30** This testimonial reinforces the type of control Mies sought to exert over the creative process that led to conflicts concerning a whole range of issues with Dr. Edith Farnsworth.

The arc of time framing the Edith Farnsworth House's private-to-public shift also encompasses a shift in architectural photography itself; from architect-directed photography that aims to fulfill their vision of a building as designed (or intended) to incorporating other viewpoints, investigating the ostensible purposes for which the building was designed, and exploring architecture as a site of encounter. This relatively new genre of photography eschews the idealized or pristine view of buildings, when architects directly guide the process onsite with the photographer or simply giving instructions from afar, in favor of personal interactions.**31** Some pioneering examples of changing approaches to photography that are simultaneously deferential to and subversive of Mies's legacy of control focus on his two most famous buildings—the Barcelona Pavilion and the Edith Farnsworth House—are found in Jeff Wall's *Morning Cleaning* (1999) and Iñigo Manglano-Ovalle's *Le Baiser/The Kiss* (1999). **[Figs. 22-23]** Wall's photograph (displayed as a transparency in a lightbox) reveals the antiheroic everyday life of the Barcelona Pavilion through the eyes of a real-life janitor in the bright light of the morning as he bends down holding a squeegee while cleaning a glass wall. Manglano-Ovalle's approach is similarly complex, despite its day-in-the-life character; he assumes the role of a voyeuristic window washer of the Edith Farnsworth House who seeks to attract the attention of a seemingly indifferent individual (channeling the aloof impersonation of Edith?) standing almost directly in front of him.**32** The task of cleaning modern and contemporary spaces, typically characterized by an abundance of glass, is an increasingly popular and mischievous embrace of the everyday, or the mundane in architectural photography and film.**33** Wall and Manglano-Ovalle also extend the experience of his buildings into a realm of the everyday by depicting the human presence. Despite the inclusion of human beings, their work is not to be understood as individual portraits. These images, whether photos or videos, are testaments to a building's uncanny ability to reveal different moods and personalities. This relatively new wave of art photographers seem to be collectively asserting that buildings, not unlike people themselves, need not always present their best and most formal or even "glamorous" side but should also be allowed to reveal a more low-key, if not contemplative, everyday life.**34**

This gradual shift in visualizing architecture was also accelerated by photographers who identify primarily with the realm of fine arts and/or commercial photography rather than architectural photography per se, coinciding with a growing interest in the built environment among a broader audience of enthusiasts. Playwright and documentary filmmaker June Finfer wrote, produced, and directed a film, *The Farnsworth House* (Filmedia, 1999), and more recently Erin Lutterbach wrote and produced (with Geoffrey Baer of WTTW as Host) *Saved from the Wrecking Ball: The Farnsworth House* (Towers Productions, 2007). Shelter magazines have used photography extensively to portray architecture, interiors, design, and garden/landscape in

22

23

terms of "lifestyle." This type of work has been augmented in recent years by the influx of self-trained photographers from different backgrounds who, in combination with professional cameras, also use their iPhones (both to capture still images and videos) and various social media outlets such as Facebook, Instagram, and TikTok to share their personal experiences of buildings and cities with an extensive social network. In sum, this eclectic cadre of image producers have considerably minimized the sole reliance upon a select portfolio of highly curated views of buildings taken by dedicated architectural photographers who dominated the profession when journals and books (and to a lesser extent personal travel accounts) were the primary vehicles of circulation of architectural knowledge. The contribution of this new wave of architectural observers and commentators is thereby broadening the visibility of the Edith Farnsworth House and ultimately reinforcing architecture as a cultural phenomenon.

Well before art photographers began to reveal the poetic potential of the everyday in the work of Mies, American cartoonists such as Alan Dunn poked fun at the seemingly authoritarian dimension of modern architecture as it sought to impose a minimalist aesthetic that did not allow those who dwelled within Mies-designed buildings (or those of his protégés) to live with their personal objects, especially those from eras with different aesthetics. Two cartoons, both published in *Architectural Record* during the late 1950s and early 1960s, demonstrate just how a certain type of European-derived minimal modernism was being playfully lampooned well before Tom Wolfe's widely popular book *From Bauhaus to Our House* (1981).**35** One cartoon from September 1958 shows an individual in the foreground holding a pair of binoculars in front of what appears to be the Mies-designed Seagram Building in New York. He points up and addresses Mies, who is heading to the entrance, with a warning: "Oh, Mr. Mies! Tenant on the 24th floor brought his own window shades!" Another cartoon by Dunn, this one from August 1961, shows a woman standing next to a closet full of personal objects that don't seem to conform with the otherwise austere modernist aesthetics of the all-glass living room. She anxiously asks her companion: "Have the photographers gone?" **[Figs. 24-25]** While there is no explicit reference to Edith Farnsworth, the humor clearly refers to the regimented, designer-driven notion that residents of modernist houses likewise had to conform to a minimalist approach to interior furnishings. Both these cartoons reinforce the idea that modern architectural photography and the buildings themselves had to adhere to a strict aesthetic in which the everyday lives, tastes, and objects of the inhabitants were perceived as intrusions that undermined the minimalist space. It is worth noting that following the sale of the Farnsworth house to Baron Palumbo, he introduced various Mies-designed objects: Barcelona Day Bed, Brno Chair, MR Adjustable

Chaise Lounge and MR Chair, Tugendhat Armchair; Dirk Lohan designed a desk, dining table, bed, and boot box. The informal atmosphere of the house during Edith's time was decisively lost in favor of a much more curated one in which Miesian aesthetics dominated the building and interiors.

House Beautiful editor Elizabeth Gordon took aim at Mies, and his followers during those years, on the pages of *House Beautiful* published in the April 1953 when she accused him (and Le Corbusier) as being at the center of a "cult of austerity" in her article "The Threat to the Next America."**36** Gordon was the first critic to publicly criticize Mies and come to Farnsworth's defense after she complained about the inadequacies of the house: "I have talked to a highly intelligent, now disillusioned, woman who spent more than $70,000 building a 1-room house that is nothing but a glass cage on stilts."**37** [Fig. 26] To be sure, the moralizing message centered around austerity at the expense of "comfort" can be traced to the socially motivated modern architects who embraced "Existenzminimum" (minimal existence), particularly within the domestic realm, while rejecting a capitalist mindset of accumulation of objects. The notion of comfort can also be extended beyond simply having access to comfortable furniture or leaving in plain view objects of everyday use; it can also be understood in terms of thermal comfort. Evidence suggests that Myron Gold-

24

"Oh, Mr. Mies! Tenant on the 34th floor brought his own window shades!"

25

"Have the photographers gone?"

22 Jeff Wall, *Morning Cleaning*, 1999.

23 Iñigo Manglano-Ovalle, *Le Baiser/The Kiss*, 1999.

24 Alan Dunn, "Oh, Mr. Mies!" *Architectural Record*, September 1958.

25 Alan Dunn, "Have the photographers gone?" *Architectural Record*, August 1961.

THE THREAT
TO THE NEXT AMERICA

By Elizabeth Gordon, *Editor*

Something is rotten in the state of design—and it is spoiling some of our best efforts in modern living. After watching it for several years, after meeting it with silence, House Beautiful has decided to speak out and appeal to your common sense, because it is common sense that is mostly under attack. Two ways of life stretch before us. One leads to the richness of variety, to comfort and beauty. The other, the one we want fully to expose to you, retreats to poverty and unlivability. Worst of all, it contains a threat of cultural dictatorship

I have decided to speak up.

In this issue, devoted to the wonderful possibilities for the better life in the Next America, I must also point out to you what I consider to be the threat to our achieving the *greater good* which is clearly possible for us, if we do not lose our sense of direction and independence.

What I want to tell you about has never been put into print by us or any other publication, to my knowledge. Your first reactions will be amazement, disbelief, and shock. You will say "It can't happen here!"

But hear me out. You may discover why you strongly dislike some of the so-called modern things you see. You may suddenly understand why you instinctively reject designs that are called "modernistic." For you are right. It's your common sense speaking. For these things are bad—bad in more ways than in their lack of beauty alone.

Here is the story, in its bluntest terms.

There is a well-established movement, in modern architecture, decorating, and furnishings, which is promoting the mystical idea that "less is more." Year after year, this idea has been hammered home by *some* museums, *some* professional magazines for architects and decorators, *some* architectural schools, and *some* designers.

They are all trying to sell the idea that "less is more," both as a criterion for design, and as a basis for judgment of the good life. They are promoting unlivability, stripped-down emptiness, lack of storage space and therefore lack of possessions.

They are praising designs that are unscientific, irrational and uneconomical—illogical things like whole walls of unshaded glass on the west, which cause you to fry in the summer, thus misusing one of our finest new materials. Or tricks like putting heavy buildings up on thin, delicate stilts—even though they cost more and instinctively worry the eye. Or cantilevering things that don't need to be cantilevered, making them cost more, too. A strong taint of anti-reason runs through all of their houses and furnishings.

No wonder you feel uneasy and repelled!

They are trying to convince you that you can appreciate beauty only if you suffer—because they say beauty and comfort are incompatible.

They are trying to get you to accept their idea of beauty and form as the measure of all things, *regardless* of whether they work, what they do to you, or what they cost.

They are a self-chosen elite who are trying to tell us what we should like and how we should live. And these arbiters have such a narrow, often ignorant, conception of the good life that only non-human, low-performance things get their stamp of approval. These arbiters make such a consistent attack on comfort, convenience, and functional values that it becomes, in reality, an attack on reason itself.

"Incredible!" you say. "Nobody could seriously sell such nonsense."

My considered answer is this. Though it *is* incredible, some people *are* taking such nonsense seriously. They take it seriously because this propaganda comes from highly placed individuals and highly respected institutions. Therein lies the danger.

For if we can be sold on accepting dictators in matters of taste and how our homes are to be ordered, our minds are certainly well prepared to accept dictators in other departments of life. The undermining of people's confidence is the beginning of the end.

Break people's confidence in reason and their own common sense and they are on the way to attaching themselves to a leader, a mass movement, or any sort of authority beyond themselves. Nothing better explains periods of mass hysteria or various forms of social idiocy than the collapse of reason, the often deliberate result of an attack on people's self-confidence.

If people don't trust themselves and their own judgment, then they turn helplessly to leaders, good or bad. And they can only recover the good, sensible life when they recover their senses and discover again that, by and large, the ultimate hope for mankind is the application of reason to the world around us. This *rediscovery* leads individuals to their own declaration of independence against the frauds, the over-publicized phonies, the bullying tactics of the self-chosen elite who would dictate not only taste but a whole way of life.

So, you see, this well-developed movement has social implications, because it affects the heart of our society—the home. Beyond the nonsense of trying to make us want to give up our technical aids and conveniences for what is *supposed* to be a better and more serene life, there is a social threat of regimentation and total control. For if the mind of man can be manipulated in one great phase of life to be made willing to accept less, it would be possible to go on and get him to accept less in all phases of life.

I can hear you say: "How can people collaborate for their own discomfort and frustration?"

Believe it or not, some people do, because their own self-confidence has been shaken. Not very many, fortunately, but enough so that I can clearly see the aberration growing. (Please turn the page)

House Beautiful, April 1953

---

smith, the architect in Mies's office who oversaw the construction of the Farnsworth House, went to great pains to assess this factor, as can be deduced by a series of studies he conducted.[38]

The modern pavilion, as exemplified by the Edith Farnsworth House, has arguably led to a paradoxical "disappearance" of architecture or, at the very least, a game-changing transformation of its relationship to landscape that is so essential to the experience of the site.[39] This transformation is not a banal issue of transparency but rather a rethinking of disciplinary premises tout court. Asked about the role of nature in the Edith Farnsworth House by influential architect, author, and phenomenologist Christian Norberg-Schulz, Mies had this to say:

One is surprised that you collect Klee pictures; one thinks that does not fit your building.
I hope to make my buildings neutral frames in which man and artworks can carry on their own lives. To do that, one needs a respectful attitude toward things.

If you view your buildings as neutral frames, what role does nature play with respect to the buildings?
Nature too shall live its own life. We must beware not to disrupt it with the colour of our houses and interior fittings. Yet we should attempt to bring nature, houses, and human beings together into a higher unity. If you view nature through the glass walls of Farnsworth House, it gains a more profound significance than if viewed from outside. This way, more is said about nature; it becomes a part of a larger whole.

I have noticed that you rarely make a normal corner in your buildings but you let one wall be the corner and separate it from the other wall.
The reason for that is that a normal corner formation appears massive, something difficult to combine with a variable ground plan. The free ground plan is a new concept and has its own "grammar," just like a language. Many believe that the variable ground plan implies total freedom. That is a misunderstanding. It demands just as much discipline and intelligence from the architect as the conventional ground plan; it demands, for example, that enclosed elements,

26 Elizabeth Gordon, "The Threat to the Next America," *House Beautiful*, April 1953.

27 Edith Farnsworth House terrace and porch photographed by Guido Guidi for *Mies in America*, April 2000.

28 Porch photographed by Guido Guidi for *Mies in America*, October/November 1999.

and they are always needed, be separated from the outside walls, as in Farnsworth House. Only that way can a free space be obtained.**40**

When prompted about color in architecture and nature by John Peter, Mies responded in a way that seems to imply that despite his differences with Edith, they both shared a common respect for nature:

In our IIT campus I painted the steel black. At Farnsworth House I painted it white because it was in the green [countryside]. I could have used any color.**41**

It is worth noting that the vast majority of the black-and-white photographs of Mies's buildings taken during his lifetime, by such American photographers as Ezra Stoller, Balthazar Korab, and G. E. Kidder Smith, did little to reveal the sensual role of nature at the Farnsworth House. The color photographs taken during and after Palumbo's ownership by a series of talented photographers from Hedrich Blessing, George Lambros, and Guido Guidi eschew black-and-white photography in favor of color.**42** [Figs. 27-28 , pp. 117-119] In particular, Jon Miller's photograph taken of the Farnsworth House in 1985 with the monumental black sugar maple in full fall color reveals and reinforces the relationship between architecture and nature pursued by Mies.

During the second half of the twentieth century, designers of pavilions simultaneously absorbed avant-garde as well as traditional approaches toward space and place while drawing upon a range of multimedia and multidisciplinary expertise. Artists, architects, and landscape architects have conceived and realized groundbreaking pavilions in the countryside and within urban settings, in the Americas, Europe, and Asia; these hybrid spaces have expanded our appreciation of what is "modern" about modern art and architecture. Whether the Farnsworth or Philip Johnson's weekend country house, the Glass House in New Canaan—discussed by Hilary Lewis, Chief Curator & Creative Director, in the afterword of this book—variations of the modern pavilion solicit a wide range of spatial and sensorial experiences both within and outside the glass walls.

Unlike the Glass House, which has no operable windows, the Farnsworth House has, at Edith's insistence, two hopper windows on the east-facing glass wall across the two entrance doors on the west side. Together with the screened porch that kept out pesky mosquitoes, the hopper windows allowed for an aural experience (to live and breathe within its natural setting) unlike the sealed glass box that Mies intended.**43** During Palumbo's ownership he introduced air conditioning and removed the screen walls on the upper terrace designed by William Dunlap upon Edith's direction.

Extending Dunn's witty questioning of the tropes of modern architecture to the visual dialogue between inside/outside, Charles Saxon's cover of *The New Yorker* (May 20, 1967) humorously depicts a homeowner as she seeks to position a sculpture outdoors based on its relationship to the views from inside her glass house, one that looks strikingly similar to Johnson's house in New Canaan. [**Fig. 29**] Over time Palumbo would follow this very same trajectory by installing outdoor sculpture in and around the

27

28

29 Cover of *The New Yorker* by Charles D. Saxon, with variation of a single-story glass house, May 20, 1967.

30 Harry Bertoia's *Untitled Sound Sculpture* (c. 1978) on lower terrace, fall 1997.

30

Farnsworth House ranging from an untitled tonal sculpture by Harry Bertoia (c. 1978), at one point placed on the lower terrace, to larger pieces located further away from the house such as Sir Anthony Caro's *Bailey* (1971) and Andy Goldsworthy's site-specific *Floodstones Cairn* (1993–2003) commemorating the 1954 flooding of the site **[Figs. 30-31]** Both of these sculptures reinforce the connection to the natural site that continues to define the experience of the Edith Farnsworth House. **[Figs. 32-36]**

Insofar as it continues to raise questions and excite the imagination of different generations of artists and architects as well as members of the general public, Mies van der Rohe's Edith Farnsworth House is a modern classic. Like Shakespeare's classical tragedies, this one-story pavilion of glass-and-steel continues to inspire competing interpretations. In the list of definitions of classics offered by Italo Calvino in *Why Read the Classics?* he states, "A classic is a book which with each rereading offers as much of a sense of discovery as the first reading." The Edith Farnsworth House should be reread and visited (and revisited) during different seasons and different times of day to fully understand the role that nature plays in experiencing it as a weekend country house. While photographs of the house across styles and eras may prove to be seductive, with this book we seek to make clear that only by engaging with the realities of the natural site and its owners over time can one hope to understand the complex relationship between architectural history, preservation, advocacy, and stewardship.

31

31 Andy Goldsworthy, *Floodstones Cairn* (1993; boulders from the Feltes Sand & Gravel Co quarry at Aurora) commissioned by Palumbo for Fox River bank near Rob Roy Creek, spring 1997.

32 Edith Farnsworth House and Fox River flooding with curtains and lights on, before flood protocol was established, August 24, 2007.

32

Representation versus Reality

33

34

The Edith Farnsworth House

33 Edith Farnsworth House, Fox River, Palumbo-era boat house (bottom left), aerial photograph by John Teich Hill, fall 2001.

34 The house and the river, aerial photograph by John Teich Hill, fall 2001.

35 Edith Farnsworth House with black sugar maple, photograph by Hedrich Blessing, fall 1951 (black-and-white version on page 66).

36 Hay field adjacent to Visitor Center and Barnsworth Gallery, fall 2023.

Representation versus Reality

Notes

1 *Sotheby's Preview* (December, 2003). The cover photo is misattributed to George Lambros. It is by François Dischinger.

2 In 1969, a new reinforced concrete bridge was completed following a path that brought it closer to the house, much to Farnsworth's chagrin.

3 David W. Dunlap, "House Proud: Personal Visions; In a Glass Box, Secrets Are Hard to Keep," *The New York Times*, June 24, 1999. Section F, p. 1.

4 Kevin Harrington and M. Sabatino, eds., *Building, Breaking, and Rebuilding: The IIT Campus and Chicago's South Side* (Minneapolis: University of Minnesota Press, 2024).

5 The threat of a "100-year flood" has already turned into reality on several occasions and continues to haunt the house and site to this very day. See Wright Water Engineers, Inc., *Farnsworth House Flood Risk and Conceptual Mitigation Evaluation. 14520 River Road Plano, Illinois*, in part. 2.2. "Flooding History," p. 11, accessed Oct 28, 2023. See also Michael Cadwell, *Strange Details: Writing Architecture* (Cambridge, MA: The MIT Press, 2007), in part. "Flooded at the Farnsworth House," pp. 92–136, https://edithfarnsworthhouse. org/wp-content/uploads/National_Trust_ Farnsworth_WWE.pdf.

6 Edith Farnsworth, *Memoirs*, ch. 11, p. 147.

7 William Cronon, *Nature's Metropolis: Chicago and the Great West* (New York: W. W. Norton, 1992).

8 Leo Marx, *The Machine in the Garden: Technology and the Pastoral Ideal in America* (1964), 2nd ed. (New York and London: Oxford University Press, 2000).

9 Kurt Soller and Michael Snyder, "The 25 Most Significant Works of Postwar Architecture," *T: The New York Times Style Magazine*, August 8, 2021, Section ST, p. 3.

10 See "The 20th-Century Architecture of Frank Lloyd Wright," accessed October 30, 2023, https://whc.unesco.org/en/ list/1496/.

11 The (Edith) Farnsworth House was designated a National Historic Landmark on February 17, 2006 by the National Park Service of the United States Department of the Interior. The plaque on the site reads: "In 1945, Dr. Edith Farnsworth commissioned architect Ludwig Mies van der Rohe to design a modern weekend house that became an icon of the International Style. Completed in 1951, the glass and steel pavilion was set five feet above ground to allow for periodic flooding of the adjacent Fox River." The (Edith) Farnsworth House was first listed in the National Register of Historic Places (Illinois) on October 7, 2004.

12 Carol Vogel, "Landmark Mies House Goes to Preservationists," *The New York Times*, December 13, 2003, Section B, p. 7; Lynne Duke, "National Trust Wins Bid for Mies Treasure," *The Washington Post*, December 13, 2003; Stevenson Swanson (with Blair Kamin), "Farnsworth House saved. Last-minute donations rescue Mies masterpiece at auction," *Chicago Tribune*, Sunday, December 13, 2003, pp. 1, 24.

13 Martha Thorne, ed. *The Pritzker Architecture Prize: The First Twenty Years* (New York: Harry N. Abrams in association with the Art Institute of Chicago, 1999); Ruth A. Peltason and Grace Ong-Yan, eds., *Architect: The Pritzker Prize Laureates in Their Own Words* (London: Thames & Hudson, 2010).

14 Jane Brown, *Lanning Roper and his Gardens* (New York: Rizzoli, 1987).

15 Paul Goldberger, ed., *Modern Views: Inspired by Mies van der Rohe Farnsworth House and Philip Johnson Glass House* (New York: Assouline Publishing, 2010) was published in conjunction with the management of the Farnsworth House shifting to the National Trust for Historic Preservation (NTHP).

16 Richard Waite, "More amazing Lego: Mies' Farnsworth House Released," *Architects' Journal* (4 April 2011); Steve Johnson, "At Home with Lego Artist Adam Reed Tucker," *Chicago Tribune*, September 14, 2016. When Google chose to celebrate Mies van der Rohe's 126th birthday on March 27, 2012 (he was born in 1886), they issued a "doodle" with S. R. Crown Hall on the IIT campus, and not one of the Farnsworth.

17 Perhaps revealing of the enduring fascination for Frank Lloyd Wright is the fact that Fallingwater, also designed by Adam Reed Tucker, had been released by LEGO Architecture in 2009, well before the kits for both the Farnsworth House and the Villa Savoye.

18 Jean-Marc Savoye and Jean-Philippe Delhomme, illus., *The Sunny Days of Villa Savoye* (Basel: Birkhäuser, 2021); Bruce Stahl, Shari Stahl Gronwald, with Kim Cross, *The Stahl House: Case Study House #22: The Making of a Modernist Icon* (Los Angeles: Chronicle Chroma, 2021); Julia Jamrozik and Coryn Kempster, *Growing up Modern: Childhoods in Iconic Homes* (Basel: Birkhäuser, 2021); Neil Levine, ed., *Frank Lloyd Wright's Jacobs Houses: Experiments in Modern Living* (Chandler, AZ: OA+D Archives Press, 2022) (with essays by Elizabeth Jacobs Aitken, Michael Desmond, William Wescott Jacobs, and Susan Jacobs Lockhart).

19 Franz Schulze and Edward Windhorst, *Mies van der Rohe: A Critical Biography* (Chicago: The Unviersity of Chicago Press, 2012), in part. ch. 10, "The Farnsworth Saga: 1946–2003," pp. 247–303; Paulette Singley, "Living in a Glass Prism: The Female Figure in Mies van der Rohe's Domestic Architecture," *Critical Matrix* 6, no. 2 (1992): 47–76. Alice T. Friedman, *Women and the Making of the Modern House* (New York: Abrams, 1998), in part. ch. 4, "People who Live in Glass Houses: Edith Farnsworth, Ludwig Mies van der Rohe, and Philip Johnson," pp. 126–59; Alex Beam, *Broken Glass: Mies van der Rohe, Edith Farnsworth, and the Fight Over a Modernist Masterpiece* (New York: Random House, 2020). Nora Wendl has written and curated a series of essays and installations about the Edith Farnsworth House including "Uncompromising Reasons for Going West: A Story of Sex and Real Estate, Reconsidered," *Thresholds* 43 (Spring 2015) and "Edith: An Architectural History," List Gallery, Swarthmore College, January 19–February 25, 2023. Detlef Mertins, *Mies* (London and New York: Phaidon Press, 2014), in part. "Farnsworth to Crown Hall: Clear Span," pp. 292–313.

20 Shortly after Palumbo purchased the house from Dr. Farnsworth two related publications appeared for the prestigious GA Global Architecture in Japan: Yukio Futagawa, *Ludwig Mies van der Rohe Farnsworth House, Plano, Illinois, 1945–50* (Tokyo: A.D.A. Edita, 1974/1983) and Dirk Lohan, *Mies van der Rohe Farnsworth House, Plano 1945–1950* (Tokyo: ADA Edita, 1976/2000). These monographs were followed by Franz Schulze, *The Farnsworth House* (Chicago: Lohan Associates, 1997); Werner Blaser, *Mies van der Rohe Farnsworth House Weekend House* (Basel-Boston: Birkhäuser Publishers, 1999); Maritz Vandenberg, *Farnsworth House: Ludwig Mies van der Rohe* (London and New York: Phaidon, 2003).

21 Published to coincide with the official name change. Nora Wendl, *Edith B. Farnsworth* (Washington, DC: National Trust for Historic Preservation, 2021).

22 See for example: Jacques Herzog and Pierre de Meuron, *Treacherous Transparencies: Thoughts and Observations Triggered by a Visit to Farnsworth House* (Chicago/New York: IITAC Press/Actar Press, 2016).

23 The Foo Dogs were subsequently donated to the University of Chicago's Smart Museum of Art.

24 John Brunetti, *Baldwin Kingrey: Midcentury Modern in Chicago, 1947–1957* (Chicago: Wright, 2004); Lisa Napoles, "'A New Outlook' Baldwin Kingrey of Chicago," August 13, 2014, accessed September 10, 2019, docomomo-us.org.

25 Jerome Nelson, State of Illinois County of Kendall, "Master's Report," *Ludwig Mies van der Rohe, Plantiff vs Edith B. Farnsworth, Defendant*, 1953.

26 To understand where the drama over curtains first unfolded see Sarah M. Dreller, "Curtained Walls: Architectural Photography, the Farnsworth House, and the Opaque Discourse of Transparency," *ARRIS: Journal of the Southeast Chapter of the Society of Architectural Historians* 26 (2015): 22–40. Especially footnote n. 11 in which Dreller cites Thomas Dyja, *The Third Coast: When Chicago Built the American Dream* (London: Penguin Press, 2013), pp. 218–19.

27 Published interview (date of interview: 27 May 1959). Source: H. T. Cadbury-Brown, "Ludwig Mies van der Rohe: An Address of Appreciation by H. T. Cadbury-Brown," *The Architectural Association Journal* 75, no. 834 (July–August 1959): 26–39. This excerpt is part of a complete collection of texts published as Vittorio Pizzigoni and Michelangelo Sabatino, eds., *Mies in His Own Words: Complete Writings, Speeches, and Interviews* (Berlin: DOM Publishers, 2024).

28 For a discussion about architecture and photography see Therese Lichtenstein, *Image Building: How Photography Transforms Architecture* (New York: Parrish Art Museum and DelMonico Books/Prestel, 2018).

29 Dreller, "Curtained Walls, Architectural Photography, the Farnsworth House and the Opaque Discourse of Transparency," pp. 22–40. Regarding Mies's approach prior to arriving in Chicago see Claire Zimmerman, "Modernism, Media, Abstraction: Mies van der Rohe's Photographic Architecture in Barcelona and Brno (1927–1931)" (PhD diss., The City University of New York, 2005), p. 44.

30 William C. Hedrich, *Oral History of William C. Hedrich/Interviewed by Betty J. Blum. Compiled under the Auspices of the Chicago Architects Oral History Project, the Ernest R. Graham Study Center for Architectural Drawings, Department of Architecture, the Art Institute of Chicago*, rev. 3d. (Chicago: Art Institute of Chicago, 2006), p. 124. For a historical overview of Hedrich Blessing see Robert A. Sobieszek, ed., *The Architectural Photography of Hedrich-Blessing* (New York: Holt, Rinehart and Winston, 1984); Tony Hiss and Timothy Samuelson, *Building Images: Seventy Years of Photography at Hedrich Blessing* (San Francisco: Chronicle Books, 2000).

31 Julius Shulman encouraged architects to be involved with the photography of their buildings. See Julius Shulman, *Photographing Architecture and Interiors* (New York: Whitney Library of Design, 1962).

32 In addition to *Le Baiser/The Kiss* (1999), Manglano-Ovalle also produced *Climate* (2000) and *Alltagszeit [In Ordinary Time]* (2000). Manglano-Ovalle has continued his exploration of Mies with his *The Krefeld Suite* (2005) and *Gravity is a Force to be Reckoned With* (2009). See Martin Hentschel, ed., *Iñigo Manglano-Ovalle: The Krefeld Suite* (Bielefeld: Kerber Verlag, 2005) and *Iñigo Manglano-Ovalle, Gravity is a Force to be Reckoned With* (North Adams, MA: Mass MoCA, 2010).

33 The recurring theme of cleaning, whether with a squeegee, mop, or vacuum cleaner, became a way of letting the everyday into modernism since a series of Alan Dunn cartoons appeared in *Architectural Record*: December 1947 (p. 7), September 1952 (p. 17), October 1958 (p. 25). See also Bêka and Lemoîne's film *Koolhaas Houselife* (2008) in which the daily life of a single-family house in Bordeaux designed by REM/OMA (1998) is seen through the eyes of the housekeeper, Guadalupe Acedo.

34 To a certain extent, even if not with the same critical attitude, the recent embrace of the everyday in architectural photography that tends to show both the heroic and less-heroic aspects of the built environment over time shares certain similarities with the protagonists of the New Topographics movement. See Robert Adams, ed., *New Topographics: Photographs of a Man-Altered Landscape* (Göttingen: Steidl, 2009).

35 Alan Dunn, *Architecture Observed* (New York: Architectural Record Books, 1970), pp. 37 and 53 respectively. For a broader discussion on architectural cartoons, especially in the context of glass houses, see Gabriele Neri, *Caricature Architettoniche: Satira e Critica del Progetto Moderno* (Macerata, 2015), ch. 9. "La casa di vetro," pp. 133–48.

36 In the article entitled "The Threat to the Next America" published in the April 1953 issue of *House Beautiful* (pp. 126–30) the editor Elizabeth Gordon published a page with view of the Tugendhat House at the top and Le Corbusier's Villa Savoye at the bottom with the following caption: "The Cult of Austerity is the product of Mies van der Rohe's cold, barren design (above) and Le Corbusier's International Style (below). See Monica Penick, *Tastemaker: Elizabeth Gordon, House Beautiful, and the Postwar American Home* (New Haven: Yale University Press, 2017), in part. ch. 8, pp. 115–28.

37 See my "Modern Houses for Modern Living in Chicago," in Susan S. Benjamin and M. Sabatino, *Modern in the Middle: Chicago Houses 1929–1975* (New York: The Monacelli Press, 2020), pp. 10–37 and Monica Penick, Tastemaker, pp. 115–28. Elizabeth Gordon, "The Threat to the Next America," p. 129.

38 See Vittorio Pizzigoni, "Reflections on the Farnsworth House," in *My Farnsworth: Journey of Discovery of a House Built for Two*, eds. Orazio Carpenzano and Cherubino Gambardella (Macerata: Quodlibert, 2019), pp. 137–45. (Pizzigoni published two of Goldsmith's notes regarding winter temperatures. CCA, 32-005-18, envelope "Goldsmith notes on Farnsworth House construction").

39 On the pavilion and windows see Jean Starobinski and Richard Pevear, "Windows: From Rousseau to Baudelaire," *The Hudson Review* 40, no. 4 (Winter, 1988): 551–60. Penelope Curtis, *Patio and Pavilion: The Place of Sculpture in Modern Architecture* (London: Ridinghouse and The J. Paul Getty Trust, 2008); Peter Cachola Schmal, ed., *The Pavilion: Pleasure and Polemics in Architecture* (Ostfildern, Germany: Hatje Cantz Verlag, 2009); Anne Friedberg, *The Virtual Window: From Alberti to Microsoft* (Cambridge: The MIT Press, 2009); "Pavilion" in Therese O'Malley, *Keywords in American Landscape Design* (Washington DC: Center for Advanced Study in the Visual Arts, 2010), pp. 479–83; Caroline Constant, *The Modern Architectural Landscape* (Minneapolis and London: University of Minnesota Press, 2012); Maria Müller-Schareck, *Fresh Window: The Window in Art since Matisse and Duchamp* (Ostfildern: Hatje Cantz, 2012); Bruno Reichlin, "Stories of Windows," in *A Window on the World: From Dürer to Mondrian and Beyond* eds. Francesca Bernasconi, Marco Franciolli, Giovanni Iovane, and Sylvie Wuhrmann (Milan: Skira Editore S.p.A, 2012), pp. 278–91; Beatriz Colomina, "Beyond Pavilions: Architecture as a Machine to See," in *Dan Graham: Beyond* eds. Bennett Simpson and Chrissie Iles (Cambridge: MIT Press, 2009); Georges Teyssot, "Windows and Screens," in *A Topology of Everyday Constellations* (Cambridge: MIT Press, 2013), pp. 251–84; Miles David Samson, *Hut Pavilion Shrine: Architectural Archetypes in Mid-Century Modernism* (Farnham, Surrey; Burlington, VT: Ashgate, 2015); Therese O'Malley and Joachim Wolschke-Bulmahn, eds., *Modernism and Landscape Architecture, 1890–1940* (Washington DC: National Gallery of Art, 2015).

40 Christian Norberg-Schulz, "Ein Gespräch mit Mies van der Rohe" [A Talk with Mies van der Rohe], *Baukunst und Werkform* 11, no. 11 (September 1958): 615–16. Available in Fritz Neumeyer, *The Artless Word* (Cambridge: The MIT Press, 1991), p. 338. This excerpt is part of a complete collection of texts published as Vittorio Pizzigoni and Michelangelo Sabatino, eds., *Mies in His Own Words: Complete Writings, Speeches, and Interviews* (Berlin: DOM Publishers, 2024).

41 John Peter, "Conversation with Mies," in John Peter, *The Oral History of Modern Architecture: Interviews with the Greatest Architects of the Twentieth Century* (New York: Harry N. Abrams, 1994), pp. 154–73. Also available in Moisés Puente, ed., *Conversations with Mies van der Rohe* (New York, 2008), pp. 49–87.

42 Guidi's photograph (along with those by Richard Pare) are part of a *Photographic Portfolio* specifically commissioned to them for the exhibition and publication *Mies in America*. See Phyllis Lambert, ed., *Mies in America* (New York: Harry N. Abrams, Inc, Publishers, 2001), in part. pp. 522–63.

43 The addition of the screen porch is explained by the son of William Dunlap who oversaw their design and fabrication. See David W. Dunlap, "House Proud: Personal Visions; In a Glass Box, Secrets Are Hard to Keep," *The New York Times*, June 24, 1999, Section F, p. 1.

The Edith Farnsworth House: Groundwork, 1945–1972

Fox River bank near the
Edith Farnsworth House
site, likely photographed by
Edith Farnsworth, mid- to
late-1940s.

Chicago - The City Beautiful,
booklet published by Curt
Teich & Co., Chicago, c. 1943.

Greetings from the Beautiful
Fox River Valley-Northern Illi-
nois, postcard printed by Curt
Teich & Co., Chicago, 1951.

Beautiful Scene at Plano, Ill.

Beautiful Scene at Plano, Ill. postcard printed by E. C. Kropp Co., Milwaukee, c. 1920s.

Bird's Eye View, Plano, Kendall County, Illinois, published by J. J. Stoner, Madison. Wisc., 1882.

Aerial photograph taken for the USDA, August 3, 1939. The future house site lies adjacent to (east of) the Plano Bridge along the Fox River. Dr. Farnsworth purchased 9.53 acres of land from Col. McCormick on December 17, 1945.

Frank Ridgway, "Tribune Farm's Plan for 1936," illus. by W.H. Wisner, Edith Farnsworth House future "Garden" site next to N. 6 (alfalfa field) and Plano Bridge, *Chicago Sunday Tribune*, May 17, 1936.

Chicago Sunday Tribune
WORLD'S GREATEST NEWSPAPER
MAY 17, 1936

Tribune Farm's Plan for 1936

WOODLAND AND PASTURE
38 ACRES

① ④

CLOVER FOR PASTURE
25 ACRES

CORN
50 ACRES ②

WOODLAND AND PASTURE
MIXTURE-LESPEDEZA, KENTUCKY
BLUEGRASS, MEDIUM RED CLOVER
& TIMOTHY FOR PASTURE } 3 ACRES
2 ACRES

⑤

SPRING WHEAT
4 ACRES

WOODLAND PASTURE
5 ACRES

CORN
3 ACRES

⑨

③

TIMOTHY AND CLOVER FOR PASTURE
8 ACRES

OATS
85 ACRES

⑧

TIMOTHY, CLOVER & ALFALFA FOR PASTURE
45 ACRES ⑦

← TO PLANO

W O O D L A N D

ALFALFA FOR HAY
12 ACRES

⑥

GARDEN
PLANO BRIDGE

⑮ ⑫ CORN FOR SILAGE
7 ACRES ⑬

WOODLAND AND NATIVE BLUEGRASS FOR PASTURE
90 ACRES

WOODLAND AND NATIVE BLUEGRASS FOR PASTURE
110 ACRES ⑩

WOODLAND & NATIVE BLUEGRASS FOR PASTURE

⑭ CORN FOR SILAGE
6 ACRES

⑪

⑯

⑰ ALFALFA FOR HAY
10 ACRES AND

CORN FOR SILAGE AND SEED
10 ACRES ⑱

HOG PASTURE
10 ACRES

OATS SEEDED WITH MEDIUM RED CLOVER
12 ACRES

22 SPECIAL ALFALFA STRAINS
5 ACRES

OATS
65 ACRES

⑲

Field Plan of
Experimental Farm
Near Yorkville, Ill.

ALFALFA FOR HAY
25 ACRES

⑳
35 ACRES
CORN

OATS SEEDED WITH MEDIUM RED CLOVER
50 ACRES

ALFALFA FOR HAY
20 ACRES

CLOVER FOR HAY
20 ACRES

SOY BEANS
30 ACRES

CORN

CORN
150 ACRES

②③ CORN
45 ACRES

②④ OATS
50 ACRES

②⑤
25 ACRES

②⑥

②① CORN
20 ACRES

②②

②⑦ CORN
80 ACRES

CORN
50 ACRES

LEGEND
FARM BOUNDARY LINES ——
FIELD BOUNDARY LINES -·-·-
FIELD DIVISION LINES - - - -
FIELD IDENTIFICATION NO. ①

CROPS
CORN | ALFALFA | SOY BEANS | OATS | OATS WITH CLOVER | CLOVER
TIMOTHY, CLOVER & ALFALFA | BLUEGRASS PASTURE | WOODLAND | TOTAL ACREAGE IN FIELDS 1,265

By
FRANK RIDGWAY

Tribune experimental farms are entering their third year of conducting tests and searching for new and superior crops, breeds of animals, and profitable methods and practices in the production of live stock and feeds.

Managers of the two farms—one of 1,332 acres near Plano and Yorkville, Ill., and the other of 1,000 acres near Wheaton, Ill.—again are combining their efforts in crop adaptation tests. The general plan followed is to first try out rare and unusual crops on a small scale at the Wheaton farm. Then crops that show promise in preliminary tests are grown on a field basis at the Yorkville farm.

Today the Yorkville farm manager announces his 1936 cropping plans, calling for the production of 1,265 acres in field and pasture crops—corn, [Continued on page eight.]

Historic single-lane Plano Bridge (c. 1897, demolished), likely photographed by Edith Farnsworth, mid- to late-1940s.

Fox River bank, likely photographed by Edith Farnsworth,
mid- to late-1940s.

View of Fox River bank looking north into Tribune Experimental Farm (alfalfa field), likely photographed by Edith Farnsworth, mid- to late-1940s.

View from the future
site of Edith Farnsworth
House looking east toward
Tribune Experimental Farm,
likely photographed by
Edith Farnsworth, mid- to
late-1940s.

PHONE DELAWARE 1059

MAR 1 1946

EDITH B. FARNSWORTH, M. D.

700 NORTH MICHIGAN AVENUE

CHICAGO 11

February 27,1946

Mr. L. Mies Van der Rohe
200 East Superior
Chicago, Illinois

Dear Mies,

The project which I mentioned to you the other
evening concerns the Fox River in Kendall County
and adjoining counties. An account in the local
newspaper of some weeks ago spoke of "improve-
emnts" of the river valley. Local rumor has it
that dams will be constructed which would raise
the level of the river. I do not know what basis
these rumors might have, but I believe it would
be wise if you were to write directly to Governor
Green in Springfield since, if damming the river
were actually comtemplated, we would undoubtedly
be unfavorably affected.

Sincerely yours,

Edith

EBF/fs

Opposite Typewritten letter from Edith to Mies following an early conversation concerning the commission for the house, February 27, 1946.

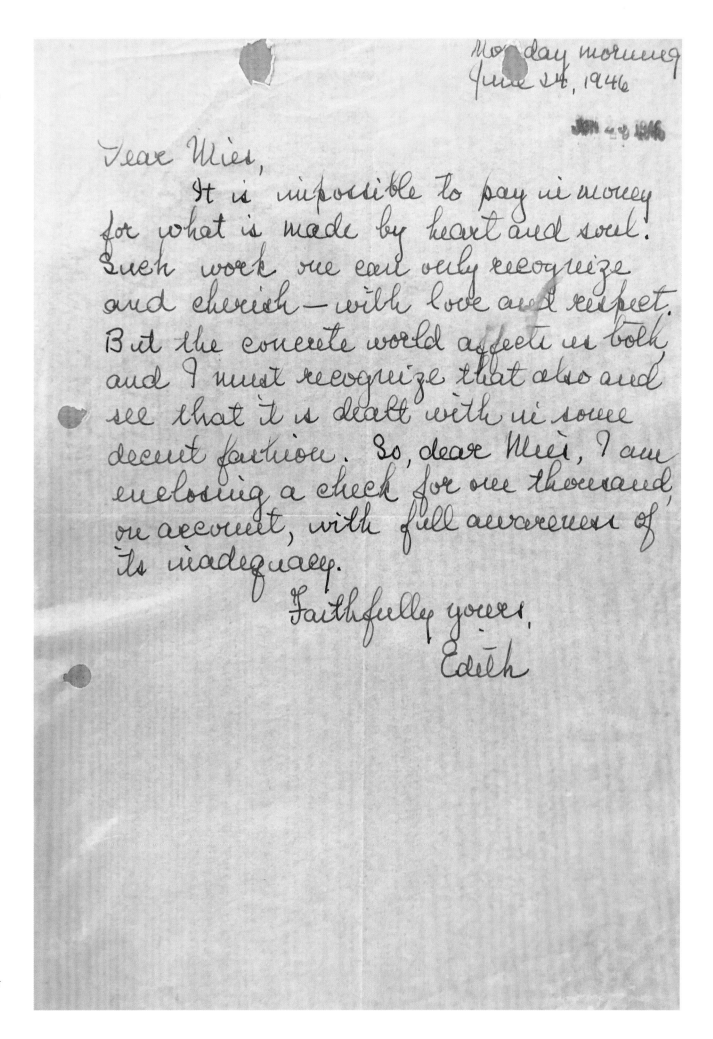

Monday morning
June 24, 1946

JUN 28 1946

Dear Mies,

It is impossible to pay in money for what is made by heart and soul! Such work one can only recognize and cherish — with love and respect. But the concrete world affects us both, and I must recognize that also and see that it is dealt with in some decent fashion. So, dear Mies, I am enclosing a check for one thousand, on account, with full awareness of its inadequacy.

Faithfully yours,

Edith

This Page Handwritten letter by Edith with retainer fee to Mies, Monday, June 24, 1946.

APPLICATION
For a Kendall County Zoning Permit

To the COUNTY SUPERINTENDENT OF HIGHWAYS,

COURT HOUSE, YORKVILLE, ILLINOIS.

Application is hereby made, and $2.00 fee enclosed, for a zoning permit involving the premises legally described as follows:

THAT PART OF THE SOUTH ½ OF SECTION 34 TOWNSHIP 37 NORTH, RANGE 6, EAST OF THE THIRD PRINCIPAL MERIDIAN, DESCRIBED AS FOLLOWS:

COMMENCING IN THE CENTER OF FOX RIVER ROAD TO A POINT 14 CHAINS SOUTH FROM THE CENTER OF SAID SECTION 34, RUNNING THENCE EAST ALONG THE CENTER OF SAID ROAD 236.13 FEET; THENCE SOUTH ALONG A LINE PARALLEL WITH THE NORTH AND SOUTH CENTERLINE OF SAID SECTION 34, 582.61 FEET TO THE NORTH BANK OF THE FOX RIVER, THENCE WESTERLY ALONG THE NORTH BANK OF THE FOX RIVER TO THE CENTER OF THE PLANO-MILBROOK ROAD; THENCE NORTHERLY ALONG THE CENTER OF SAID PLANO-MILBROOK ROAD TO WHERE THE SAME INTERSECTS THE CENTERLINE OF SAID FOX RIVER ROAD; THENCE EASTERLY ALONG THE CENTER OF SAID FOX RIVER ROAD TO THE PLACE OF BEGINNING; ALL IN THE COUNTY OF KENDALL AND STATE OF ILLINOIS.

The dimensions of the lot-tract of land-building plot, the exact location of all existing and proposed buildings, structures and highways and such other information as may be required by the enforcing officer, are shown on the drawing marked "A" attached to and made a part of this application.

The proposed uses of the above premises and its buildings and structures are: RESIDENCE

The estimated cost of the proposed improvements are $ 60,000.00 .

The contractor or builder is (name) CARL FREUND (address) ALGONQUIN, ILL

I hereby declare that the above and attached information is correct, and agree, in consideration of and upon issuance of a zoning permit, to do or allow to be done only such work as herewith applied for, and that such premises and its existing and proposed buildings and structures shall be used or allowed to be used for only such purposes as are set forth above or other uses permitted in the RESIDENCE district.

Owner
~~Lessee~~   DR. EDITH B. FARNSWORTH

Address 198 E ONTARIO Phone SU 7-8809
         CHICAGO, ILL

Signed by Ludwig Mies van der Rohe
LUDWIG MIES VAN DER ROHE
Address 37 S. WABASH AVE Phone ST 2-8388
         CHICAGO
Who hereby declares that he has been duly authorized by the Owner-~~Lessee~~ to make the above application and agreement.

Dated Oct 17 , 19 49

Drawing "A"

Part of zoning application of _DR. EDITH B. FARNSWORTH_ dated __OCT 17__, 19_49_
The dimensions of the lot or tract of land, the exact location of all existing and proposed buildings and structures, dimensions, distances to center of road and to property or tract lines and buildings within 10 feet of property lines are shown on the drawing below. Existing buildings and structures are marked "X." Proposed buildings and structures are marked "P".

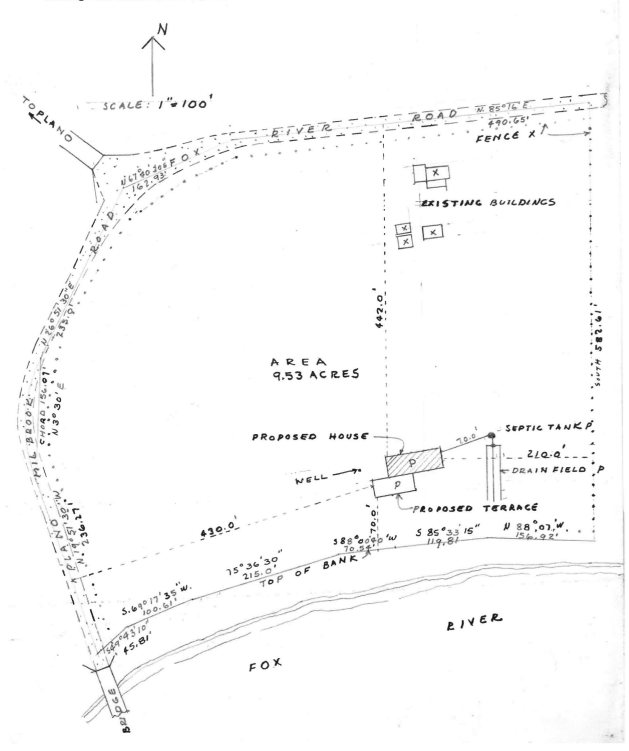

Kendall County Zoning Permit, Drawing "A" with proposed house and existing buildings that were later demolished, Oct. 17, 1949.

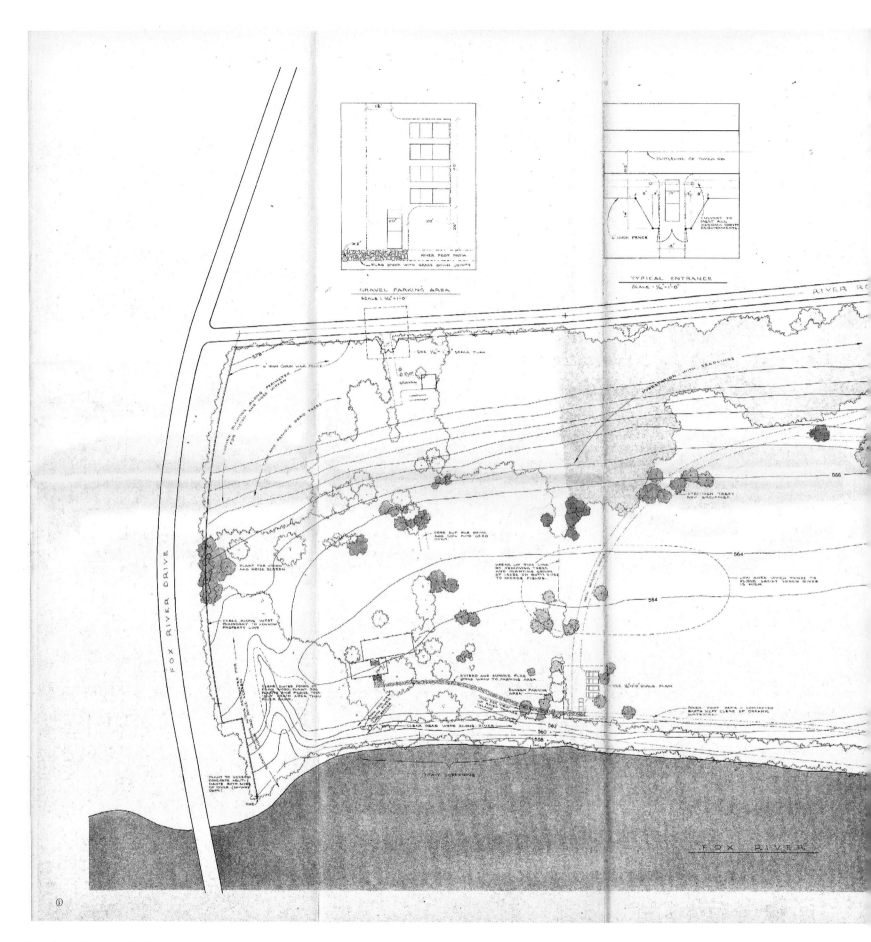

Palumbo-era "Proposed Planting
Partial Plan," with modified Fox
River Drive and all three parcels
previously purchased by Edith
Farnsworth, Office of Mies van
der Rohe, April 16, 1973.

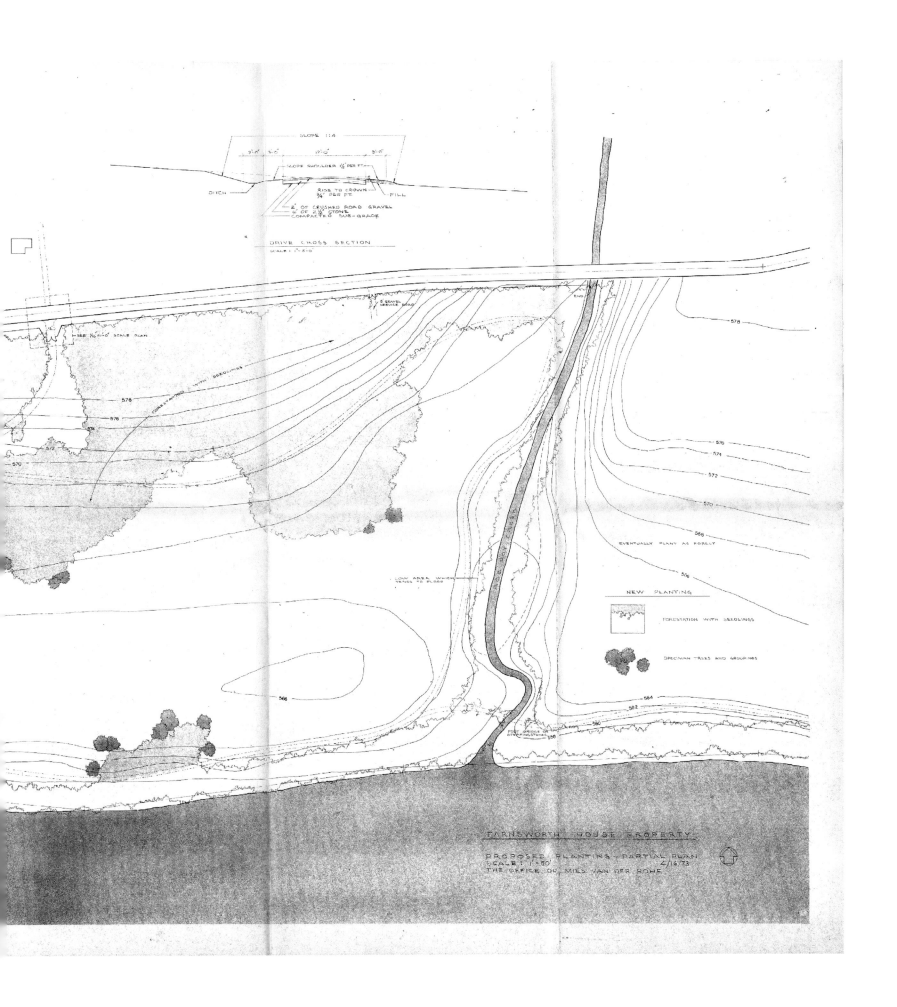

SLOPE 1:4

DITCH

SLOPE SHOULDER 1½" PER FT.
RISE TO CROWN
¾" PER FT.
FILL

2" OF CRUSHED ROAD GRAVEL
6" OF 2½" STONE
COMPACTED SUB-GRADE

DRIVE CROSS SECTION
SCALE: 1"=5'-0"

FARNSWORTH HOUSE PROPERTY

PROPOSED PLANTING - PARTIAL PLAN
SCALE: 1"=50'   4/16/73
THE OFFICE OF MIES VAN DER ROHE

NEW PLANTING

FORESTATION WITH SEEDLINGS

SPECIMAN TREES AND GROUPINGS

EVENTUALLY PLANT AS FOREST

LOW AREA WHICH
TENDS TO FLOOD

FOOT BRIDGE OR
STEPPING STONES

MoMA presentation model of Edith Farnsworth House with screened porch with trees and without lower terrace steps, no longer extant, photographed by Hedrich Blessing, c. 1947.

Early study model without trees and with lower terrace steps, no longer extant, photographed by Y.C. Wong, mid-1940s.

The Edith Farnsworth House

From detailed recollections shared by Myron Goldsmith to Betty Blum and recorded in the Chicago Architects Oral History Project (1990/2001), it is clear that Mies was deeply committed to the design and realization of the Edith Farnsworth House. However, he also relied on teamwork in addition to Goldsmith, who superintended the on-site building, a handful of employees—all IIT graduates Alfred Caldwell, Bruno Conterato, Edward A. Duckett, William (Bill) E. Dunlap, R. Ogden Hannaford, Gene Summers, and Y. C. Wong—and local builders such as Carl Freund assisted in various capacities throughout the extended process. These employees occasionally photographed the design process, including rarely seen models, and construction progress across the seasons. Taken together, these informal photos reveal the careful implementation of Mies's lofty and sometimes inscrutable vision.

Betty Blum There were some brilliant buildings done while you were there. For instance, the Farnsworth house. It's my understanding that Mies did a small model and a watercolor for that house. Then it sort of sat unattended for a while, apparently not ready to begin. When he was ready to begin, he asked you to make the working drawings. Would you talk about that project?

Myron Goldsmith There isn't any mystery I think in all this or any special significance. Let me put it differently, when I came into the office in 1946, that watercolor already existed. He had done it, not very long before. Over the years until we started again on it in the 1950s, we saw much of Dr. Farnsworth. She would come into the office and there would be numerous picnics out to the site. Why Mies never started on it again I'm not quite sure, because the building that was finally started on was as close to the original concept as possible. I'm not quite sure why they never started, maybe nobody was in a hurry. Finally it was decided to go ahead with it. I was put in charge of it in the office. I did the structural engineering on it. Mies followed it very closely. Other people worked on the drawings.

Blum Who else worked on the drawings with you?

Goldsmith I remember I think Bill Dunlap developed the moveable windows on the end. There were quite a number of drawings—I can't remember who else worked on the drawings, whether it was Y. C. Wong who worked on it. Finally we built, and Mies did something very unusual, we did all the drawings in the office, all the engineering. There was a consulting structural engineer, Bill Goodman, who did the heat and ventilating. We acted as the general contractor in the office.

Blum You were clerk of the works?

Goldsmith I think more than that. I think the clerk of the works was beneath what I was. I superintended the building on the site, checked the engineering drawings, actually got the bids, did everything for the contracts. I ordered stuff that had to be ordered for the house.

Blum Is it fair to say that Mies designed the building and then it was up to you and the others in the office, primarily you, to see to its execution?

Goldsmith Oh no. There is no other building in the American work that Mies followed so closely. He examined every visible detail. He told us how he wanted the windows detailed. He personally went to the plywood warehouse to pick the panels for the primavera panels. When the travertine came he was on the site and looked at every piece. If they were different quality than what was first quality, what was second quality went into the corners and into unimportant places, and what was to be discarded. He absolutely enjoyed it, was fascinated by it, followed everything. When the steel was almost erected he came out and squinted along the beams. I think once he said, "Goldsmith, this corner is low, fix it." I think it was the cantilever corner on the terrace.

Blum So he was very much involved, beyond the design stage

Goldsmith Oh, yeah. When I got the prices together I gave them to Mies and we discussed them. I think he had great fun with this. I think Dr. Farnsworth said, "Mies, build it as if you were building your own house." The understanding was that she would let him use it sometimes. I think that was the spirit of the whole thing.

Alfred Caldwell also shared his recollections about Edith and the Farnsworth House with Betty Blum, recorded in the Chicago Architects Oral History Project (1987/2001).

Blum Did you work in Mies's Office?

Caldwell No. I did it at home. One time I worked part of one summer. Dr. Farnsworth, Mies, and I met many times. She called me up one time and she said, "Caldwell, how can I get Mies to do my house? Every year it's postponed by Mies, he says he's too busy." She is the same woman that talked about Mies so badly. She said, "That man, I can't get him to do anything, I love the house, I want it. He keeps putting it off. Will you talk to him about it?" I did.

I said to Mies, "Why don't you do the Farnsworth house? She called me up and she said I should talk to you about it." He said, "Ya, we have a lot of work and I can't get my mind on it because I got so much work. There is nobody in my office who can draw that plan, nobody can do the actual drawing. If I had somebody to do it, I would do it." I said, "All right, I'll do it, the summer's coming on." He said, "Fine." So we started. I spent two or three weeks and Mies was busy on other things. I drew as much as I could. With something so personal for Mies one can only go so far. The big trouble with Mies was to find out what he wanted. Everybody wanted to give him what he wanted, but he wouldn't tell you what he wanted.

Bruno Conterato

Presentation model with screened porch, photographed in the Mies van der Rohe Office, May 1, 1950.

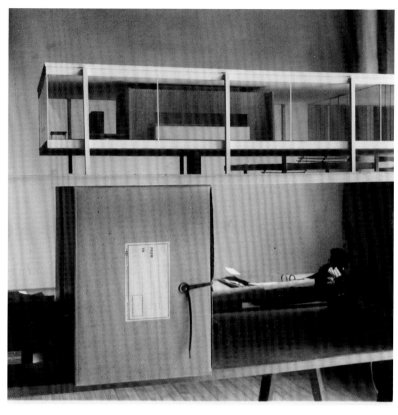

Presentation model with the galley kitchen and primavera core visible, photographed in the Mies van der Rohe Office, May 1, 1950.

Interior of the house under construction, May 29, 1950.

The plumbing in center core in process of being installed, May 29, 1950.

The house under construction with white structural steel frame awaiting the installation of single-pane polished plate glass, seen from meadow, May 29, 1950.

Edith Farnsworth House under construction close-up, May 29, 1950.

Under construction with single-pane polished plate glass installed, fall 1950.

Mies (left) with cigar in hand, on terrace steps visiting during construction, fall 1950.

William E. Dunlap

Under construction with steel frames before being painted (original photographic print dated but not signed), March 1950.

Beth I. Dunlap and Myron Goldsmith standing on unfinished lower terrace, spring 1950.

Opposite Page Contact sheet with sequence of construction views (photo on right-hand column second row shows existing farm buildings subsequently demolished), spring 1950.

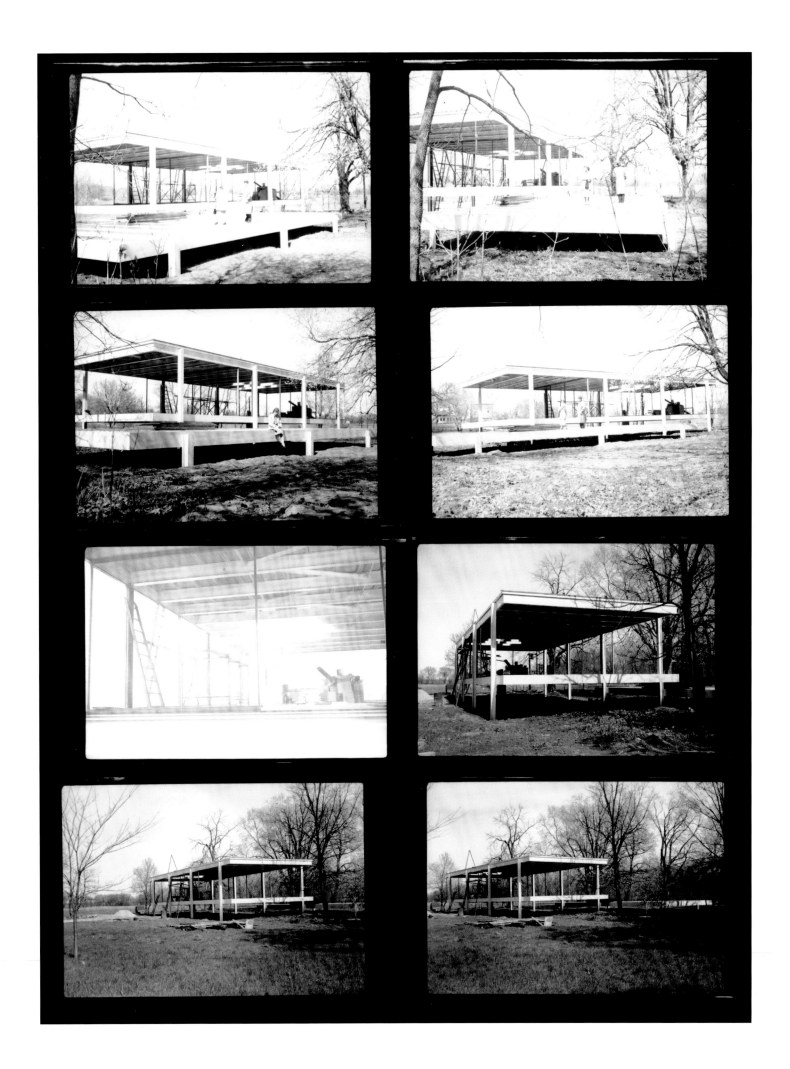

Mies visits construction site with project supervisor Myron Goldsmith and Y.C. Wong, fall 1950.

Construction view with painted steel frame and screen porch mullion mock-up (left), summer 1950.

Construction views with
unpainted steel stops for
plate glass, summer 1950.

The Edith Farnsworth House

Opposite top Mies visiting construction site with project supervisor Myron Goldsmith and Y.C. Wong, fall 1950.

Opposite bottom The completed house with curtains installed and garden in bloom, summer 1951.

This page top Contractor/builder visit, possibly Carl Freund on steps, fall 1950.

This page bottom Lower terrace steps during construction, fall 1950.

Mies inspects a travertine slab while workers install another slab. Installation of hot water radiant floor heating system using an oil-fired boiler, summer 1950.

Grouting travertine floor, installing travertine core wall between living area and bathroom, with Mies on site, summer 1950.

Groundwork, 1945–1972

Screened porch
with rotating-hinge
painted monel
metal-frame doors
under construction
with farm buildings in
the background (right),
spring 1952.

63

THE MAGAZINE OF BUILDING

HOUSES ISSUE

The Edith Farnsworth House

Opposite *Architectural Forum*, October 1951 (Houses Issue), cover photograph by Bill Hedrich/Hedrich Blessing.

Top First post-completion photographic overview of the Edith Farnsworth House by Chicago-based Hedrich Blessing in preparation of publication in *Architectural Forum*, October 1951.

Living room with curtains and midcentury furniture (set of Gugliemo Pecorini chairs and Angelo Lelli Triennale floor lamp), summer 1951.

Bottom Left House, photographed by Bill Hedrich, summer 1951.

Bottom Right House, photographed by George H. Steuer, summer 1951.

Opposite House with black sugar maple, photographed by Bill Hedrich, fall 1951.

This page The house from meadow, photographed by Bill Hedrich, fall 1951.

Groundwork, 1945–1972

View of living room with midcentury furniture (Jens Risom's Model 650 and Angelo Lelli's Triennale floor lamp), with Edith's dog at entrance, summer 1951. Photographs on this page and opposite by Bill Hedrich.

View of entrance with two sets of Gugliemo Pecorini dining chairs with curtains installed, summer 1951.

View of galley kitchen with stainless steel counter by Elkay Mfg. Co, and farmland in the background, summer 1951.

View of primavera core with fireplace and makeshift daybed, with Edith's dog at entrance, summer 1951.

House Beautiful

APRIL · 50c

How you will live in the <u>next</u> America

FEBRUARY, 1952

House & Garden

THE AMERICAN IDEA, 1952

WELL-PLANNED HOUSES   LIVABLE KITCHENS   EASY-UPKEEP GARDENS

THE DU PONT MUSEUM

50 Cents

House & Garden,
February 1952,
with the included
feature about Edith
Farnsworth House
described as "A
glass shell that
'floats' in the air."

"Travertine terrace for outdoor living also serves entrance" (original caption), photographed before the installation of porch screen, by André Kertész for *House & Garden*, February 1952.

"Double glass doors at front entrance are as simple and unpretentious as house" (original caption), photographed by André Kertész for *House & Garden*, February 1952.

Chicago Daily Tribune
THE WORLD'S GREATEST NEWSPAPER
Neighborhood Section

Thursday, June 21, 1951   Part 5—Page 1   S

I. I. T. Architect Gives Chicago Another 'First'—Glass and Steel Towers of Homes

---

LINKS SURVIVE 40 ROUGH YEARS AT MARQUETTE

Park Fairways Beckon to Pros and Duffers

BY GORDON WINKLER

Supervisors of the golf course at Marquette park, Marquette rd. and Kedzie ave., have had their nicks and slices during the 40 year history of the course but always have managed to get out of the rough.

Everything is as well as can be expected, commented the present supervisor after the original 9 hole course, which had been opened Memorial day of 1912, had been extended to 18 holes.

Crawfish Holes a Problem

His opinion was a bit off the fairway. The grounds were littered with crawfish holes which called a devilish recovery shot from a ball rolled into one.

Because of inadequate drainage the course was reduced after a year to 18 well laid out swamps. It was unplayable for weeks. To add to troubles the golf shelter, erected in 1912, burned to the ground.

In 1917 a new shelter was erected on the Kedzie av. entrance to the park near 67th st. at a cost of more than $50,000. A concrete building, 250 by 113 feet, it included locker rooms, showers, a lunch room. A cinder drive to the building was surfaced.

Divots Fall Everywhere

The course attracted a large number of players during the next years but because many of them were beginners, upkeep became a staggering financial problem. Unfilled divots were found everywhere.

All those difficulties were remedied in 1923 when the South park board decided to abandon the 9 hole course to make way for a lagoon. After the lagoon was completed a new course was built and opened May 22, 1926, with public officials attending the great fanfare.

Entirely on Island

The course was unique among municipal courses in that it was located entirely on an island. Its setup always has been popular with small boys of the area. There were 10 official possibilities of a ball going into the water and retrieving business was lucrative.

This insular arrangement went along nicely until 1933 when the area was reduced to nine holes. It seemed that the city found it necessary to extend Kedzie av. thru the park. In 1936 adjustments on the course were completed and the present Marquette course was established.

Anyone for tennis?

America's first steel and glass apartment building of 26 stories completed at 860 Lake Shore dr., was designed by Ludwig Mies van der Rohe, well known modern architect. *(Story on page 6.)*

Gene Summers, a student at Illinois Institute of Technology until he received his master's degree in architecture, is one of a number of promising young architects starting their careers in Mies van der Rohe's office.
(TRIBUNE Photos by Russell V. Ramm)

KIWANIANS' PUMP TO SLAKE YOUNG CAMPERS' THIRST

The 200 boys and girls who will enjoy the facilities of Camp Hinge, near Michigan City, Ind., this summer will have the Kiwanis Club of South Chicago to thank for their fresh drinking water.

Steve Bubacz, 3104 E. 83d st., a member of the club and also of the Russell Square Community committee, a group of neighborhood residents and business men who support the camp, said the Kiwanians responded immediately when informed that the camp needed a new water pump and reservoir tank. The need had not even anticipated in the camp's budget.

The pump and an 80 gallon capacity tank, for drinking and cooking water, recently was presented to the committee by Charles Gaugl, 7625 Kingston av., president of the Kiwanis club, to Michael's Boys club, 3106 E. 91st st., which also is supported by the Russell Square Community committee. The equipment cost $175, Bubacz said.

FOUR SOUTH SIDERS GO TO CLEVELAND FOR 'Y' CONVENTION

Hyde Park Y. M. C. A., 1400 E. 53d st., has four youths as delegates at the International convention being held in Cleveland, O., today thru Sunday. The convention marks the 100th anniversary of the Y. M. C. A. movement in the United States.

Hyde Park delegates and the clubs they represent are Miss Susan Weitzel, 1501 E. 68th st., Sorelle Tri-Hi-Y; Miss Nina McMillan, 5011 Blackstone av., Calliope Tri-Hi-Y; James West, 1436 Marquette rd., Beta Hi-Y; and Dave Nakaya, 6321 Ingleside av., Alpha Hi-Y.

President Truman and Prime Minister St. Laurent of Canada

12 SOUTH SIDERS RECEIVE WESLEY NURSE DIPLOMAS

Twelve south and southwest side girls were among 99 student nurses awarded diplomas recently by the Wesley Memorial hospital school of nursing. The diplomas were presented by Dr. J. Roscoe Miller, president of Northwestern university, of which the hospital is an affiliate.

The graduating class included Mary Lou Byers, 8724 Wabash av.; Marilyn Christian, Harvey; Nancy Erickson, 9028 Ada st.; Mary Golos, 6532 S. Rockwell st.; Mary Galvin, 532 W. Marquette rd., and Lois Hemstra, Blue Island.

Also Haruc Kawano, 5723 Ellis av.; Ellen Kay, 8807 Ashland av.; Dolores Peterson, 8938 Union av.; Carol Warrington, 9536 Lowe av.; Waneta Wood, 9753 Maryland av.; and Betty Zimmerman, Harvey.

Hold Outing for Blind Sunday in Glen Ellyn

The annual outing for the blind sponsored by the Catholic Blind administration will be held Sun-

In his office at 37 S. Wabash av. Mies van der Rohe inspects model of glass house he designed which is now a family residence at Plano. The architect is known as "the friend of steel" and uses steel and glass primarily in many of his structures. He says the Chicago area and Florida are leading the way in modern architecture. He heads architecture department at Illinois Tech.

The chemistry building on the Illinois Tech campus, 33d and Federal sts., is one of the many purely functional buildings designed by Mies van der Rohe. Architect's biggest project is designing the 20 research, laboratory, office, and residence buildings on the campus.

The architect looks at plans for small homes to be constructed of glass and steel. Models of home units are on desk.

Beverly Sends Delegates to National Hi-Y Congress

Joan Hoeglund, 1652 W. 104th pl., and Richard Haynes, 9131 Damen av., are delegates to the sixth national Hi-Y congress at Cleveland, O., today to Sunday. From Sunday to Tuesday they will be at Oberlin college for other meetings.

Final Term Bell to Ring for Miss Lucy

(Picture on page 7.)

"Remember me, Miss Lucy, you taught me at Gresham."

"I think I remember your face, but I'm sorry I can't recall your name."

Such a conversation often has led to a renewed friendship for Miss Florence E. Lucy, 9206 May st., whose "second home" for the last 45 years has been Gresham school.

Last Class Tomorrow

"I think I have taught at least one person from every family in the area," said the retiring 2d grade teacher who will dismiss her last class tomorrow afternoon.

"When I meet people on the street I don't always remember who they are but the chances are good that they were in one of my classes," she said. "That is the greatest reward. I never tire of having people greet me with a smile and stop for a few minutes to talk about the old days."

Miss Lucy has no idea how many second generation pupils she has had "but there have been a great deal of them," she said. "Once a girl in the class said I taught her grandfather, but I don't think that is correct. At least I can't remember back that far."

Plans to Travel

Miss Lucy has been absent from her classes only once when she took a three week leave several years ago, at her father's death. "And I have never gotten around to taking a sabbatical," she added. Now she plans to travel and the first place will be Florida for a good rest.

Besides the smiles from former pupils, it does not take much to keep Miss Lucy happy. She speaks with pride of the Kimball hall concert given by pupils of her music class in 1933. And she thought it was fine when the Gresham PTA gave her a silver tea set at a special party recently.

COUPLES WED BY DR. COX TO RENEW VOWS

The Rev. Clinton C. Cox, pastor of Drexel Park Presbyterian church, 64th st. and Marshfield av., has invited the approximately 5,000 couples he has united in marriage during his 36 years of ministry on the south side—33 years of which have been spent at Drexel Park in a vow renewal service at 8 p. m. Sunday in the church.

Each couple will be given a souvenir and special gifts will be presented the couple married longest, the couple having the youngest child, and the couple traveling the farthest to attend the service.

There will be a special musical program and refreshments will be served.

South Shore Toastmasters to Get Charter Tuesday

South Shore Toastmasters club will receive its charter in the Toastmasters International at a banquet Tuesday evening at South Shore Y. M. C. A., 71st st. and Bennett av. Emmit Holmes, district governor of the parent group, will present the charter to Louis Eichenfeld, 2049 E. 68th st., the club's first president.

HALSTED, 79TH SHOPPERS GET PARKING RELIEF

Provide for 1,000 Cars at Five Lots

(Picture on page 6.)

Business men of the Auburn Park area have instituted a cooperative parking lot project which they hope will alleviate the parking pinch in the vicinity of 79th and Halsted sts. Four lots are open now and a fifth will open next week.

Michael A. Dwyer, executive secretary of the Auburn Park Chamber of Commerce, said parking area will be provided for almost 1,000 cars in the business district. The chamber has spent more than two years working on the project and studying the offstreet parking setups of other cities.

Put Cost at Million

"We found," Dwyer said, "that merchants in smaller cities can take their parking problems to their city governments, but in a city of Chicago's size this is almost impossible. So we decided that if anything was to be done we would have to do it ourselves."

The chamber has contracted with the Capitol theater for the daytime use of its parking areas. This lot has a total capacity of approximately 500 vehicles—at 82th and Halsted sts. These lots will be open to shoppers until 6 p. m. every day except Mondays and Thursdays when they will be open until 9 p. m.

Under the agreement the chamber will pay for an attendant at the lots during the hours they are in general use. Capitol theater patrons will be allowed to park at any time in all of the parking lots opened by the chamber for shoppers.

New Lot at 81st-Halsted

These include the 60 car capacity lot of the Mutual National bank at 79th st. and Union av., the chamber's present 60 car capacity lot at 7920 Emerald av., and a new lot at 81st and Halsted sts.

This new lot, leased from an estate, will have a capacity of about 300 cars, Dwyer said. Grading operations are expected to be completed in a week and lights will be installed. Attendants will be on duty during business hours in all lots and will give motorists checks to be stamped by merchants or the theater.

Dwyer said grading of the large area and installation of lighting on it and the other chamber lot will cost approximately $10,000. The funds have been contributed by the area merchants.

All Lots Insured

All the lots will be insured for personal liability and property damage, Dwyer said the chamber has not yet considered opening the lots to overnight parking by residents of the community because of the possible liability involved. He said he would ask the chamber to study the question.

Others who have been active in the project, Dwyer said, include August Van Daele, president of the chamber; Maurice Blackman, vice president; Albert Dykema, chairman of the chamber's parking committee, and Joseph Frank, a chamber director.

THE LIND SHOPS

WOMEN'S APPAREL
INDIVIDUALLY YOURS

SUMMER SALE

Starting Thursday, June 21, through
Saturday, June 23rd

"I.I.T. Architect Gives Chicago Another 'First'–Glass and Steel Towers of Homes," *Chicago Daily Tribune*, Thursday June 21, 1951, Part 5, Page 1.

Edith Farnsworth House
following 1954 flood with
basswood roll up blinds,
May 16, 1959.

View from meadow, shortly
after the removal of the
screened porch by new owner
Peter Palumbo, June 1972.

Edith Farnsworth with Beth I. Dunlap (right) on porch steps with dogs before the screens were installed, c. 1951.

Beth I. Dunlap at entrance with Edith and Mies in conversation on steps, c. 1951.

Beth I. Dunlap seated in midcentury slipper chair, summer 1951.

Screened porch with plants and midcentury furniture (Bruno Mathsson, Model 36, slipper chair, and Guglielmo Pecorini dining chair) photographed by Edward A. Duckett, early 1950s.

Living room looking toward wardrobe with traditional furniture and basswood roll-up blinds in the place of curtains, likely photographed by Edith Farnsworth, late-1960s.

Living room with traditional furniture, likely photographed by Edith Farnsworth, late-1960s.

Screened porch with view
out to meadow, likely
photographed by Edith
Farnsworth, mid-1950s.

View of primavera core with three Asian architectural fragments hanging on panels, likely photographed by Edith Farnsworth, mid-1950s.

West bathroom with shower and door to mechanical room, Crane Diana lavatory (sink) with Temple "Dial-ese" trim (controls and faucets), Crane toilet, photographed 2009.

East bathroom, Crane Oxford recess bathtub and Crane Diana lavatory (sink) with Temple "Dial-ese" trim (controls and faucet), Crane toilet, photographed 1997.

Beth I. Dunlap inside
the house seated in
midcentury slipper chair,
photographed by William E.
Dunlap, summer 1951.

Edith's friend Jenny Geer-
ing in daybed on a winter
day, likely photographed
by Edith Farnsworth, early
1950s.

Groundwork, 1945–1972

1951 GOOD DESIGN EXHIBITION

SPONSORED BY THE MUSEUM OF MODERN ART AND THE MERCHANDISE MART

DESIGNED BY FINN JUHL

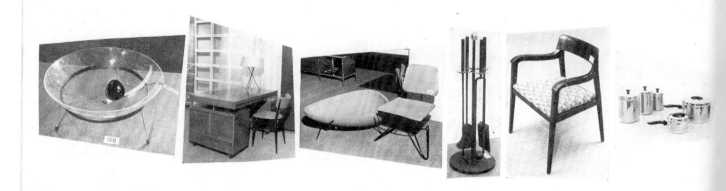

1951 *Good Design* exhibition, cosponsored by the Museum of Modern art and Chicago Merchandise Mart, with Franco Albini desk in lower right corner, *Arts & Architecture*, April 1951.

Sponsored jointly by the Museum of Modern Art, and The Merchandise Mart, the 1951 showing begins the second year of the "Good Design" exhibtion, which runs continuously at The Mart, with special selections on display each autumn at the Museum. Director of "Good Design" is Edgar Kaufman, Jr., of the Museum of Modern Art, who also serves as the chairman of the Selection Committee. Other members on the committee were: William Friedman from the Walker Art Center in Minneapolis and Hugh Lawson of Carson Pirie Scott & Co., Chicago.

Backgrounds and architectural installations for the new "Good Design" exhibition are the work of Finn Juhl, Danish architect and designer. Stressing architectural elements in partial partitions of glass or bamboo, and the use of bright colors, Mr. Juhl's settings have employed the use of sharp contrasts of spacious areas to adjoin more crowded portions.

Furniture has a major role in this year's selections, with outstanding design in new chairs of every type and more fine storage pieces and tables than were shown in 1950. Chairs range from the simplest metal frames with canvas seats and backs, to all-wood molded designs of walnut veneer, and a luxurious lounge chair with tapered metal legs, upholstered in a muted plaid. A simple birch chair has a curved spindle back shaped to provide maximum comfort for three sitting postures. Foam rubber upholstery or cushions is used with a black cast iron frame for one group and white lacquered steel for another.

The selected knock-down pieces are: a handsome Swedish-de-

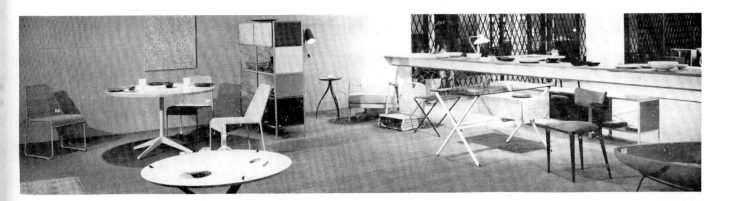

signed arm chair of birch, a casual chair with seat and back of laced cotton cord on a wooden frame, and four stacking stools with bright colored tops.

Table designs run from low-cost to luxury exhibits, including a magnificent oval-topped drop-leaf design in natural walnut to a knock-down coffee table of natural birch with black trim. Included is a circular table with top of gray and white plastic and a lazy susan center. Glass and metal combinations proved effective in a large round coffee table with black iron base utilizing variations of the practical triangular support and a top of clear heavy glass. Micarta and ebony are combined in another coffee table with a gray micarta used for the top. The "door" table, with the top a simple slab of oak set on tripod legs of chrome is surprisingly light in weight.

Housekeeping equipment, includes fine tableware, and a new line of silver flatware done in what is considered the first really contemporary design. One set of coordinated pottery and glassware makes use of a snow-glass for the tumblers and repeats this material in plates of various size, cups and saucers, to be used in combination with pottery pieces of a variety of colors.

Sectional cooking equipment makes a new appearance in a four burner cooking top and an "In-A-Wall" oven of stainless steel. There is a portable bar and portable buffet server, both composed of bright colored covered porcelain containers set in a tray-like frame of black wrought iron.

From Italy, India, England, Denmark, France, Finland, Sweden and Germany, foreign imports make noteworthy contributions to this year's "Good Design."

Edgar Kaufmann, Jr., at the *Good Design* exhibition, standing next to a Franco Albini steel desk (originally produced in 1928 and introduced to the US by Knoll in 1949).

Chicago Merchandise
Mart, *Good Design in
New Home Furnishings*,
designed by Charles and
Ray Eames, opened on
Monday, Jan. 16, 1950.

East elevation with two opened hopper windows for ventilation, required by Farnsworth, and historic Plano Bridge in background, likely photographed by Edith Farnsworth.

House site flooding while under construction, photograph by Hedrich Blessing, spring 1950.

Groundwork, 1945–1972

Index of Witnesses, Ludwig Mies van der Rohe (Plaintiff) vs. Edith B. Farnsworth (Defendant), May 23–July 3, 1952. The trial ended with Special Master in Chancery Jerome Nelson's recommendation that Edith pay Mies, after which she countersued. [*Chicago Tribune*, June 9, 1953, Part 1, Page 20F]

Felix Bonnet
  (Dep. -
    Bohrer) July 2, 1952 Vol. 24 .... *3390-3397*

Wallace Evans
  Direct   June 26, 1952 Vol. 20 2755-2763
  Cross   June 26, 1952 Vol. 20 2764-2766
  Redirect June 26, 1952 Vol. 20 2767

Dr. Edith B. Farnsworth
  Direct   June 25, 1952 Vol. 19 2610-2650
  Direct   June 26, 1952 Vol. 20 2652-2669
  Cross   June 26, 1952 Vol. 20 2669-2686
  Redirect June 26, 1952 Vol. 20 2686-2694
  Recross   June 26, 1952 Vol. 20 2694-2696

John P. Francis
  Direct   June 27, 1952 Vol. 21 2880-2940
  Cross   June 27, 1952 Vol. 21 2940-2958
  Redirect June 27, 1952 Vol. 21 2958-2964
  Recross   June 27, 1952 Vol. 21 2964-2965
  Redirect June 27, 1952 Vol. 21 2966-2969

Lillian J. Francis
  Direct   June 27, 1952 Vol. 21 2859-2871
  Cross   June 27, 1952 Vol. 21 2872-2875
  Redirect June 27, 1952 Vol. 21 2876-2879

Myron Goldsmith
  (Dep. -
    Bohrer) July 2, 1952 Vol.24 .... *3398-3403*
                                            3424-3437

Warren Henning
  Direct   June 26, 1952 Vol. 20 2768-2775

Carl Linder
  Direct   July 1, 1952 Vol. 23 3222-3253
  Cross   July 1, 1952 Vol. 23 3254-3286
  Redirect July 1, 1952 Vol. 23 3286-3300
  Recross   July 1, 1952 Vol. 23 3300-3302

Georgia Lingafelt
  Direct   June 26, 1952 Vol. 20 2745-2749
  Cross   June 26, 1952 Vol. 20 2749-2752
  Redirect June 26, 1952 Vol. 20 2752-2754

Clifford McKirgan
  Direct   June 26, 1952 Vol. 20 2740-2744
  Cross   June 26, 1952 Vol. 20 2744

Ludwig Mies van der Rohe
  (Sec. 60)-
    Cross   June 26, 1952 Vol. 20 2697-2739
  (Sec. 60)-
    Cross   June 26, 1952 Vol. 20 2776-2827
  (Dep. -
    Bohrer) June 27, 1952 Vol. 21 2829-2856
  (Dep. -
    Bohrer) July 2, 1952 Vol. 24 .... *3403-3423*
  Recross   July 2, 1952 Vol. 24 .... *3439-3441*

Mrs. Carl Reguse
  Direct   July 2, 1952 Vol. 24 .... *3381-3389*

Harry Theisen
  Direct   July 1, 1952 Vol. 23 3303-3334
  Cross   July 1, 1952 Vol. 23 3345-3357
  Redirect July 1, 1952 Vol. 23 3357-3367
  Recross   July 1, 1952 Vol. 23 3367-3369
  Redirect July 1, 1952 Vol. 23 3369-3371
  Recross   July 1, 1952 Vol. 23 3371-3374
  Redirect July 1, 1952 Vol. 23 3374-3375
  Recross   July 1, 1952 Vol. 23 3375

Defendant's Exhibits Introduced:
        June 24, 1952 Vol. 18 2478-2489,
                                             2495-2500
        June 27, 1952 Vol. 21 .... 2857, 2936-2937
        July 1, 1952 Vol. 23 3339-3343,
                                             3376-3379
                      Vol. 24 (?)   *3437-8, 3441-4*

Defense Rested   Vol. 24 .... *3445*

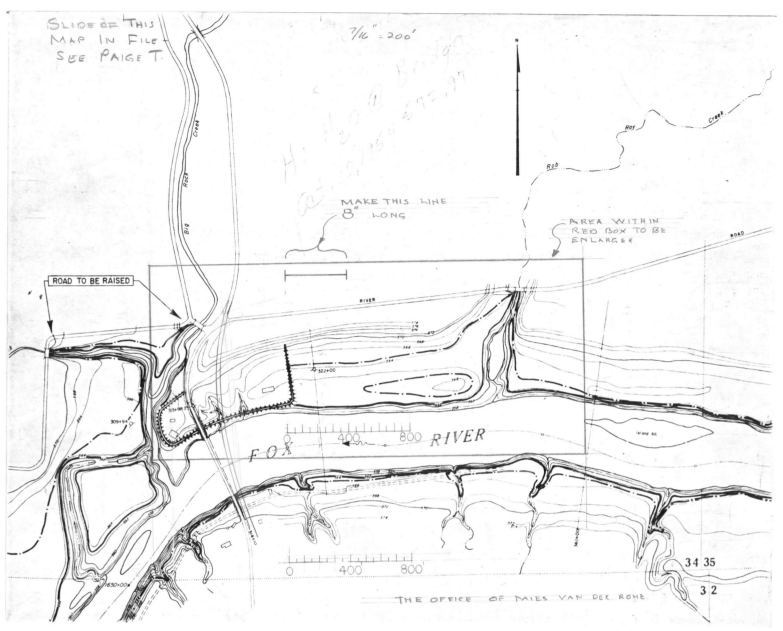

Plan with historic Plano Bridge (bottom left) and new Fox River Drive Bridge (overlaid in red) whose construction resulted in the appropriation, by way of eminent domain, of a part of Farnsworth's original property. Note annotation regarding first post-construction flood: "Hi H2O @ Bridge. Oct, 10, 1954 5.72,97." Office of Mies van der Rohe, n. d., early 1970s.

Historic Pratt truss Plano Bridge with horse-drawn carriage, likely photographed in the late nineteenth century.

Chicago Tribune article by Ann McFeatters, "Fox River Bridge Issue to Be Settled by Court," Thursday, May 2, 1968, 2 – Section 3A, W. ("In an attempt to allow exploration of the ancient settlements, Dr. Farnsworth offered the two acres condemned by the county to the Illinois Department of Conservation.")

Protest letter addressed to the Kendall County Board of Supervisors written by Phyllis Lambert, October 20, 1967.

October 20, 1967

The Kendall County Board of Supervisors
Yorkville, Illinois

Gentlemen:

Pollution of towns and the countryside and large tracts of subdivision developments spread every day. Not only is this loss of natural resources a loss of our heritage, visually and ecologically, but, also, economically. Programs requiring vast sums of money have been proposed to rectify these conditions. How, then, can we continue this devastation?

The Farnsworth House in Plano, Illinois is a clear illustration of lack of planning and foresight. This area around the Fox River is one of the loveliest in the state. An old bridge crosses the river near the Farnsworth House, a house that is one of the masterpieces of architecture in the world. To turn this small road into a highway would render this area useless for habitation and leave the Farnsworth House stranded, a relic of a very recent past.

It seems hard to understand that our society overweighs real values with pseudo technological efficiency. The Farnsworth House is an expression of our technology at its highest level. A multi-lane highway in close proximity to it would be an expression of the brutality of technology.

Sincerely,

Phyllis Lambert

Fox River Bridge Issue to Be Settled by Court

BY ANN McFEATTERS

Indians, long since gone from the area, an architectural landmark, and a new $400,000 bridge are the ingredients of a controversy in Kendall county, southwest of Chicago.

The principals include county highway officials, the superintendent of the Illinois department of conservation, and a lady doctor with an interest in archaeology. The argument began more than a year ago and courts from Yorkville to Washington may be involved before the issue is settled.

The Fox River road bridge, built 83 years ago, is only one lane wide. Everyone agrees that it must be replaced. The question is where to put the new bridge.

Eliminate Sharp Curve

The Kendall county department of highways wants to eliminate a dangerously sharp s-curve north of the present bridge, bringing it into line with the state-set standard for curve radius. The easiest way to do this, they decided, was to move the location of the bridge further to the east. An engineering survey of the proposed site was made and the county moved to obtain the necessary land.

County residents opposed to the new location suggested two alternatives. One involved a site west of the present structure, the other rebuilding the bridge at the same location. Proponents of the latter felt that the troublesome s-curve could be removed by other means.

On Sept. 1, 1967, the county filed a condemnation suit against three property owners. The strongest opposition has come from Dr. Edith Farnsworth who is semi-retired from her north-side practice.

Owned by Col. McCormick

Dr. Farnsworth, an assistant professor of medicine at Northwestern university and on the staff of Passavant hospital, bought her property in 1943. It had been owned by Col. Robert R. McCormick, late editor and publisher of the TRIBUNE. She owns 60 acres. The county has condemned slightly more than two acres.

Mies van der Rohe, a noted architect, was commissioned by Dr. Farnsworth to design her house. The low, glass-walled building is considered a prime example of his style.

The privacy and quiet of her home will be shattered by the new bridge, Dr. Farnsworth said. "It will pass within 180 feet of the house. Just think, any of these Hell's Angels who seem to be riding around could shoot right into the house—it's all glass."

But Dr. Farnsworth, who has had an amateur interest in archaeology for many years, also objects to the new bridge because it will destroy pre-historic Indian sites which have been found on her land. After the new bridge location had been set, a local conservation officer mentioned that Indian relics had been found on her property. Concerned, Dr. Farnsworth enlisted the aid of several archaeologists from Illinois Institute of Technology and Northwestern university. Experts confirmed that the sites are definitely pre-historic, probably at least 2,000 years old and "very significant." No sites were found on the other condemned properties.

Offered to State

In an attempt to allow ex-

gested that the county's hard line stemmed from financial causes. The new bridge, wherever it is built, will cost at least $400,000. In attempting to keep costs down, it is felt, the county decided to survey only one possible location—the one involving Dr. Farnsworth's land.

Ron Brandau, an assistant to Kendall county highway superintendent David Sharkey, emphasized the importance of replacing the present structure. He refused to comment on the legal aspects of the controversy. On suggestions to build the bridge elsewhere, he said, "this is settled, this is the site."

State conservation official Arnold Kugler said that the state

could not accept Dr. Farnsworth's offer because it was made after the county had filed its condemnation suit. "According to our legal authorities, the state cannot overrule the county in this matter." An expert on state law commented, "That means they don't want to overrule the county."

Told of Kugler's statement Dr. Farnsworth said, "This is very interesting. It is the first word I've had from the conservation people. And, you see the condemnation suit does not affect my right to transfer my own property." She also said that it did not affect her earlier decision to go to Springfield to see Superintendent Lodge, in person, to demand a reply.

Historic Sites Being Ruined, Professor Says

"Pre-historic sites are unreplenishable natural resources and they are being destroyed—without restriction—by industry, by residential building in the suburbs, and by the growth of the highway system," said Stewart Struever, Northwestern university anthropology professor and one of the most vocal defenders of Illinois' Indian heritage.

Member and past president of the Illinois Archaeological survey, Struever commented on the sites threatened by the proposed Fox River road bridge in Kendall county. He said the sites were left by the Hopewell Indians, whose civilization is dated 200 B. C. to 500 A. D. This culture spread thru Illinois' river valleys. The Kendall county sites are related to already excavated downstate locations, he said.

The State Archaeological survey, Struever's organization, is a private group which attempts to locate and explore ancient

sites. The Illinois State museum, whose duties include archaeological exploration, is a public body but it is hampered by lack of funds and manpower.

Struever said that Illinois has no laws to prevent the destruction of important archaeological sites. The state does not have adequate facilities to explore significant areas, he said, nor are there any provisions to preserve sites for future excavation.

In this regard, Illinois lags behind the federal government which surveys and excavates, if necessary, before it builds. But the United States as a whole lags behind the rest of the world in protecting its heritage according to Dr. Struever. He points out that the European nations—and even Asian nations without economic resources—recognize the importance of and protect the evidence of their national history. The United States, he said, is destroying her past.

GIFT TO STATE—House, designed by Mies van der Rohe, is surrounded by 60 wooded acres and has a view of the Fox river. Dr. Edith Farnsworth, owner, has offered the

In 1968 Lord Peter Palumbo offered to purchase the house and paid Edith Farnsworth a deposit; due to UK currency transfer restrictions during that time, he could not purchase the house outright. Edith Farnsworth likely kept the house on the market until Palumbo's payments were complete; he obtained the title in 1972.

"Home-Designed and Built by: MIES VAN DER ROHE On 60 Acres Along the beautiful Fox River," real estate advertisement by realtor Grover Gauntt with Baird & Warner, *Wall Street Journal*, June 26, 1970, (midwestern regional edition, p. 12).

View of Edith Farnsworth
House site next to Fox
River Drive Bridge with
surrounding farmland, na-
ture preserves, and parks,
fall 1990s.

Groundwork, 1945–1972

Technological Sublime: Designing and Building the Edith Farnsworth House

Dietrich Neumann

One of the most fateful encounters in Ludwig Mies van der Rohe's career happened one winter evening in 1945, in the Irving Apartments (1885–1887) at Oak and North State Street in Chicago, a short walk from Mies's home at 200 East Pearson Street. **[Fig. 1]** He had been invited to dinner by the journalist, book dealer, and accomplished cook Georgia Lingafelt and her friend Ruth Lee. Also present was Dr. Edith Farnsworth, a doctor at Chicago's Passavant Memorial Hospital, specializing in kidney diseases, who had just bought a parcel of land on the Fox River in Plano Illinois, an hour and a half west of downtown Chicago. She was 42 at the time, seventeen years younger than Mies. Apparently,

Mies had been mostly silent during the dinner–perhaps due to boredom, perhaps due to the fact that speaking English still caused him considerable effort, even seven years after his arrival in the United States and having just received his citizenship.

After dinner, when Georgia and Ruth were out in the kitchen doing dishes, Edith Farnsworth asked Mies if "some young man" in his office could design "a small studio weekend-house" for her newly acquired property. As Edith Farnsworth recalled in her unpublished memoirs many years later: "The response was the more dramatic for having been preceded by two hours of unbroken silence. 'I would love to build any kind of house for you.' The effect was tremendous, like a storm, a flood or other act of God."**1** This first conversation was followed by countless others and many visits to the site. **[Figs. 2-3]**. The resulting Edith Farnsworth House represented the culmination of a decades-long search on Mies's side, a rethinking of architectural and domestic conventions driven by a radical reductivism that sought to reduce architectural elements to their assumed essence. Traces of this search can be found throughout his earlier work. At the same time, Mies established here new structural paradigms that constituted the DNA for the rest of his American career. The taciturn German had immigrated to the US in 1938; the offer two years earlier from Chicago's Armour Institute (later Illinois Institute of Technology, IIT) to head its architecture school, had come at the right moment. The Nazi dictatorship had begun in 1933, the famous Staatliches Bauhaus in Dessau, of which Mies was the director, had been closed, and four years later Mies was forced out of the Preussische Akademie der Künste (Prussian Academy of Art). Any hopes for continued work under the new regime had been dashed.

While having built comparatively little, Mies had been widely considered one of the most prominent architects in Germany. After apprenticeships in Aachen and Berlin, his independent work had begun modestly with a series of unremarkable, if competent, houses in Berlin's suburbs, fitting squarely into the fashion of "Reformarchitektur," inspired by the rural vernacular around 1800 and less ostentatious than the historicist neo-Gothic or neo-Renaissance palaces popular before. It also lacked any of the flourishes of art nouveau that Belgian, French, and Spanish architects would have routinely applied to their residential architecture at that time. His first house, finished in 1909, a

1

2

3

4

5

4 + 5 Mies van der Rohe, Riehl House, Potsdam Babelsberg, 1908–09. Main facade towards rose garden and interior hall. From *Innen-Dekoration* 21 (July 1910).

6 Mies van der Rohe, Urbig House, Potsdam Neubabelsberg 1914–17.

7 Mies van der Rohe, Mosler House, Potsdam Neubabelsberg, 1924–26.

6

7

weekend house for prominent philosophy professor Alois Riehl, was praised by a contemporary critic as so "simply impeccable that one would never suspect it to be the first independent building by a young architect."**2** Its key innovation was a multipurpose central hall, which could serve both as a living room and a space for occasional gatherings of Riehl's students. **[Figs. 4-5]** Two adjacent open alcoves could be separated by curtains and used as intimate sitting or dining spaces. Nine conventional villas followed in and around Berlin until 1926, mostly for a prosperous clientele of bankers and civil servants. Among them a dominant type emerged—a symmetrical facade with a tall hip roof. On its first floor it would contain the typical bourgeois enfilade of representational rooms along an axis—salon, dining room, library. Prominent examples include the Urbig House in the Berlin suburb of Potsdam Babelsberg (1915-17), the Kempner House in Berlin (1921-23) and the Mosler House (1924-26), also in Potsdam Babelsberg. **[Figs. 6-7]**

While still designing such conventional villas, after adding the vaguely aristocratic-sounding "van der Rohe" to his last name, from 1922 on Mies began to reinvent himself as a member of the architectural avant-garde. Over the course of two years, he created five visionary designs of office buildings and country houses to great

public acclaim. Mies turned out to be adept at self-promotion and made sure that these visually striking projects—usually produced by skilled draughtsmen in his office on exceptionally large sheets of paper—were widely exhibited and published. There were two versions of glass-clad high-rises for the center of Berlin, a starkly proto-brutalist office building in reinforced concrete, and two expansive country house designs, one in concrete and one in brick. **[Figs. 8-9]** Both skyscraper designs were clad in a glass skin—a revolutionary, radical idea—seemingly impractical and impossible to realize at the time. The office building and both country houses had openly connected interior spaces. The brick country house project, developed under the influence of Dutch colleagues including Theo van Doesburg and Cornelis van Eesteren, Mies described in 1924: "In the ground plan of this house, I have abandoned the usual concept of enclosed rooms and striven for a series of spatial effects rather than a row of individual rooms. The wall loses its enclosing character and serves only to articulate the house organism."**3**

In his usually terse statements, Mies always emphasized simplicity, clarity, honesty, and essentialism—qualities which to him and many others seemed the only logical responses to the tumultuous and confusing era. The interwar

8

8 Mies van der Rohe, Concrete Country House, 1923. Perspective view. Charcoal and crayon on paper, 54 1/2 × 9 ft. 5 3/4 in. (138.8 × 289 cm). This is one of two versions of the same perspective, the other one, more frequently published, uses grey for the concrete color.

9 Mies van der Rohe, Brick Country House, 1924. Gelatin silver photo of lost drawings, 6 11/16 × 7 1/2 in. (17 × 19.1 cm). "Mies van der Rohe: Design for Country House: Neubabelsberg" (Neubabelsberg is part of Potsdam).

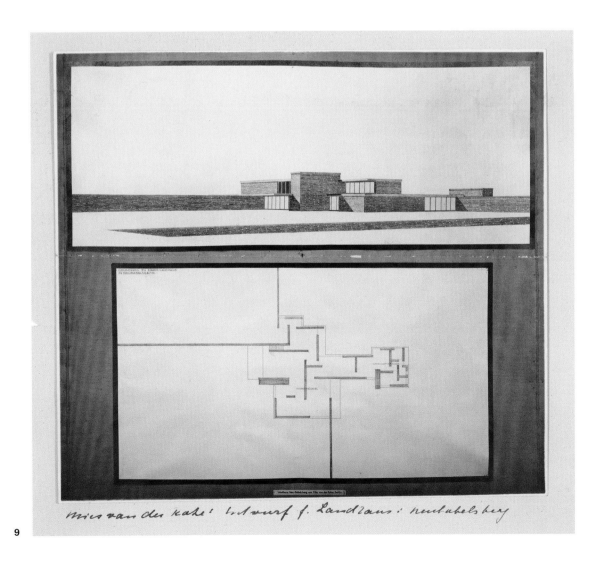

9

period in Germany was marked by the painful aftermath of the catastrophe of World War I: the devastating sanctions imposed on Germany and the economic turmoil they produced, as well as continuous political unrest. Prominent architect and critic Heinrich de Fries had written in 1924 that now, "after this unfathomable cultural catastrophe... to build means leaving out everything that is not strictly necessary for the inner essence of a vibrant structure.[4] At the end of the period, in early 1933, Mies summarized: "Only now can we articulate space freely, open it up and connect it to the landscape. Now it becomes clear again what a wall is, what an opening, what is floor and what ceiling. Simplicity of construction, clarity of tectonic means, and purity of material reflect the luminosity of original beauty."[5]

From 1925 to 1927 Mies built his first modern house, the Wolf House in Guben (now Gubin, Poland), a cubic brick structure with flat roofs. Here he realized the spatial effects that he had described in 1924—open connections between the representational and living rooms replacing the traditional linear enfilade. [Figs. 10-11] Parts of his success in realizing this building can be attributed to his recent partnership with Lilly Reich, a talented and experienced interior designer with whom he would work closely from 1925 until his departure to the United States in 1938. Reich was a board member of the prominent design advocacy group Werkbund. While the Wolf House in Guben was destroyed in World War II, two immediate successors, the Esters and Lange Houses in Krefeld (1928–30), still exist and demonstrate the next step in the evolution of Mies's dogged pursuit of his vision of open spatial connections and transparent outside walls. In these designs, large spans of plate glass were lowered into the ground, creating glazed walls that stopped short of reaching the floor to accommodate heating elements. [Figs. 12-13]

Despite having built comparatively little (and probably thanks to Lilly Reich), Mies was entrusted with the leadership of the Werkbund exhibition in Stuttgart of 1927 and its model housing estate. He succeeded in bringing sixteen international modern architects together and crowned the estate with an apartment block of his own design. The defining characteristic of Mies's steel frame structure was the flexibility of its interior layout. Only the stairs, kitchens, and bathrooms were fixed, while all interior walls could be easily moved and allowed for unprecedented spatial flexibility.

10 Mies van der Rohe, Wolf House, Guben, 1925–27, garden side.

11 Mies van der Rohe, Wolf House, Guben, 1925–27. Floor plan (the walls surrounding the spatial sequence of library, living, and dining room have been slightly enhanced by Hassan Bagheri for visibility), 2012.

12-13 Mies van der Rohe, Lange House, 1928-30. Garden facade with single-pane retractable windows on the first floor and open verandas on the eastern and western end and interior view toward the garden with retractable windows.

10

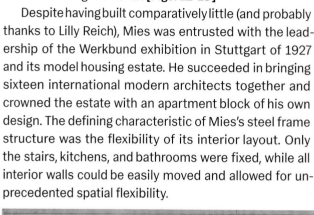

11

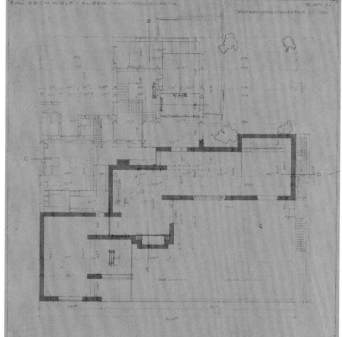

12

13

14 Mies van der Rohe, Werkbund Exhibition Glass Room, Stuttgart, 1927.

15-16 Mies van der Rohe, German Pavilion at the Barcelona World's Fair, 1929.

17 Mies van der Rohe, German Pavilion at the Barcelona World's Fair, 1929, rebuilt 1986.

14

15

16

17

In a display room for the German glass industry at the Stuttgart exhibition, Mies and Lilly Reich experimented with a vaguely domestic environment surrounded entirely by walls of plate glass—some transparent, some translucent—an important harbinger of things to come. **[Fig. 14]** The public success of the Werkbund Exhibition led to Mies's and Reich's appointment as directors of the German presence at the World's Fair in Barcelona in 1929, which would result in the iconic pavilion where Mies innovated more spatial and material concepts. While not equipped to serve the traditional functions of a national pavilion (such as exhibitions and receptions), it again presented a vague vision of future domestic environments, based on generous, openly connected—flowing—spaces. **[Figs. 15-17]** The eight cruciform columns that carried the ceiling were covered in polished, reflective nickel in order to be as invisible as possible. All walls consisted of glass, travertine, or marble—the precious stones a nod towards the representational nature of the pavilion (and a demonstrative profligacy that almost bankrupted the German commissioner Georg von Schnitzler, who had prefinanced Mies's pavilion when additional government funds were not forthcoming).**6** A building that invited critical and public fascination, the German Pavilion became the most critically acclaimed building of its time. The exhibition pavilion had been taken down in January 1930 and was rebuilt in the same location in 1986.**7**

Immediately after the World's Fair, Mies had a chance to test a similar concept in an actual villa, the Tugendhat House in Brno (in today's Czech Republic) for a couple of wealthy textile merchants. The main living room on the lower floor combined dining and sitting areas, a study, and library in one continuous space—divided only by a wall-high section of golden onyx and a semi-circular Makassar wood screen around the dining table. The southwestern facade consisted entirely of floor-to-ceiling panes of plate glass, two of them retractable into the floor. **[Figs. 18-19]** The double-layered southeastern glass facade contained a green house. After Philip Johnson, then architecture curator at the Museum of Modern Art, had seen the house in 1930, he told the Dutch architect J. J. P. Oud: "I wish I could communicate the feeling of seeing the Brünn house of Mies. I have only had similar architectural experiences before...with old things [like] the Parthenon."**8** Others, however, were critical of the openly displayed luxury at a time of great hardship for many during the Depression. "Can one live in the Villa Tugendhat?" a provocative essay by critic Justus Bier asked, initiating one of the most succinct discussions about the responsibility of modern architecture.**9** Mies's answer to his critics was a small and modest house in the Berlin suburb of Friedrichshain, for the printer Karl Lemke and Martha, his wife. The simple brick house consisted of merely a living/dining room and a bedroom, connected by a wide corridor, whose L-con-

18

19

20

21

figuration cradled a paved courtyard, toward which the floor-to-ceiling windows of the dining room and corridor looked. **[Figs. 20-21]**

Mies van der Rohe had become director of the Bauhaus art school in Dessau in 1930. When the Nazis reached a majority in the Dessau city council, the school was terminated there in 1932. After moving it to Berlin as a smaller, private institution, Mies again faced aggressive scrutiny in 1933, when the Nazis took over the Reich's government and the school was temporarily closed by the secret police. Mies's appeals to reopen the Bauhaus emphasized its apolitical nature, but also its apparent compatibility with the new ideology. Just as the Nazis signaled their willingness to let the school continue, Mies closed it due to a lack of funds. In his three years as leader of the school, Mies, for the first time, turned the art school into a true architecture school, as its name Bauhaus (House for Building)

suggested. In studio classes, his students developed variations of Mies's own work, where he continued to explore ideas of the Tugendhat and Lemke Houses, via countless variations of so-called courtyard houses. Both in Mies's sketches and in those of his students we find examples of glass-enclosed living rooms—however with an almost indiscernible structure **[Fig. 22]**. After the Bauhaus had closed, Mies taught a summer course for several former students in the Swiss Alps in 1933. Here, a small sketch for a mountain house from Mies's hand showed a suspended steel structure with two enclosed ends and cross-bracing visible behind glass in its open center. **[Fig. 23]**

Ultimately, the decade that followed, from 1933 to 1943, was the least fruitful of Mies's career—marred by a long series of unexecuted projects under the Nazi dictatorship, inconsequential patent applications for furniture designs and wallpaper manufacturing, and finally his decision to immi-

18-19 Mies van der Rohe, Villa Tugendhat, Brno, Czech Republic, 1930–31, garden facade and living room.

20-21 Mies van der Rohe, Lemke House, Berlin 1932–33, garden facade and view from corridor towards dining room.

22 Heinrich Siegfried Bormann, Ceph House, court house interior designed for Mies van der Rohe's studio class at the Bauhaus, 1933. Watercolor and pencil on heavy stock, 22 7/8 × 16 in. (58 × 40.8 cm).

23 Mies van der Rohe, Mountain House Design, 1933. No intended site known (possibly Merano, South Tyrol, Italy). Ink on paper, 4 1/2 × 8 in. (10.7 × 20.3 cm).

grate to a foreign country whose language he did not speak, to an institution without a modern campus, dispersed over twenty-two locations in the vast, industrial city of Chicago. Creatively, Mies seemed trapped in a loop—unable, for those ten long years, to move beyond the vocabulary he had created for the Barcelona Pavilion in 1929. That short-lived building had triggered the most sustained amount of praise of his career, and this success might have made it hard to let go of its central elements. A vacation home in Wyoming, commissioned by advertising executives Helen and Stanley Resor, is a case in point. It never managed to shed the earlier formal vocabulary, while trying to respond to the rural environment in the foothills of the Rocky Mountains (and possibly trying to fend off the pervasive imagery of Frank Lloyd Wright's Fallingwater, which was widely published and celebrated in an exhibition at MoMA while Mies was working on the Resor design). After the project had been cancelled by the Resors, it lived on in Mies's imagination, and evolved, much simplified, into a wooden box with a central, glass-enclosed open space. It was shown as a model, alongside that of the Farnsworth House, at Mies's first major exhibition at MoMA in 1947. **[Fig. 24]**

Things began to change in 1943 when Mies finished his first building on IIT's campus, the Minerals and Metals building, erected in great haste to aid in IIT's wartime production. While clearly designed under the influence of the industrial architecture of Albert Kahn, a German émigré to the US of the previous generation, Mies introduced a number of refinements, such as welded and polished steel connections on the main facade, and a proportioning system of regulating lines for its windows. More buildings for IIT, whose urban plan Mies had developed, followed in 1945, such as Wishnick Hall and Alumni Memorial Hall. The Second World War finally ended with the German and Japanese surrenders in May and September of 1945, respectively.

A Glass House

When work on the weekend house for Edith Farnsworth began, Mies was eager to see some of his earlier ideas of multiuse, light-flooded rooms come to fruition. In fact, it is here that he managed to guide the idea of open spatial connections and multifunctionality that he had pursued in his first project already, to its final conclusion. He would

22
23

combine not just spaces for dining, conversation, and work, but he added to the continuously open space a kitchen and sleeping area. He also pushed radical new interpretations of relationships of walls and windows, which he had begun to explore at the Stuttgart glass room and the Tugendhat House, to their extreme. Windows could function as walls and walls could be understood as windows. What was radically new in his oeuvre at this moment, though, was the artistic attention to the appearance of certain structural details (more on which below).

Sometime in early 1946, Mies's collaborator Edward Duckett developed elevation drawings for the Farnsworth House. He described how Mies would give his drawing the final touch: "He put a wash on two different sketches of the house with Edith Farnsworth standing right there watching. One scheme was on the ground and the other was with it raised up, the way it was eventually built."**10** Only the version of the drawing hovering above ground has survived—it

24 Mies van der Rohe, Resor House, 1937–43 (model dated 1947).

25 Drawing, Edith Farnsworth House, 1946. North elevation; preliminary version. Pencil, watercolor on tracing paper, 13 × 25 in. (33 × 66.5 cm).

25

was clearly Mies's favorite and already close to the final result. [Fig. 25] No drawings of alternative versions have been found. Mies resisted suggestions to move the building out of the floodplain to higher ground, as that would have eliminated the justification of the hovering volume.11 His impeccable sense of proportions (and not for potential flood levels) dictated the distance from the ground. A simple rectilinear glass box, sited roughly east-west, 77 feet, 3 inches long and 28 feet, 8 inches wide, held aloft by eight heavy I-beams, the large glass panes are divided by vertical mullions. There is an open terrace on its southern side towards the river and a covered entrance area towards the low western sun. The design was conceived in 1946; additional design work was done in the summer of 1947 for two upcoming exhibitions; ground was broken in 1949 (estimates for the house ran around $40,000 at that point); and it was finished in 1951.12

Noticing the abundance of mosquitoes close to the river, Mies planned a screened-in porch on the western end, rendered it as such and exhibited the model at the 1947 MoMA exhibition. [Fig. 33] It rendered the overall volume opaque and considerably less elegant. When the house was photographed in 1951 by Bill Hedrich of the renowned Chicago agency Hedrich Blessing, the mosquito screens had not yet been installed, enhancing its lightness and structural clarity.13 Once they were in place, the building lost some of its visual appeal, and many years later its next owner, Lord Peter Palumbo, removed them again. Thanks to the freestanding, tall central block encompassing the core elements—fireplace, two bathrooms, and kitchen—four distinct, but flexible, spaces emerged. In procession, these were progressively less public—the entrance area, the main living area in front of the fireplace, and at the end, facing east, the private sleeping quarters.

Both the kitchen section on the northern side and the fireplace directed the gaze and focus inward, rather than out toward the surrounding landscape.

Discovering Structural Poetry

According to Mies, at first, the building's construction was meant to be much simpler, "a steel construction, not welded, but bolted and on a more simple house—we were thinking even if we could do a lot of the work with the students on it....[And] at this time, we were thinking about a concrete floor [and plywood for the core]."14

In the end, the structure represented Mies's decisive step towards a new direction. An exoskeleton of eight rolled 8-inch flange steel beams held both floor plate and ceiling. The self-effacing reflective slenderness of the supports in Barcelona had given way to assertive, heavy piers, proudly testifying to the rolling process in the foundry. In an enthusiastic 1951 review, *Architectural Forum* noted that their size was determined by formal considerations, as they were strong enough "to support a much heavier structure, and some have misinterpreted their use as a functional impurity. They have not realized, perhaps, that there are demands of architectural expression quite as compelling as the demands of pure engineering, that the visual relationship of column thickness to depth of fascia and of column thickness to thickness of mullion can make or break a work of art as precise as this house."15

As there are no visible screws, bolts, or welding seams, the glass house seemed "suspended...as if by magnetic force," the article noted.16 This magic trick was accomplished with so-called "plug welds." All invisible steel connections (inside the terrace, floor, and roof structures) are bolted, but all visible connections on the outside are accomplished by a particular type of welding. While ordinarily seams would show up along the line where two metal parts had been merged under heat, plug welds made the connection invisible. Once the steel columns and floor and ceiling frames were fixed in place, welders would carefully target pre-drilled circular holes in the I-beam, and melt enough of the surface of the adjacent frame and the edge of the hole in the column to fuse them together with additional metal. This needed to be done with skill and care, as too much focused heat could burn through the frame, too little could result in a weak connection. As a result, these welds were hard to calculate as their strength varied from case to case (and was, in any event, weaker than that of rivets or bolts). The "welding marks were ground flush after assembly. Mies did not like the texture of the structural steel next to the grinding marks and so the entire steel frame was sandblasted down to a smooth, matte silver..."[17] Thus, Mies applied the same method of sanding and polishing that he, a trained stonemason, would have used to reveal the essential quality of a piece of marble. He would have preferred to show the actual metal color, but the recently invented stainless steel was not yet affordable, and so he tried a coat of rustproofing zinc, which would have provided a color similar to that of brushed steel, but finally settled on four coats of white enamel paint. [Figs. 26-27]

These meticulous design decisions were lost on the average observer but would excite visiting architects. Philip Johnson wrote to Mies: "The steel connections are so in-

evitable, so clean, so beautifully executed, that I believe no one will ever improve on them. Their problems are solved once and for all. Their execution is also a wonder to me. I am amazed that you found workmen to execute them so well. I cannot be specific, because each one is as good as the next. It exhausts me to even imagine what work you have been through."[18]

A profound artistic breakthrough of great originality had happened here: while Mies had made an oversized steel frame the determining factor of the design, he went to great length to hide its structural particularities from view. The industrial gravitas of the rolled I-beam—forged under enormous pressure in its Pennsylvania foundry while moving back and forth, red hot, between ever tightening steel drums—was complemented by meticulous craftsmanship on site. The result was a unique formal solution, anticipating minimalist sculpture. Of course, this only applied to the visible part of the building; everywhere else, the conventional connections were applied. [Fig. 28]

To make all of this possible, equipment for gas welding, sandblasting, and appropriate energy sources had to be brought to the site, which was far from the center of Plano. New electric lines had to be connected and made invisible by being placed underground, just like the waterline and oil and septic tanks. Interestingly, while Mies had commissioned Hedrich Blessing to photograph the construction of the Promontory Apartments and the details of Alumni Memorial Hall and other buildings on IIT's campus, there are very few photos of the Farnsworth House under construction, and they are all taken after the frame's plugs were already welded.

It is important to note that this approach was developed hand-in-hand with facade solutions at other contemporary projects, such as the two residential towers at 860-880 Lake Shore Drive (1949-51) and buildings on IIT's campus (1947 onwards) in Chicago. At his first high-rise building, the Promontory Apartments in Chicago (1947-49), Mies had articulated the decreased load of the ascending concrete skeleton. The piers are deeper at the bottom, and then recede by about four inches above the sixth, eleventh, and

26 Edith Farnsworth House, 1945-51. Steel support at lower terrace.

27 Edith Farnsworth House, 1945-51. Steel support at terrace. Pencil and color pencil on note paper showing positions of plug welds.

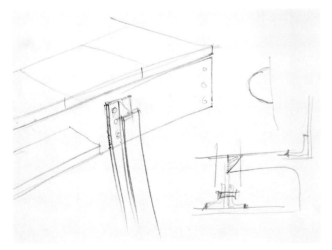

28 Edith Farnsworth House under construction, 1950.

29-30 Mies van der Rohe, 860-880 Lake Shore Drive Apartments, Chicago, 1949–51. Photographs by Hassan Bagheri, 2012.

sixteenth floors. In oblique sunlight, a staggered shadow line becomes visible. This was still a straightforward representation of structural realities, as Mies's head designer Joe Fujikawa remembered: "If you look at Promontory, the columns step back. That was one of Mies's fundamental efforts in architecture, to express the structure of a building, and this did it very, very neatly. It's kind of Gothic in its character, the way it's stepped back; the buttresses reduce in size as it goes up."[19]

While working on the Promontory in 1947, however, Mies developed an alternative structural model in steel which introduced a facade solution that became his trademark approach for the rest of his career and reflects the same shift in philosophy that had led to the solution at the Farnsworth House. Rather than truthfully reflecting the structural realities, as at the Promontory Apartments, here Mies aimed at powerful, photogenic imagery. A sequence of slim I-beams (with no structural function) would be attached to the outside, representing the much larger, structural I-beams, which were invisible, as they had to be encased in concrete for fire protection. The system would be applied first at the two apartment towers at 860-880 Lake Shore Drive. These slim I-beams suggested structure, while being purely ornamental. They

were pedagogical devices, signifiers, representing the structure inside. **[Figs. 29-30]**

How little that coincided with Mies's intentions became obvious when he applied the same system to the facades of pure concrete-frame structures (which had no I-beams inside) in the following years to several housing projects and the Seagram Building (1956–58). Here, the small I-beams experienced their apotheosis—they were not made of steel anymore, but brass. Brass is a softer

31-32 Mies van der Rohe, Seagram Building, New York City, 1956–58. Photographs by Hassan Bagheri, 2012.

material, which would not be rolled under pressure in the foundry, but extruded—a method that allowed more formal variety. To make this point visible, Mies introduced an additional lip on the flange. [Figs. 31-32]

Mies's interest in structural poetry added significantly to the cost of the house. The transportation of equipment to the site and underground service connections contributed to the house's finished cost of $70,000, almost ten times that of the median home price in the United States in 1950, and more than twice what Walter Gropius' House in Lincoln, Massachusetts had cost over a decade earlier (however, Philip Johnson's Glass House came in close at $60,000 in 1949).

Mies's office organization and accounting was notoriously chaotic, as demonstrated by the rather puzzling claim that Mies and his collaborators had racked up an astonishing 5,884 billable hours for the design of the house—more than twice the amount billed for the two high-rise towers of Lake Shore Drive Apartments.[20] Compared to the amount of care devoted to the appearance of the columns, other areas at the house remained woefully unsolved. Since double-pane Thermopane glass did not come in the required sizes, the single-pane glass that was selected predictably led to streams of condensation water inside in the winter. The fireplace had draft problems in the hermetically sealed house, working only when the front door was opened—allowing cold air in, undermining its purpose. The oil heating system produced a considerable output of soot, and the flat roof leaked almost immediately. On the river-facing southern side, the midday sun hit the large glass expanses without protection. For its formal strength and visual delicacy, the house that Edith Farnsworth moved into in 1951 was impractical to live in.

Mies vs. Farnsworth

The troubles that became inseparable from the legacy of the house unfolded with a series of unfortunate events as it was nearing completion. While Edith Farnsworth had greatly enjoyed being part of the design process and supporting Mies's experiments towards a new relationship between architecture, craft, and industry, the mood had finally soured when costs continued to spiral out of control, and decisions were made without her consent, such as the selection of furniture by Mies. She eventually stopped payments and chose her own furniture by contemporary designers such as Florence Knoll, Bruno Mathsson, and others.[21]

At that time, in the spring of 1951, Philip Johnson noticed the financially unsustainable way in which Mies' Chicago office was run, and extended help in the form of his own business manager Robert C. Wiley, for whom he was designing the magnificent Wiley House in New Canaan. Going over the books, Wiley noted $4,500 of outstanding construction costs at the Farnsworth House and approached Edith Farnsworth. Unhappy with some unsolved issues, Edith Farnsworth offered $1,500 instead. A settlement somewhere in the middle was never reached.

Instead, Wiley contacted a major Chicago law firm, Sonnenschein, Nath & Rosenthal, and set up a meeting between senior partner David Levinson and Mies. Perhaps not surprisingly, Levinson recommended a lawsuit and Mies decided to go ahead. "I think this was one of the most unfortunate things that could have happened," Myron Goldsmith, a young architect and engineer in Mies' office during the construction, noted later.[22] Over time, Mies came to greatly regret this decision, as he ended up deeply worried about the ensuing publicity, which often

31

32

33

swung in favor of Dr. Farnsworth, and the possibility of losing his license during the four years that it took for the case to be solved in the courts.

Guided by Levinson, Mies sued Edith Farnsworth for an outstanding electrician's bill and his own fees (never before quoted or discussed), totaling roughly $33,000. In response, Farnsworth countersued for $30,000—the difference between the $70,000 she had already paid and Mies's initial estimate, years earlier, of $40,000.

A complicated and drawn-out legal proceeding commenced, involving the expert opinion from a "special master" and a new judge appointed halfway through; a settlement was finally reached in 1955, four years after it had commenced, with Edith Farnsworth paying Mies $2,500. She arguably ended up with the better deal; her lawyer was a patient of Farnsworth and had worked pro bono, while Mies was stuck with the bill from David Levinson. Ultimately Mies did not receive the architect's fee that he had demanded.

Edith Farnsworth continued to spend weekends at the house for the next twenty-one years, often making it available for visitors. She sold it in 1972 to British property magnate Lord Peter Palumbo for a reported $120,000 and retired to Italy where she wrote her memoirs and translated Italian poetry; she died in 1977. A collector of modern art and architecture, Palumbo had commissioned Mies in July 1962 to design a 19-story office building in London, which he still hoped to execute after Mies's death, as initially not all of the required properties and titles at the site had been available (see below). Palumbo executed several important changes to the house, notably installing air conditioning and removing the mosquito screens, as well as to the property, notably installing sculptures by Alexander Calder, Richard Serra, Henry Moore, and others on the grounds.

Palumbo inherited a key threat to the house: flooding. The Fox River flooded the house in 1954, but there were serious floods during Palumbo's time in 1996 and 1997 (as well as in 2008 and 2013). In 1996 the water inside the house was several feet high, and destroyed most of the woodwork. Lord Palumbo undertook a thorough restoration and intermittently opened the house to the public. After an incident of significant vandalism to the house and the erosion of relations between the Palumbos and former civic backers and allies in Chicago, they sold it in 2003 to the National Trust for Historic Preservation for $7.5 million (see the Oral Histories with Peter and Hayat Palumbo, pp. 166–75). While Edith Farnsworth didn't quite double her investment, Palumbo multiplied his by a factor of 62.5. While these ratios will be lower when adjusted for inflation and factoring in the costs of restoration and repairs, they nevertheless reflect the different levels of appreciation for Mies the first time the house was sold in the early 1970s versus 2003, in the wake of two monumental exhibitions at MoMA and the Whitney Museum in 2001.

For the four years that it was underway, the legal case threatened to derail Mies's career and to inflict major financial losses against the losing party. Both parties launched media campaigns in attempts to bolster their complaints in the court of public opinion. Several fawning profiles of Mies appeared as soon as the lawsuit had been filed in the summer of 1951, and just before dispositions were taken, and then again in time for the final report of the appointed special master. In June 1951, for instance, the *Chicago Tribune* described Mies's "devotion to simplicity" and him as "a friend of steel." He was shown in deep contemplation looking at a model of the Farnsworth House, "now a family residence in Plano."**23** [Fig. 33]

In October of that year, the house was featured on the cover of *Architectural Forum* under associate editor Peter Blake, another émigré friend of Mies (born in Berlin in 1920 as Peter Blach): "To some it may look like 'nothing much'–just a glass-sided box framed in heavy, white steel; but...the Farnsworth House near Chicago has no equal in perfection of workmanship, in precision of details, in pure simplicity of concept." Blake praised the "jewel-like perfection" of the house, comparable to the craftsmanship of the finest Japanese cabinet-makers. Blake slyly suggested that Edith Farnsworth simply might not have what it takes, as "such serenely beautiful spaces make heavy demands upon those who live in them;" they are not for everybody, but "for those who are willing to enter Mies van der Rohe's world, there are [few] experiences as rich and rewarding." It is worth quoting the final paragraph of the essay:

> For while Mies subtracts and keeps on subtracting until all is skin and bones, the result is much like the reduction of a substance, in chemical analysis, to its crystalline parts. What remains after Mies' subtraction is a concentration of pure beauty, a distillation of pure spirit. Mies' buildings only seem to have a kind of nothingness at first glance; as time goes on, their subtle, indirect influence becomes increasingly apparent...this subtle influence is likely to remain–the influence of a great artist, of a great work of art, of a great discipline, of a great belief that man in architecture should be free.[24]

When MoMA presented its exhibition on postwar architecture in 1953, Mies naturally played a major role, and the Farnsworth House was celebrated as showing most clearly "the relation between conspicuous space and the structure that generates it...indeed, a quantity of air caught between a floor and a roof."[25]

While Mies was busy presenting his arguments in the press, the other litigant was by no means idle. Elizabeth Gordon, prominent editor of *House Beautiful* magazine, published a lengthy piece titled "The Threat to the Next America" in the April 1953 issue. It coincided perfectly with the issuance of the report of the special master, issued on May 7, 1953. Gordon had interviewed Edith Farnsworth twice and started her piece with a photograph of the Tugendhat House, illustrating "The Cult of Austerity... the product of Mies van der Rohe's cold, barren design" and reported that Edith Farnsworth, "a highly intelligent, now disillusioned woman, who spent more than $70,000 building a one-room house that is nothing but a glass cage on stilts."[26] It belonged to a movement, she declared, that promoted "the mystical idea that 'less is more'" and thus "unlivability, stripped-down emptiness, lack of storage space and therefore lack of possessions." Behind this, she claimed, was "a self-chosen elite who are trying to tell us what we should like and how we should live." And,

she declared ominously, "accepting dictators in matters of taste" would lead to accepting "dictators in other departments of life." The fact that Mies was German was certainly part of the intended smear. Executive editor Joseph Barry followed suit in the May issue of *House Beautiful* with his "Report on the American Battle between Good and Bad Modern Houses," featuring the Farnsworth House as "a particularly fine example of a bad modern house." He quoted Edith Farnsworth, who felt unsafe and restless, and hemmed in by the design's stringency: "Mies talks about 'free space' but his space is very fixed. I can't even put a clothes hanger in my house without considering how it affects everything from the outside."[27]

Edith Farnsworth was well aware of the impact of the well-timed positive pieces about the house. In her unpublished memoir, she noted with frustration how her visitors' perceptions were colored by what they had read about her house: "The big glossy reviews polished up their terms and phrases with such patience that the simpler minds that came to have a look expected to find the glass box light enough to stay afloat in air or water, moored to its columns and enclosing its mystic space. So 'culture spreads by proclamation'"–a phrase, apparently, from Mies himself[28]–"and one got the impression that if the house had had the form of a banana rampant instead of a rectangle couchant, the proclamation would have been just as imperative....Perhaps, as a man," she summarized, "he is not the clairvoyant primitive that I thought he was, but simply a colder and more cruel individual than anybody I have ever known."[29]

While awaiting the judgment of the lawsuit, Mies tried applying key elements of his essentialist concept elsewhere, in an attempt to show its validity. When approached by businessman Leon Caine in 1950, who wanted to build a home in Winnetka, Mies presented a design that essentially scaled up the Farnsworth House for a family with three children and a maid. The result was a large open glass volume with the same outside I-beams, four columns inside, and larger plates of glass. Its domestic landscape evolved from the earlier "court house" studies, providing an open, central area flanked by the children's and parents' bedroom wings. The house was meant to sit on a wide and deep podium over uneven terrain. It remained unexecuted.

Aiming for a flexible type for mass production, Mies then designed a house of a comparable size, but on a square plan of 50 x 50 ft., yielding 2,500 square feet. The interior provided space for a couple with two children, two bathrooms, and a central fireplace. In his ongoing quest for thinking problems through to their absolute, radical end, Mies came up with the idea of having just one column in the center of each wall, thus bringing their number down to four (instead of eight at the Farnsworth House). The corners would be column-free, offering closer communion with nature. Of course, structurally, this was a terrible idea. Two 25-foot-long cantilevers from a single point would have met under a 90-degree angle at each corner. Any snow load, for example, would have pressed particularly hard onto those unsupported glass corners. Mies appointed Myron Goldsmith in his office to work out the details, but Goldsmith had difficulties "calculating it out…trying all kinds of modifications to make it work." He drew several deflection diagrams to explain to Mies the effect of the center columns. At some point he sketched a diagonal grid instead, which would have been slightly advantageous, but he "didn't know if [Mies] would stand for it."

Published in *Architectural Forum*, the magazine's editors were not entirely convinced: "Besides placing emphasis truly on the tensile qualities of steel, this approach removes the visual problem of the corner post–although at the same

commissioned at the same time, but only built in 1955.**33**

As a prototype for mass production, both houses had to forego expensively crafted details such as the plug welds, or the enormous panes of glass. Given their sites, there was also no reason to lift these buildings off the ground. Substantial white I-beams were still applied to the facade, but in much closer vicinity to each other, due to the smaller window size. Their structural role was different here as well, not touching the ground, but merely transferring the weight of the roof beams to the steel frame surrounding the concrete floor. **[Fig. 35]** They were shorter and their dense sequence was visually unappealing. Mies noticed that himself, and made the unlikely claim that "proper steel sections for vertical members were not available at the

34

35

time it enlarges the structural problem of connections....The steel frame, for a house 50' x 50' would cost about 40% more than a steel frame with corner posts, but it looks as if might be well worth it."**30** About ninety sketches, thirty technical drawings, and photographs of a model exist in the archive.**31** **[Fig. 34]** An extensive article in the *Chicago Tribune* about the "core house" (later often called 50x50 House) emphasized its flexibility (it came in three versions 40 x 40, 50 x 50 and 60 x 60 feet) and multifunctionality: "Dinner in Yesterday's Bedroom: It's Possible in This Flexible Plan."**32**

Also, while the court decision was pending, two commissions realized for clients in Mies's immediate orbit used elements of the Farnsworth House to demonstrate their validity for future mass production. One was for Robert H. McCormick III, one of the investors behind Lake Shore Drive 860-880 (executed in Elmhurst, Illinois, 1951–52); the other one was for Morris Greenwald, the brother of Herbert Greenwald, the developer Mies worked with on the Promontory, Lake Shore Drive, and other apartment projects. Morris Greenwald's house in Weston, Connecticut, was

36

37

time of construction" and that, therefore, the sections in place were "one inch larger than was specified."**34** The ceiling showed the I-beams openly, and the plywood partition walls were not load-bearing. **[Fig. 36]** The houses did not attract sufficient interest and remained the only ones like them ever built.

The failure to attract any clients for these projects weighed particularly heavy at the postwar moment when the prefabrication of houses experienced a boom with about seventy active firms and 200,000 units manufactured annually.**35** Their aesthetic might not have appealed to the middle-class clients usually targeted for prefabricated houses. Apart from their heavy-handed appearance, the other reason they didn't find interest might have been their high costs due to the abundant application of steel in the houses. The simple McCormick House, out of two base units, had cost $45,000.

Others were better at adapting Mies's central idea. Philip Johnson, famously, had seen the model of the Farnsworth House at the MoMA show, and built his own version within a year. By May 1949, his new home was featured on New Canaan modern house tours, and it was widely published that fall.**36** While Johnson not only stole Mies's thunder by publishing his glass house first, he also solved the spatial flow more elegantly, as his house was wider and shorter than Mies' design. The row of kitchen appliances remained low, and the cylinder with the bathroom/fireplace combination obstructed the view less than the central, wall-high

installation at the Farnsworth House. Johnson solved concerns about privacy, which had plagued Edith Farnsworth, by building a separate, almost windowless brick box nearby as the bedroom, thereby compromising the purity of the initial concept. Johnson's house was, in any event, no match to the visual radicalism of Mies's hovering box, whose stark white frame underscored the notion of detachment from ground and context.

Richard Kelly's lighting installation had helped Johnson prevent the glass walls from appearing as reflective black voids at night by lighting the immediate perimeter outside from above and selected bushes and trees nearby from below. Inside, uplights on the floor used the ceiling as a diffuse reflector. **[Fig. 37]** Mies, who according to Johnson, "was absolutely no good at...lighting" had simply provided curtains for privacy all around, and relied on individual light sources to leave the ceiling plane uninterrupted.**37**

The photographer André Kertész, who had probably seen images of the stunning appearance of Johnson's glass house at night, fixed the situation for Mies.**38** One of his photographs showed a nocturnal Farnsworth House aglow with no visible light sources.**39** This was, in all likelihood, achieved by the European technique of "wandering light:" during a long exposure, an assistant would walk through a building and shine a portable light towards ceiling, floor and walls. In the resulting image, the moving assistant remained invisible, while the surfaces reflected the light they had received. **[Fig. 38]**

The Farnsworth House was ahead of its time. It became more comfortable after Lord Peter Palumbo introduced air conditioning and addressed other shortcomings. Mies had been less interested in building a perfectly functioning, livable house, than in working through a formal and structural paradigm: the fascinating idea of reducing a project to its absolute essence in an age and in a country of highly developed technology—resulting in a simple glass box, whose floor and ceiling slabs were suspended between mighty steel beams. At the same time, Mies was eager to create a *technological sublime,* a formal application of the steel frame so elegantly crafted that it lifted it from the realm of industrial production into the refinement of abstract sculpture. Both concepts would dominate the rest of his career and become crucial undercurrents in modern architecture worldwide.

38

Notes

1 Franz Schulze and Edward Windhorst, *Mies van der Rohe: A Critical Biography* (Chicago: University of Chicago Press, 2014), p. 248.

2 Anton Jaumann, "Vom künstlerischen Nachwuchs" *Innen-Dekoration* 21 (July 1910): 265–73.

3 Mies van der Rohe, "Lecture" (1924). Quoted from Fritz Neumeyer, *The Artless Word: Mies van der Rohe on the Building Art* (Cambridge: MIT Press, 1991), pp. 250–51, quote 251.

4 Heinrich de Fries, *Modernen Villen und Landhäuser* (Berlin: Wasmuth, 1924), pp. vi, xii.

5 Mies van der Rohe, "What Would Concrete, What Would Steel Be without Plate Glass?" quoted in Neumeyer, *The Artless Word*, pp. 313–14.

6 See Robin Schuldenfrei, *Luxury and Modernism: Architecture and the Object in Germany 1900–1933* (Princeton: Princeton University Press, 2018), pp. 157–222.

7 See Dietrich Neumann with David Caralt, *An Accidental Masterpiece: Mies van der Rohe's Barcelona Pavilion* (Basel: Birkhäuser, 2020) and *The Barcelona Pavilion by Mies van der Rohe: 100 Texts since 1929* (Basel: Birkhäuser, 2020).

8 Terence Riley, "The Curator as a Young Man," in *Mies van der Rohe and the Museum of Modern Art*, ed. John Elderfield (New York: Abrams, 1998), pp. 34–69, quote 36.

9 Justus Bier, "Kann man im Haus Tugendhat wohnen?," *Die Form* 6, no. 10 (October 1931): 392–93.

10 Edward Duckett, quoted in William S. Shell, Interview with Edward A. Duckett and Joseph Y. Fujikawa, *Impressions of Mies: An Interview on Mies van der Rohe: His Early Chicago Years 1938–1958* (n.p. 1988), p. 18. (quoted in Schulze and Windhorst, *Mies van der Rohe,* p. 451).

11 Several severe and destructive floods over the years proved right those who had warned Mies about the threat.

12 Schulze and Windhorst, *Mies van der Rohe*, p. 252.

13 See the review of the arrival of the screened-in porch, https://curtainedwallstimeline.hcommons.org/static-timeline-with-large-images/.

14 Mies van der Rohe during court proceedings, quoted in Alex Beam, *Broken Glass: Mies van der Rohe, Edith Farnsworth, and the Fight Over a Modernist Masterpiece* (New York: Random House, 2020), p. 150.

15 "This is the First House Built by Ludwig Mies van der Rohe," *Architectural Forum* 95 (October 1951): 156–61.

16 "This is the First House Built by Ludwig Mies van der Rohe," pp. 156–61, quote 159.

17 "This is the First House Built by Ludwig Mies van der Rohe," pp. 156–61.

18 Johnson to Mies, June 4, 1951. MoMA, MvdR., quoted in Beam, *Broken Glass*, p. 147.

19 Joseph Fujikawa, *Oral History of Joseph Fujikawa/interviewed by Betty J. Blum, Compiled Under the Auspices of the Chicago Architects Oral History Project, Ernest R. Graham Center for Architectural Drawings* (Chicago: Art Institute of Chicago, 1995/2003), p. 18. https://artic.contentdm.oclc.org/digital/api/collection/caohp/id/3571/download.

20 Schulze and Windhorst, *Mies van der Rohe*, p. 252. Beam, *Broken Glass,* p. 135.

21 Edith Farnsworth's furniture selection was reassembled at the house on the occasion of its re-naming as Edith Farnsworth House. See Nora Wendl, *Edith Farnsworth House* (Chicago: National Trust for Historic Preservation, 2021), https://issuu.com/edithfarnsworthhouse/docs/edithbook_nov.

22 Myron Goldsmith, *Oral History of Myron Goldsmith/interviewed by Betty J. Blum, Compiled Under the Auspices of the Chicago Architects Oral History Project, Ernest R. Graham Center for Architectural Drawings* (Chicago: Art Institute of Chicago, 1990/2001), p. 67. https://artic.contentdm.oclc.org/digital/collection/caohp/id/4086/.

23 Leigh Atkinson, "Architect finds beauty lies in 'skin and bones': Proud of Simplicity in Gold Coast Building," *Chicago Daily Tribune*, June 21, 1951, S6.

24 "This is the First House Built by Ludwig Mies van der Rohe," pp. 156–61, quotes 157, 160.

25 Arthur Drexler, "Post-war Architecture," in *Built in USA: Post-war Architecture*, eds. Henry-Russell Hitchcock and Arthur Drexler (New York: Museum of Modern Art, Simon & Schuster, 1952), pp. 20–37, quote 20–21.

26 Elizabeth Gordon, "The Threat to the Next America," *House Beautiful*, April 1953, pp. 126–30, 250–51.

27 Joseph A. Barry, "Report on the Battle between Good and Bad Modern Houses," *House Beautiful*, May 1953, pp. 172–73, 266–72.

28 Edith Farnsworth quoted in Franz Schulze, *Mies van der Rohe* (Chicago: University of Chicago Press, 1986), p. 155. Edith Farnsworth, *Memoirs,* Chapter 13, n.p. Edith Farnsworth Papers (boxes 1 and 2) at the Newberry Library, Chicago, https://ia903004.us.archive.org/24/items/mms_farnsworth/mms_farnsworth.pdf. See also pp. 136–59 in this book.

29 Edith Farnsworth, *Memoirs*, quoted in Schulze, Mies, p. 193.

30 "Mies van der Rohe," *Architectural Forum* 97 (November 1952): 93–111, quote 110.

31 Luciana Fornari Colombo, "Mies van der Rohe's Core House, a Theoretical Project on the Essential Dwelling," https://vitruvius.com.br/index.php/revistas/read/arquitextos/11.130/3782/en.

32 Anne Douglas, "Dinner in Yesterday's Bedroom: It's Possible in This Flexible Plan," *Chicago Daily Tribune*, August 24, 1952.

33 Summers to Fujikawa, Mai 31, 1955, McCormick House Museum Archive. https://www.150southcottagehillave.net/2019/03/23/greenwald-house-planning/.

34 "Mies van der Rohe," pp. 93–111, quote 108.

35 Gilbert Herbert, *The Dream of the Factory-Made House: Walter Gropius and Konrad Wachsmann* (Cambridge: MIT Press, 1984).

36 Mary Roche, "New Canaan Holds Modern House Day," *The New York Times*, May 14, 1949, p. 10. "Glass House. It consists of just one big room completely surrounded by scenery," *Life Magazine*, September 26, 1949, pp. 94–96. Mary Roche, "Living In a Glass House," *The New York Times*, August 14, 1949, Section M, p. 34.

37 Ludwig Glaeser and Philip Johnson, "Epilogue: Thirty Years Later," in *Mies van der Rohe*, 3rd ed. by Philip Johnson (New York: Museum of Modern Art, 1977), pp. 205–11, quote 207.

38 For instance, Richard Kelly, "Focus on Light: New Techniques Inspire Exciting Use in Décor." "Romantic Lighting for a Glass House" *Flair* 1, no. 1 (February 1950): 66–69.

39 "The American Idea in Houses: A Glass Shell that 'Floats' in the air," *House & Garden*, February 1952, pp. 44–49, 96, photo 46.

Dream in the Shade of the Black Sugar Maple

Ron Henderson

In her memoirs, Dr. Edith Farnsworth recounted an early visit to the site of her future house, in the summer of 1944, with her friend Sue Brill. She wrote, "We...walked down to the riverbank where we found the most inviting easy chairs between the swelling roots of two immense black sugar maples whose shade was repeated and extended by the hackberries, the lindens, and the walnut trees grouped about us. In the water, close to the shore, a milk-white heron stood, motionless at the foot of his rippling image." (See pp. 138, 142 in this book.) Based on an obvious knowledge of tree taxonomy, Dr. Farnsworth was enthralled by these maples, and, as the commissioning client, she likely directed the attention of her architect to them. In a subsequent paragraph, she wrote of the impact these trees had on her and Sue, "I imagine that we both dreamed in the shade of the black sugar maple that night." (See p. 138.)

Black sugar maples, *Acer saccharum subst. nigrum*, are riverine trees native to Illinois, as their native range stretches from the northern shore of Lake Ontario to middle Tennessee and from the western slope of the Appalachian Mountains to the shortgrass prairies of Iowa and Missouri. Their scientific identification is contested; some identify it as *Acer saccharum*, others identify it as its own species, *Acer nigrum*, and others—including the current preference with the Edith Farnsworth House administration—identify it as a subspecies of *Acer saccharum* known as *nigrum*. Like most maples, it has a dense, rounded crown and furrowed bark. The black sugar maple is differentiated from sugar maple, in part, by darker bark and darker green three-lobed leaves.

The black sugar maple appears on the earliest surveys as well as repeatedly in sketches, additional surveys, and drawings of the house. As apparent to visitors, the Edith Farnsworth House was certainly sited to nestle around this specimen tree. The fireplace stands directly opposite to it so that the sitting area is framed by the fire and tree through which one looks out to the larger landscape and the Fox River. The terrace descends alongside the tree such that the terrace and house enclose the tree on two sides—a kind of open-sided one-tree courtyard.

A Jon Miller/Hedrich Blessing photograph from the mid-1980s captures the chromatic vitality of the golden leaves and the intense permeation of fall color in the house;

white house, black tree, yellow-orange foliage, and blue sky. Mies van der Rohe's gouache elevation sketch from sometime in early 1946 (see Dietrich Neumann's essay p. 106 in this book) looking at the rear of the house toward the river predicts this seasonal experience with a golden yellow mass towering over the house and provides further evidence of the intention to pair the house and this tree in the landscape.

Much has been written about the relationship of the house to the floodplain and clearly, the house is situated on a shallow ridge as the floodplain rises away from the river. However, the house could have been situated anywhere along that ridge. The consistent portrayal of the tree in early studies supports the notion that it was this black sugar maple that influenced the final resolution of the house's relationship to the site.

This tree was in decline but carefully sustained with pruning, fertilizing, and cabling prior to being removed in 2013 and replaced with a sugar maple, *Acer saccharum*, in 2021. This replacement tree was planted about five feet south of the location of the original black sugar maple, which keeps it in alignment perpendicular to the house but a few feet further away, and a bit closer to the river.

The deep shade cast by the dense canopy of the tree obstructed the southerly summer sun, and the vibrant yellow-orange fall foliage reverberated in reflections on the windows, plaster ceiling, and white-painted steel columns of the house. Its stout black trunk, heavy branches, and thick stems cast skeletal shadows on the snowy winter ground. This broadly spreading maple gathered the Edith Farnsworth House around it.

This page Edith Farnsworth House photograph by Jon Miller/Hedrich Blessing, commissioned by the Museum of Modern Art's Arthur Drexler for the 1986 Mies van der Rohe centennial, October 1985.

Next Page Edith Farnsworth House with black sugar maple, Jon Miller/Hedrich Blessing, October 1985 (leader removed early 1980s, tree removed summer 2013, new tree planted in fall 2021).

The author thanks Scott Mehaffey and Michelangelo Sabatino for their insights and knowledge of this specimen tree and relevant archival resources.

The Edith Farnsworth House

Dream in the Shade of the Black Sugar Maple

The Modern House in Chicago: Organic and (not or) Modern

Michelangelo Sabatino

Although the Edith Farnsworth House has been celebrated as one of the most consequential modern houses to be built during the second half of the twentieth century in America and beyond, it was not greeted with universal acclaim upon its completion and the circulation of photographs in professional journals and magazines. For some it was a daring demonstration of a powerful dialogue between design and cutting-edge building technology. For others, Mies's modern minimalist pavilion revealed the emergence of two seemingly irreconcilable approaches: *organic* and *modern*. In Chapter Eleven of her unpublished memoirs presented in this book, Edith recounts Frank Lloyd Wright's reaction to the MoMA retrospective exhibition about Mies's work held in New York (September 16, 1947–January 25, 1948) and curated by Philip Johnson. While it is not clear if Wright, America's foremost advocate of organicism, explicitly referenced the Farnsworth House in his letter to Mies, it is unlikely that he could have missed the house model prominently on display:

> The art critics and the architects who attended the opening of the Museum exhibit found themselves dwarfed by the immense blow-ups of old photographs which covered the walls: the Barcelona Pavilion, the Tugendhat House with its onyx wall. The little Fox River house was set up on a table and I was distressed that the handmade trees standing around it gave the observer no idea of the great lindens, the maples and the hackberries under which it was to stand. But it was the pivotal point of the exhibit, and I was happy as I boarded the train back to Chicago, reflecting that our project might well become the prototype of new and important elements in American architecture.
>
> I do not remember what the New York critics wrote about the Van der Rohe exhibit. But there was one visitor who let fall a comment which found its way to Mies, not in minutes but in seconds. That visitor was Frank Lloyd Wright. The comment was pithy: "Negation is not enough."
>
> Back in Chicago, a day or two later, we gathered at Mies's to consider what should be done about that comment. After long deliberation during which he sat in his black chair and puffed his cigar, inarticulate and huffy, we drafted a dignified complaint having a dim bearing upon negation. This was approved with one or two minor corrections, signed, addressed and mailed. The answer came promptly: "Sorry old chap," it said, "that my comment offended you. I apologize. But negation just isn't enough."

The differences between organic and modern may seem obvious: the "organic" being an embrace of traditional materials such as brick, wood, and stone, whereas the "modern" being more experimental and open to the use of new industrial materials such as steel and glass. One could also extend the comparison to address different approaches to designing in plan, elevation, and section. More importantly, however, is that the categories of organic and the modern represent concepts more than mere styles. A brief survey of Chicago's modern houses built between the 1930s and the early 1970s reveals how architects in this midwestern city, shaped by the ideas and works of both Wright and Mies, eschewed simplistic dichotomies between organic and modern in favor of a more nuanced approach with a dialogue with "nature" as a unifying spatial and material ideal.[1] As attests the first set of photographs taken of the house, whose importance was discussed in the Introduction, the Edith Farnsworth House was designed by Mies with a deep sense of awareness of the agrarian site along the Fox River. Its deference to the site demonstrates that the organic and the modern need not live in an antagonistic relationship. This is especially true if one understands that nature can play very different roles depending on the individual architect and client. A conjunctive "and," rather than a polarizing "or," can go much further in revealing the subtle differences to approaches to houses of all sizes realized by architects, for and with their clients, during the twentieth century.

Despite its identification with a towering skyline, Chicago's abundant parks and founding motto *Urbs in Horto* ("City in a Garden") describe a special relationship of its inhabitants with nature as a source of beauty and well-being. Wright's Robie House, completed in 1910 for an entrepreneur and his family in the Chicago neighborhood of Hyde Park, is a highpoint in an important episode of organic architecture in America that historians have long established as the Prairie School.[2] [Fig. 1] Since the late nineteenth century, Wright and like-minded architects and designers pioneered an approach in the "Middle West" based on a dialogue with nature (i.e., prairie landscape) that eschewed explicit references to classicism and historicism.[3]

Mies arrived in Chicago in 1938, nearly three decades after the completion of the Robie House, on the eve of World War II, when the tenets of the Prairie School no longer yielded the same fascination despite ongoing interest in organicism among newer generations of "modern" architects. Less than a decade after establishing a bold new curriculum at Armour Institute (later known as IIT) celebrating "the potentialities of organic architecture," Mies began designing a country weekend house for Dr. Farnsworth.[4] Together, the Robie and the Farnsworth houses, albeit with entirely different approaches to space and the integration of modern materials and structure, established Chicago and surrounding cities and villages (the broader "Chicagoland") as a laboratory for architectural innovation in residential architecture during the first half of the twentieth century.

As various articles about the Farnsworth began to be published after the house was completed—the first ap-

1

The Edith Farnsworth House

peared in *Architectural Forum* (October 1951), *House & Garden* (February 1952), and *Harper's Bazaar* (June 1952)—Mies was repeatedly asked questions about his design philosophy, to which he replied with thoughtful and concise statements (a selection of his own remarks specifically regarding the Edith Farnsworth House are gathered in this book, p. 162). Graeme Shankland, an English town planner, conducted a radio interview with Mies for the BBC in 1956, shortly after the Farnsworth House was completed. During this interview he mentioned that "Bruno Zevi said this was not a house at all but a museum."[5] Zevi was at the time one of Italy's foremost architectural critics and the most well-known internationally; he made his reputation in and outside of Italy as a staunch advocate of organic architecture.[6] To Zevi's comment Mies replied:

> No, that is not a fact. It was a house for a single person. That made the problem more simple. Later, I made a house in glass with five bedrooms and five bathrooms, and even a room for the help. That is really a difficult problem. From my point of view, the open plan, when it is possible, makes you work really much harder. Well, Farnsworth House is, I think, not really understood.

In America, various writers and journalists, mostly based on either the East or West Coasts, began to offer their own critiques that combined outright praise with more candid observations. A case in point is the article published in *Architectural Forum* in October 1951, which declared: "...it is the most important house completed in the U.S. since Frank Lloyd Wright built his desert home in Arizona a dozen years ago. For the Farnsworth House near Chicago has no equal in perfection of workmanship, in precision of detail, in pure simplicity of concept." This description was part of a longer overview in which other houses were discussed, dedicated to "Houses—Architect and Client"; the author, who did not sign the article, continued:

> Quite obviously that concept is very special and selective in its appeal. It has little to say to those whose ideal is an informal setting for family living, or to those who seek first to express the individual personality of a client, or finally to those who concentrate on devices of climate control and scientific management of environment. The Farnsworth House was designed for something else to which all these things are equally irrelevant.[7]

In March 1952, the Los Angeles-based *Arts & Architecture* dedicated an entire issue to Mies van der Rohe. The Farnsworth House is discussed within a broader coverage of a number of Mies's buildings and still-to-be realized projects. The author, Hugo Weber, a Swiss-born artist and educator based in Chicago, wrote in general terms about "Space to Space." He credits Wright for laying the groundwork on which Mies could follow: "Mies obtains the flowing space, the totality of space. The articulation of space is achieved subtractively by means of free intermediate walls. Wright has already opened the unity spaces, eliminated the strict separations and accented passages and connections."[8] After a general discussion about Mies, Weber wrote more specifically about the Farnsworth House: "The first detached house Mies could build in America was a country house for a lady doctor. It is a glass house in a wide field with beautiful trees. The house is built and lived in to enjoy the calm of the country and greenery."[9] Today, it is hard to imagine that such a dismissive and generic description as "lady doctor" would be used in reference to a patron and client of modern architecture of the caliber of Edith B. Farnsworth, MD.

In a themed issue of *House & Garden* published in February 1952 dedicated to "The American Idea," Editor-in-Chief Albert Kornfeld wrote in much more respectful terms fully recognizing the role played by the client:

> Dr. Farnsworth decided she wanted a place in the country to relax from her professional duties. She wanted a house that would be aesthetic in terms of today. She submitted her problem to Mies van der Rohe, the pioneering purist who wrote, "architecture is the will of an epoch translated into space." The translation as expressed in Dr. Farnsworth's house is a structure of implacable clam, precise simplicity, and meticulous detail. It could not be built in any age but our own since its realization depends on today's building methods.[10]

This article, as well as one published by *Harper's Bazaar* titled "The Grand Old Men of Modern Architecture" (June 1952), reveals the importance of looking beyond "professional" journals, read primarily by architects, to understand reactions to modern architecture by a general audience.[11] It is perhaps not a coincidence that the *House & Garden* article, sympathetic to both the house and Dr. Edith Farnsworth, was illustrated with a series of intriguing photos by Hungarian-born photographer André Kertész. Significantly, this article contains the only known published photograph—at least until now—of Farnsworth in her house. A handful of more straightforward black and white photos by Hedrich Blessing are also included in this multi-page article.

Additional space to showcasing Farnsworth's contribution as well as voicing her frustrations, something that can also be found in excerpts from her unpublished memoirs, was given by Elizabeth Gordon, in the April 1953 issue of *House Beautiful*. Gordon, the magazine's editor from 1941–64, was a midwesterner with an undergraduate degree from the University of Chicago, and one of Frank Lloyd Wright's greatest champions in the media. In Farnsworth's "defense," she published an article entitled "The Threat to the Next America."[12] Significantly, this article appeared shortly after Mies initiated a lawsuit against Edith Farnsworth ("In Equity General No. 9352").[13] Gordon began her article by taking aim at Mies, by inference rather than name by citing "less is more," an expression typically associated with him: "There is a well-established movement, in modern architecture, decorating, and furnishings, which is promoting the mystical ideal that 'less is more.'"[14] Later on, likewise without naming Farnsworth, Gordon wrote, "I have talked to a highly intelligent, now disillusioned, woman who spent more than $70,000 building a 1-room house that is nothing but a glass cage on stilts."[15] Unfortunately, articles like this contributed to establishing an antagonistic relationship between the organicism started by Louis Sullivan and continued by Wright and the Modern architecture associated with Mies and a number of European émigrés.[16] To be sure, the Farnsworth house is raised on "stilts," however, this is in response to the adjacent Fox River and not for merely aesthetic reasons. Wright designed his buildings by anchoring them, when possible, into the ground. Regarding his ongoing architectural and education experiment at Taliesin, located just outside Spring Green, Wisconsin, Wright wrote: "I knew well that no house should ever be on a hill or on anything. It should be of the hill. Belonging to it. Hill and home should live together each the happier for the other."[17]

Whether in plan, elevation, or section, Wright's organicism took a more aggressive design stance than Mies's modern geometric abstractions. For examples, Wright tended to perforate walls with groupings of windows (both horizontal and vertical, which he often filled with stained glass) to allow light to enter and the viewer to glimpse and visually engage with the outdoors. Wright generally used windows to curate views of the surrounding landscape. Mies deployed floor-to-ceiling glass to provide expansive and uninterrupted views. In his modern European houses designed before arriving to Chicago, Mies used large picture windows (as in the Krefeld Villas) and floor-to-ceiling glass (in the Tugendhat Villa) to let in light and provide interrupted and expansive views. He spoke about this in the following way: "Nature, too, shall live its own life. We must beware not to disrupt it with the color of our houses and interior fittings. Yet we should attempt to bring nature, houses, and human beings together into a higher unity."[18] Despite their differences, Mies's preference for one-story residential pavilions shares more in common with Wright's Usonians than might first appear, especially since this type of building engages visually and spatially with the setting.[19]

Just as the definition of "organic" changed throughout the late-nineteenth and twentieth centuries, so too did the definition of "modern," as either an adjective or noun, shifting considerably depending on the country and language. The use of the variants *modernization*, *modernity*, and *modernism* helps clarify an ever-changing landscape of meaning, insofar as these terms differentiate among technical, philosophical, and aesthetic innovations. Even Frank Lloyd Wright, who took issue with the term, delivered a series of lectures at Princeton University in 1930, subsequently published as *Modern Architecture*.[20] Within this evolving and fluid landscape of definitions, the questions that beg asking are: Is designing and building modern houses for Chicago different from other major cities in the US and beyond? What makes a single-family house modern and/or organic? Why did nature and site play such a consistently important role in the design of modern and/or organic houses? What are Chicago's most significant modern and/or organic houses? And what role did the suburbs play in encouraging the development of the modern and/or organic house in Chicago? The houses discussed in this brief overview chapter, aimed at putting the Edith Farnsworth House into context, reveal that the answers to these questions are not so straightforward, falling more into a gray area than into easily characterized black and-or white zones.

The reasons behind an enduring fascination for the "modern" Edith Farnsworth House are interconnected: awe for the architectural qualities and its site, as well as the controversial client-architect relationship that has generated intrigue among generalists and specialized observers.[21] This country house was designed as a weekend getaway on the banks of the Fox River in Plano, a small city to the west of Chicago.[22] Insofar as it was a house commissioned by a cultivated and independent woman, its client has generated interest among historians seeking to bring visibility to the pioneering role that women played during the twentieth century in shaping modern architecture and design.[23] These contributions have also countered a barrage of unflattering characterizations of Farnsworth contained in first- and secondhand accounts over the years, articulated mostly by men. For example, about twenty years ago, the house's second owner, Lord Peter Palumbo, referred to her in print as a "difficult" woman.[24]

The neighborhoods, cities, and villages surrounding Chicago where these modern and/or organic houses are located were first established in the nineteenth century and considered part and parcel of its metropolitan identity early on.[25] The interconnected identity among the city and its suburbs is evident from a number of guidebooks produced from the late-nineteenth century to the first decades of the twentieth century.[26] Just as the designs of modern and/or organic houses differed, so too did the social fabric of where they were located. What many of these houses share in common is the fact that architects and their adventurous clients introduced "bespoke" architecture (as opposed to the great variety of mail order or builder-driven houses) in places where none was previously found. Especially starting in the 1930s onwards, these communities still had available affordable and desirable parcels of land, unlike within the city itself which had been mostly taken up by houses or apartment buildings.

What makes the Edith Farnsworth House remarkable is its deep connection to the surrounding farmland on the edges of Plano and previously owned by Colonel Robert R. McCormick. Most of the modern houses of note in Chicago functioned as primary residences for their owners, who commuted daily to Chicago for work, and were generally not weekend country houses utilized for leisure.[27] The two most prominent Chicago exceptions are Farnsworth's country weekend house and Adlai E. Stevenson II's house in Libertyville (1938), designed by Philip Will Jr. (Perkins, Wheeler & Will). In Chapter Eleven of Edith's *Memoirs*, she reveals the motivations in commissioning Mies to design her country house on a parcel of farmland:

On Sunday afternoon I used to stretch out on the sofa and listen to the N.Y. Philharmonic on the radio. Often I dropped to sleep during the program, and wakened to the gripping timbre of Msr. Sheen, as he worked his vineyards. As Spring came on one year. I came to the conclusion that something would have to be done about those tired, dull Sundays.

A spot in the country which could be reached in an hour, from which important calls could be taken, patients could be hospitalized if advisable and, at the worst, I could get back to town. With the wife of one of the younger surgeons who had left with his unit, I explored the country about 50 miles west of Chicago one day and crossed the Fox River at Yorkville. Taking the dirt River Road on the west side we came to an abandoned frame farmhouse from which the land sloped down to the river, and to the great views which bordered it. As we stood at the farm gate, a girl came down the road on a Piebald pony. The house was unoccupied, she said, and the place was part of the Tribune Farms, and belonged to Col. McCormick.

Perhaps the most iconic pair of weekend "country" houses in America commissioned by the same patron in two different parts of the country are: Fallingwater in Mill Run, Pennsylvania (1936) designed by Frank Lloyd Wright for the Liliane and Edgar Kaufmann family, and the Kaufmann Desert House in Palm Springs, California (1946) designed by Richard Neutra.[28] The acclaimed International Style house on Long Island (1938) designed by Edward Durell Stone for A. Conger Goodyear and his spouse at the time, Mary Martha Forman, was conceived as a weekend retreat for the industrialist and art collector who was appointed as MoMA's first president in 1929.[29] During the postwar years, the town of New Canaan, Connecticut,

along with Cape Cod and its surrounding areas, became preferred sites for New Yorkers and Bostonians in search of either permanent or weekend houses.[30]

While Philip Johnson's Glass House in New Canaan (1949), which has deep connections to the Farnsworth, functioned as a weekend retreat, architects like Marcel Breuer and Eliot Noyes experimented with designs for permanent residences during those same years for their own families in New Canaan, and in so doing established it as a progressive enclave for modern architecture.[31]

Architectural Forum, cited earlier, described the Farnsworth house as a synthesis between modern and classical: "Mies van der Rohe's house is *modern* and *classical;* he has embraced industry, translated the steel skeleton frame into a house 'language,' provided impersonal but beautiful space to be personally arranged by those willing to live in the modern equivalent of the Doric order."[32] Lord Palumbo, the Farnsworth's sophisticated second owner, also spoke repeatedly about this quality.[33] In the interview included in this book, conducted during the author's research and writing phase, Palumbo stated about his years at Eton College:

And so, when we came to the actual study time, which was one hour every Sunday, the class was done with photographs and descriptions of the artist, his life, and his work. We did Jackson Pollock and it was shortly thereafter, he showed us photographs of the Farnsworth House. When we saw the photographs, I thought to myself, "I've never seen anything as beautiful as this–or as historic." I mean, it was like the contemporary version of the Temple of Paestum, or somewhere like that, springing up out of the meadow.

Palumbo references one of three temples at Paestum and not, for example, the Acropolis. The Greek temples are located on the West Coast of Italy just south of Naples, and modern-day visitors to the archaeological site like Palumbo would have viewed them within a field and not within a densely "urban" portion of a city like Athens.

The *Architectural Forum* writer also discusses differences between the Farnsworth and the Glass House, describing the latter as "symmetrically balanced" and the Farnsworth house as "asymmetrical, dynamically balanced."[34] Unlike Johnson, who had the structural elements painted dark grey, Mies's choice of white-painted steel echoes classicism, while allowing for contrast with the surrounding nature throughout most of the seasons except after a winter snowfall.[35] Unlike the Glass House, which rests on the ground, the Farnsworth has eight I-beams/columns to sustain both the ceiling plane and the floor, which is elevated from the ground to accommodate the periodic flooding of the Fox River.[36] This practical decision confers to the house an otherworldly dimension as it floats above the meadow. In addition to responding to the floodplain, Mies strategically sited the house around the monumental black sugar maple tree in order to exploit the shading capabilities of this natural "architecture" (see Ron Henderson's essay, p. 116). These two responses to siting conditions alone speak to an architect who reacts to specific site-contextual cues, despite the abstraction typically associated with modern architecture or the International Style, which some critics claimed deprived architecture of a site-specific quality.

Unlike Johnson's frontal symmetrical entrance, the Farnsworth House is accessed indirectly through a side entrance at the covered "porch" (upper terrace) that is reached by five stairsteps from the lower terrace. The open-plan configuration—only the two bathrooms and utilities are concealed in the primavera wood-clad freestanding core flanked by a galley kitchen, "bedroom," as well as a living and dining area—confers a sense of airiness that is further reinforced by the unobstructed views on all sides of the rectangular floor plan. Through a magisterial dialogue of the modern materials glass and steel, contrasted in part by the organic qualities of the primavera wood and the travertine floor, Mies sets up a relationship with the surrounding nature that is simultaneously deferential and participatory. The constant change of seasons made visible through the floor-to-ceiling glass "walls" ensures that the experience of this architectural space is always different for inhabitants and visitors alike.

Rather than viewing organic principles associated with the Prairie School in opposition to modern functionalism or rationalism, Chicago architects who arrived from elsewhere or who trained in America absorbed cues from *both* traditions throughout the course of their careers. It is with this exchange of ideas and approaches in mind that one can understand Mies's enthusiastic reaction to the exhibition and publication of Wright's Wasmuth portfolio (1911) in Berlin:

> We young architects found ourselves in painful inner conflict. We were ready to pledge ourselves to an idea. But the potential vitality of the architectural idea of this period had, by that time, been lost. This, then, was the situation in 1910. At this moment, so critical for us, there came to Berlin the exhibition of the work of Frank Lloyd Wright. This comprehensive display and the extensive publication of his works enabled us really to become acquainted with the achievement of this architect. The encounter was destined to prove of great significance to the development of architecture in Europe. The work of this great master revealed an architectural world of unexpected force and clarity of language, and also a disconcerting richness of form. Here finally was a master-builder drawing upon the veritable fountainhead of architecture, who with true originality lifted his architectural creations into the light. Here, again, genuine organic architecture flowered.[37]

Mies's comments point to the growing dialogue between modern architects who were arriving to the United States and transforming architectural practice and education. Two important books published in the early 1940s and coauthored by architect James Ford and sociologist Katherine Morrow Ford—*The Modern House in America* (1940) and the companion volume *Design of Modern Interiors* (1942)—acknowledge the changes to the American house and its interiors following the arrival of European émigrés:

> Then came the hegira to America. In their relative youth came Belluschi, Lescaze, Neutra, Schindler, and Soriano, each prior to 1930. In more recent years arrived such already established leaders as Gropius—the founder of that pioneering school, the Bauhaus—and his associates, Breuer and Moholy-Nagy; also Mies van der Rohe from Germany, Saarinen from Finland, and Ruhtenberg from Sweden.

> These men have been quick to catch the spirit of America, to appraise its opportunities for new rationales and mediums, and for new uses of materials. They are now making their own performance essentially American. They and their students are producing, not an "international style," but a new American architecture, cosmopolitan in spirit, but native both in form and detail—a genuine expression of American individuality.[38]

The Fords' anthology includes, among others, Chicago-based architects: William F. Deknatel, Keck & Keck (George Fred and William), and Philip B. Maher. In a subsequent publication written by Katherine Ford and Thomas H. Creighton entitled *The American House Today: 85 Notable Examples Selected and Evaluated* (1951), the authors reflect on the dissemination of modern houses beyond the coasts:

> So it was not until the late thirties and early forties that anything which could be reasonably called a contemporary movement in architecture had developed in the United States. In contrast to the choice of material available for this book, when one of the present authors collaborated on a book about residential architecture in 1940 it was a matter of discovering unrecognized talent, of searching for little-known work. And discovering that not very much worth consideration existed except in a few parts of the country, chiefly on the east and west

2 George Fred Keck, the
Irma Kuppenheimer and
Bertram J. Cahn House,
1937, Lake Forest.

coast. However, many architects in others sections of the country were feeling their way toward the new objectives.**39**

Together, these three books did much to promote modern architecture in America and the growing awareness of how different perspectives could enhance rather than limit its transformation.

A decade before the Farnsworth House revolutionized Chicago's postwar modern architectural identity, America was showing signs of embracing modern architecture. Just two months before Germany's invasion of Poland would trigger the beginning of the Second World War, the July 1939 issue of *Architectural Forum* dedicated the entire volume to "Modern Houses in America." The first paragraph of the opening editorial reads:

3 Philip B. Maher, the
Madeleine Michelson and
Philip B. Maher House,
1938, Lake Bluff.

> It is thirty years since Frank Lloyd Wright built the Coonley house, fourteen years since Le Corbusier's pavilion disrupted a Paris fair, nine since Miës van der Rohe produced the Tugendhat plan. Long enough, one might think, for the modern house to come of age in an epoch of swift development. But the new dwellings in the 1939 U.S. landscape are still predominantly traditional."**40**

Out of the fifteen featured houses that cumulatively demonstrate the coming of age of American modern residential design, two were designed by Chicago-based architects for cities and villages that are part of the greater Chicago metropolitan area. These houses include George Fred Keck's Irma Kuppenheimer and Bertram J. Cahn House in Lake Forest (1937) and Philip B. Maher's own house (with Madeleine Michelson Maher, his spouse at the time) in Lake Bluff (1938). [Figs. 2-3] In the Cahn House, Keck used large picture windows and glass block for his one-story, crescent-shaped pavilion. Maher's elegant two-story L-shaped volume also made abundant use of "glass block walls," plus large panes of glass, in order to take advantage of the views of Lake Michigan. These two modern houses reveal how different generations of Chicago-based architects during the 1930s—who were at the time mostly in their thirties and forties—were rethinking residential architecture in response to a rapidly modernizing American society still grappling with the challenges of the Great Depression.

In this 1939 issue of *Architectural Forum*, the editorial introducing the fifteen houses asserts that change is in the air: "There are the recent polls, which show a consistent consumer opinion of 40-odd percent favorable to the modern house, some four times the figure of a few years back," and goes on to assert that, "The modern house today is no longer the frigid white symbol of a small cult, and in changing it has immeasurably broadened its appeal."**41** Without explicitly identifying an architect,

building, or country, the editors' reference to "frigid white symbol of a small cult" seems to target certain examples of modernist architecture of the late 1920s through the early '30s. To be sure, some of these buildings were on display at *Modern Architecture: International Exhibition* (Exhibition 15), curated by Henry-Russell Hitchcock and Philip Johnson, at the Museum of Modern Art in 1932, and later that year shown in the galleries of the Sears flagship store in Chicago's Loop.**42** The curators and authors of the accompanying catalog—which bore the new title that provided the shorthand phrase for this new architecture, *The International Style: Architecture Since 1922*—single out three Chicago-based architects: Howard Fisher, George Fred Keck, and Henry Dubin.**43** Despite the fact that an entire section was dedicated to Frank Lloyd Wright, this traveling exhibition seems to have contributed to the American public's understanding (or misunderstanding) of modernism as "frigid white" buildings that all looked alike regardless of client, climate, or site.**44**

Also a year after the MoMA exhibition was displayed in New York and traveled to Chicago, the midwestern city hosted the hugely popular Century of Progress International Exposition (1933–34), which did much to distract Depression-era citizens from their daily challenges. George Fred Keck's House of Tomorrow (interiors by Irene K. Hyman and J. Leland Atwood) and Crystal House drew considerable interest. The range of

model houses on display at the "Home and Industrial Arts Exhibit" promoted both modern materials alongside traditional building materials used in new ways (for example the Brick Manufacturers Association House by Andrew Rebori) as well as furnishings for the single-family house.**45** [Figs. 4-5]

In a bid to correct the perceived "modernistic" shortfalls of Chicago's Century of Progress Exhibition, which in his opinion was not modern enough, Philip Johnson offered a polemical curatorial campaign by launching his own counter-exhibition entitled *Work of Young Architects in the Middle West* at the Museum of Modern Art in the spring of 1933.**46** Johnson wrote in the catalog:

It seems appropriate in the year that Chicago is the cynosure of architectural eyes that there should be an exhibition of work of men whose attitude toward architecture is newer and younger than that of those in charge of designing the buildings for the Century of Progress Exposition. Some of these young men are working for the Exposition but their work will be lost in the midst of the official architecture which dominates the main pavilions.

This exhibition is a logical successor to the International Exhibition of Modern Architecture held by the Museum in 1932. The young generation, now beginning their independent practice, have broken away from academic design. They have not as much opportunity to build as their predecessors, but more to observe and study. As a result this exhibition consists mainly of projects, but projects which show not only research into new problems but great strides away from the Beaux Arts classical (not to mention the Beaux Arts "modernistic").**47**

For reasons not necessarily ascribable to the curators of MoMA's International Style exhibition, the expression "International Style" became synonymous with promoting an idea of modern architecture as a static set of formal characteristics rather than a source of ideas and ideals. For example, Sigfried Giedion's *A Decade of New Architecture,* published in 1951, offers a summary of significant architecture covering the years 1937–47; in this overview he discusses a number of Chicago-area houses by George Fred Keck, Ralph Rapson, Robert Paul Schweikher, and Winston Elting. Giedion's book attempted to communicate with his readers that "modern" in architecture was very much in constant transformation. The American architectural historian and critic William Jordy offers a similar insight: "If, however, one interprets Hitchcock and Johnson very narrowly—more narrowly than they would wish—and if one seeks the outstanding buildings designed after 1932 which continue in the image of the Style described in their book, few are to be found."**48**

It is against the backdrop of an evolving debate shaped by complementary and sometimes competing ideas about modern architecture that Chicago's contribution to the single-family house in America should be understood. Alongside the single-family house, we understand that a variety of other building types ranging from schools to religious buildings played important roles in creating livable neighborhoods within cities and villages while promoting acceptance of modern architecture. For example, the

4 George Fred Keck, Chicago Century of Progress, House of Tomorrow, 1933.

5 George Fred Keck, Chicago Century of Progress Exposition, Crystal House, 1934.

6 Howard T. Fisher, the Katherine Dummer and Walter T. Fisher House, 1929, Winnetka, photographed for *Architectural Record.*

7 Pereira & Pereira, the Charles Dewey Jr. House and Beach House, 1940, Lake Bluff.

8 William Deknatel, the Ellen Newby and Lambert Ennis House, 1942, Evanston.

9 George Fred Keck, the Vine Itschner and Herbert Bruning House 1936, Wilmette.

10 Henry Dubin, the Anne Green and Henry Dubin House, 1930, Highland Park, photographed for *Architectural Forum*.

Katherine Dummer and Howard T. Fisher House (1929) introduced modern architecture to Winnetka nearly a decade before Perkins, Wheeler & Will collaborated with Eliel and Eero Saarinen to design one of America's first truly progressive educational buildings, the Crow Island School (1940). Henry-Russell Hitchcock, cocurator of the MoMA International Style exhibition, would go on to state the following about the Fisher House, "it is nearly the first [house] in America to which the most rigid international standards of contemporary architectural criticism may be applied."**49** [Fig. 6]

Along with professional journals and anthologies organized around themes or types, Chicago's modern houses were occasionally selected to be part of national and international marketing publications and shelter magazines aimed at architects, builders, and homeowners.

For example, William Pereira's Charles Dewey Jr. House (1940) in Lake Bluff was featured on the cover of George Nelson and Henry Wright's *Tomorrow's House: A Complete Guide for the Home-Builder* (1945). [Fig. 7] A number of Chicago houses including Paul Schweikher and Winston Elting's Gertrude Stevens and Philip S. Rinaldo Jr. House in Downers Grove (1940, demolished) and William Deknatel's Ellen Newby and Lambert Ennis House in Evanston

(1948) were featured in the 1948 book *Windows in Modern Architecture* by Geoffrey Baker & Bruno Funaro.**50** [Fig. 8]

From the 1930s onward, picture windows (as well as awning and casements windows) were frequently showcased in residential architecture advertisements, as they were seen as key to the pursuit of "spaciousness" in the modern American house.**51** The Libbey-Owens-Ford Glass Company (Toledo) published a brochure titled "Glass-As an Architectural Medium in 9 Small 'Modern' Houses at the Century of Progress 1933–34," and they used the Vine Itschner and Herbert Bruning House designed by George Fred Keck in Wilmette (1936) in an advertisement about Insulux Glass Block in *Architectural Record* (November 1938).**52** [Fig. 9]

While glass was most often associated with modernism, the materials and building technologies deployed in the Chicago houses of this period are quite eclectic. Architect Henry Dubin's "fireproof" Battledeck House in Highland Park (1930) abandoned wood as a conventional structural building material in favor of a hybrid steel and load-bearing brick-and-concrete-block system. [Fig. 10] The strikingly "cubist" Josephine Topp and De Forest S. Colburn House in Highland Park designed by Gilmer Vardiman Black and completed in 1937, was advertised as a "fire-

safe concrete home."[53] [Fig. 11] The first house designed by Howard T. Fisher in 1935 for Ellen Borden and Adlai E. Stevenson II in Libertyville was prefabricated; it burned to the ground in 1938 and was replaced by another, more conventionally built house designed by Perkins, Wheeler & Will. Schweikher and Theodore Warren Lamb's brick masonry Flora Francis and David B. Johnson House in the Chicago neighborhood of Jackson Park Highlands (1936) reveals a debt to the city's architects' deep commitment to building in brick as a material that bridged modern with organic approaches.[54] [Fig. 12]

Exceptions, however, to the use of brick did exist especially amongst the architects trained at IIT. In addition to Mies's steel-and-glass Farnsworth House, he designed a one-story house for Robert Hall McCormick III and poet Isabella Gardner, his spouse at the time, in Elmhurst (1952). This experimental house, Mies's response to Wright's Usonian House, was conceived as a prefabricated glass and steel modular pavilion that that could be easily replicated.[55] [Fig. 13] The Frances Landrum and Ben Rose House designed by A. James Speyer, one of the first students to train with Mies upon his arrival to Armour, designed the steel-framed one-story main house with infill cypress vertical boards; these complement the wooded setting and

created a beautiful synthesis between organic and modern materials and structure. [Fig. 14] While some of Mies's students deployed steel construction in a handful of modern houses in Chicago, the American residential building industry has remained somewhat conservative; elsewhere in America, despite their best efforts, many architects who participated in the Case Study House program, whose epicenter was mainly Los Angeles, were unable, despite the vigorous campaign by *Arts & Architecture* magazine, to convince the majority of Americans that modern houses should be built of steel.[56]

Conversely, largely thanks to the wood buildings of George Fred Keck that were on the forefront of passive solar experimentation, the greater Chicago area received a considerable amount of national and international press from the 1930s to the '60s.[57] For example, the house that he designed and built for renowned sociologist Hugh Dalziel Duncan in 1941 marked an important moment in his development of the passive solar house. It, like the McCormick House, was one story, but it deployed wood (and glass) instead of steel (and glass). The design of the Minna Green and Hugh Duncan House in Flossmoor was linear, with the major spaces—the bedroom and combined living, dining, study, and kitchen—of this small house all

11 Gilmer Vardiman Black, the Josephine Topp and De Forest S. Colburn House, 1937, Highland Park.

12 Paul Schweikher and Theodore Warren Lamb, the Flora Francis and David B. Johnson House, 1936, Jackson Park Highlands, Chicago.

13 Mies van der Rohe, the Isabella Gardner and Robert Hall McCormick III House, 1952, Elmhurst.

14 A. James Speyer, the Francis Landrum and Ben Rose House, 1953, Highland Park.

facing south to capture sunlight. The walls on the southern exposure were floor-to-ceiling glass sheltered by a deep roof projection that took into account the seasonal angles of the sun. **[Fig. 15]**

Emblematic of a synthesis of lessons, regarding nature and organicism learned from Wright and Mies, is Paul Schweikher's House (1938) and Studio addition (1947) in Schaumburg. **[Fig. 16]** Schweikher used natural materials (unfinished redwood) for interior paneling and exterior siding, and employed large panes of glass. In addition, he seems to replicate the House and Studio mixed-use model first used by Wright in Oak Park.**58** Before partnering with Schweikher, Winston Elting designed a house for himself and his wife, Marjorie Horton, and their family in 1940, in the affluent city of Lake Forest. It blends modern attitudes toward massing, plan, and siting with organic materiality.**59** **[Fig. 17]** Winston Elting's Lake Forest House was designed shortly after completing the Sylvia Valha and Frances J. Benda House in Riverside (1939); this two-story flat-roof house blends modern attitudes toward massing, plan, and siting with organic materiality. **[Fig. 18]** Edward Humrich combined Wrightian with midcentury modernist cues in his numerous one-story ranches such as the Eleanor Gray and Saul Lieberman House designed for the planned community of Graymoor Residential Park in Olympia Fields (1956).**60** **[Fig. 19]**

Even just the proximity to Mies and Wright buildings in Chicago's neighborhoods and suburban villages and cities served as a catalyst for younger architects in the city in search of a synthesis between organic and modern cues. For example, Ralph Rapson, speaking about his commission for the modern Adele Bretzfeld and Willard Gidwitz House in Hyde Park (1943) admitted that the proximity of the site to Wright's Robie House just a few blocks away prompted him to "work at that level."**61** **[Fig. 20]** Whereas Mies exerted considerable influence upon architects who trained at Armour/IIT and who chose to remain in the city to work, Wright sponsored his own laboratory at the School of Architecture at Taliesin he founded in nearby Wisconsin in 1932 and subsequently in Arizona in 1937.**62**

The range of houses realized during the first half of the twentieth century such as the Fisher House in Winnetka (1929), or the mid-sized Duncan House I, Flossmoor (1941), points to fact that the income status of many of the clients who commissioned the houses were in the middle- to upper-middle class range. Commissioning clients of modern houses, such as Edith Farnsworth herself, tended to be professionals who identified with progressive values.**63** Although many had some wealth, they were not the super-affluent who had commissioned the nineteenth- and early twentieth-century mansions along Prairie Avenue, the Gold Coast, Lake Shore Drive, and areas of the North Shore.**64**

15 Keck & Keck, the Minna Green and Hugh Duncan House I, 1941, Flossmoor.

16 Paul Schweikher, the Dorothy Miller and Paul Schweikher House, 1938 with studio addition in 1949, Schaumburg.

17 Winston Elting, the Marjorie Horton and Winston Elting House, 1940, Lake Forest.

18 Winston Elting, the Sylvia Valha and Francis J. Benda House, 1939, Riverside.

During the second half of the twentieth century this trend continued. A number of modern houses in Chicago were designed by architects for their own families, especially since they tend to fall into the category of middle-class professionals. Examples include Sheila Adelman and David Haid's House in Evanston (1969), as well as Doris Curry and Jacques Brownson's House in Geneva (1952), located along the very same Fox River Valley where the Farnsworth House is found. [Figs 21-22] Both of these one-story houses were designed by graduates of IIT, and they pay direct homage to Mies's deep interest in the design of pavilion and courtyard houses. Combining natural materials like brick with industrially-produced ones like steel and glass, both Haid and Brownson demonstrate the extent to which the "organic," or "modern" for that matter, are less about style and more about the experience of nature.

Simplistic characterizations, flat roof or pitched roof, two-story "boxy" house versus a land-hugging one-story pavilion, do not sufficiently capture the complex interplay between the organic and the modern in twentieth century houses in Chicago. To be sure, Chicago is a particularly interesting city to study the development of a modern architecture that developed in part due to the arrival from Europe of émigrés after Frank Lloyd Wright and the Prairie School architects had already developed a uniquely

"American" architecture with an international following. By understanding the different trajectories of Ludwig Mies van der Rohe in Chicago—in comparison to Rudolph Schindler and Richard Neutra (both of whom worked in Chicago before moving to Los Angeles), Walter Gropius in Cambridge, and Eliel Saarinen (who moved to Evanston after a sojourn in Chicago) in Bloomfield Hills, Michigan—one can better understand how the arrival of émigrés offered opportunities for exchanges that contributed significantly, along with other aspects of everyday American culture, toward a new approach to designing modern single-family houses. It is not surprising that as battles were raging in Europe for a war that was jump-started by the rise of nationalist collective ideologies, increasingly the focus turned to modern architecture with "American individuality" and more importantly, the single-family house, which promoted the traditional family nucleus. By absorbing cues from modern architecture (associated with Mies and other Bauhaus émigrés such as Walter Gropius) with an organic architecture (associated with Wright's Prairie School), architects of different generations designed innovative modern houses that transformed Chicago into a veritable laboratory of design.

19 Edward Humrich, the Eleanor Gray and Saul Lieberman House,1956, Olympia Fields.

20 Ralph E. Rapson and John van der Meulen, the Adele Bretzfeld and Willard Gidwitz House, 1946, Chicago.

21 David Haid, the Sheila Adelman and David Haid House, 1969, Evanston.

22 Jacques C. Brownson, the Doris Curry and Jacques C. Brownson House, 1952, Geneva.

Notes

1 This essay is based upon my Introduction "Modern Houses for Modern Living in Chicago," published in Susan S. Benjamin and Michelangelo Sabatino, *Modern in the Middle: Chicago Houses 1929–75* (New York: The Monacelli Press, 2020), pp. 10–37.

2 On the Robie House see: Donald Hoffmann, *Frank Lloyd Wright's Robie House: The Illustrated Story of an Architectural Masterpiece* (New York: Dover, 1984); Joseph Connors, *The Robie House of Frank Lloyd Wright* (Chicago: University of Chicago Press, 1984).

In terms of dialogue between modern and organic, recall that before and during the realization of her country house, Dr. Farnsworth consulted with Chicago-based architects George Fred Keck and Harry Weese, whose design approaches took cues from both Mies and Wright. Note the following two quotations in Schulze and Windhorst, *Mies van der Rohe: A Critical Biography, New and Revised Edition* (Chicago: University of Chicago Press, 2012). On page 248 (quoting from trial transcript Van der Rohe v. Farnsworth, No. 9352 Ill. Cir. Ct., Kendall County, p. 313): "Mies added that he learned that before she met him, Farnsworth had asked Chicago architect George Fred Keck to design the house. Keck, said Mies, would undertake the project only on condition that he "can do what he wants, and she didn't seem to like that." On page 255 (quoting from Myron Goldsmith in his Oral History interview with Betty J. Blum, 2001, p. 68) in the context of discussions over the color of the curtains: "She said something like "I don't like the Shantung natural silk color. I discussed it with Harry Weese and he thought it should be brown." Farnsworth likely met Harry Weese in the context of Baldwin Kingrey, a design store specializing in midcentury modern design, open between 1947–1957, co-owned by Kitty Baldwin Weese and Jody Kingrey. In addition to the Good Design exhibitions held at the Merchandise Mart during the 1950s, Farnsworth most likely purchased some of her midcentury furniture from Baldwin Kingrey. Zach Mortice ("A Second Look at Edith Farnsworth and Her Mies van der Rohe-Designed Retreat," *Architectural Record* (July 15, 2020): 85) "traced the likely design lineage of Edith's daybed back to Harry Weese."

3 H. Allen Brooks, *The Prairie School: Frank Lloyd Wright and His Midwest Contemporaries* (Toronto: University of Toronto Press, 1972). In 1908 Wright wrote: "We of the Middle West are living on the prairie. The prairie has a beauty of its own and we should recognize and accentuate this natural beauty, it's quiet level. Hence, gently sloping roofs, low proportions, quiet sky lines, suppressed heavy-set chimneys and sheltering overhangs, low terraces and out-reaching walls sequestering private gardens." First published as "In the Cause of Architecture," *Architectural Record 23*, no. 3 (March 1908) and republished in Frederick Gutheim, ed., *Frank Lloyd Wright in the Cause of Architecture* (New York: Architectural Record, 1975), 53–119.

4 In the architecture curriculum launched in 1939 by Mies at the Armour Institute (subsequently the Illinois Institute of Technology) he wrote in a section entitled "Planning and Creating" about "The obligation to realize the potentialities of organic architecture." See Rolf Achilles, Kevin Harrington, and Charlotte Myhrum, *Mies van der Rohe, Architect as Educator* (Chicago: Mies van der Rohe Centennial Project, Illinois Institute of Technology, 1986). See also Alfred Swenson and Pao-Chi Chang, *Architectural Education at IIT, 1938–1978* (Chicago: Illinois Institute of Technology, 1980).

5 Graeme Shankland, Radio Interview: BBC Third Programme (aired on October 6th, 1956). Published in Vittorio Pizzigoni and Michelangelo Sabatino, eds., *Mies in His Own Words: Complete Writings, Speeches, and Interviews* (Berlin: DOM Publishers, 2024).

6 The source of Zevi's comment about the Farnsworth House, cited by Graeme Shankland, is unclear. During those years, Zevi published the following article in English: Bruno Zevi, "The Reality of a House is the Space Within," *House Beautiful*, November 1955, pp. 254–57; 373–76. However, he makes no mention the Farnsworth House. This article appeared shortly after the publication of: Bruno Zevi, *Towards an Organic Architecture* (London: Faber & Faber, 1950) (orig. Italian edition, *Verso un'architettura organica; Saggio sullo sviluppo del pensiero architettonico negli ultimi cinquant'anni* (Turin G. Einaudi, 1945).

7 "Houses-Architect & Client," *Architectural Forum* 95, no. 4 (October 1951): 156–61, 157.

8 A note in the table of contents states "This material arranged by Konrad Wachsmann," but the article is signed with the initials H. W. (presumably Hugo Weber). "Mies Van der Rohe," *Arts and Architecture* 69, no. 6 (March 1952): 16–31, 17.

9 "Mies Van der Rohe," *Arts and Architecture*, pp. 16–31, p. 38. The Farnsworth photographs are found on pp. 22–25.

10 Albert Kornfeld, "The American Idea in Houses," *House and Garden*, February 1952, pp. 44–49.

11 "The Grand Old Men of Modern Architecture," *Harper's Bazaar*, June 1952, pp. 68–71. The portrait of Mies in this article is by renowned photographer Harry Callahan whereas Wright was portrayed by Richard Avedon.

12 Elizabeth Gordon, "The Threat to the Next America," *House Beautiful*, April 1953, pp.126–30; 250–51.

13 Franz Schulze and Edward Windhorst, *Mies van der Rohe: A Critical Biography* (Chicago: The Unviersity of Chicago Press, 2012), in part. Ch. 10, "The Farnsworth Saga: 1946–2003," pp. 247–303.

14 Gordon, *House Beautiful*, p. 126.

15 Gordon, *House Beautiful*, p. 129.

16 For an analysis of Gordon's career and contributions see Monica Penick, *Tastemaker: Elizabeth Gordon, House Beautiful, and the Postwar American Home* (New Haven: Yale University Press, 2017).

17 Frank Lloyd Wright, "Taliesin," in Edgar Kaufmann and Ben Raeburn, *Frank Lloyd Wright: Writings and Buildings* (New York: Horizon, 1960), p. 173.

18 Christian Norberg-Schulz, "A Talk with Mies van der Rohe," *Baukunst und Werkform* 11, no. 11 (1958), reprinted in Fritz Neumeyer, *The Artless Word: Mies van der Rohe on the Building Art*, trans. Mark Jarzombek (Cambridge: MIT Press, 1991), p. 235. On Mies and nature see: Albert Kirchengast, *Das unvollständige Haus: Mies van der Rohe und die Landschaft* (Basel: Birkhäuser, 2019); Albert Kirchengast, "Mies's Organic Order," in *Nature Modern: The Place of Landscape in the Modern Movement*, eds, Christophe Girot and Albert Kirchengast (Berlin: Jovis, 2017), pp. 149–68.

19 Neil Levine, ed., *Frank Lloyd Wright's Jacobs Houses: Experiments in Modern Living* (Chandler, AZ: OA+D Archives Press, 2022).

20 Frank Lloyd Wright, *Modern Architecture: Being the Kahn Lectures for 1930* (Carbondale: Southern Illinois University Press, 1987).

21 For accounts aimed at general readers see the book written by journalist Alex Beam, *Broken Glass: Mies van der Rohe, Edith Farnsworth, and the Fight Over a Modernist Masterpiece* (New York: Penguin Random House 2020). At one point a film, *Farnsworth House*, written and directed by Richard Press with Maggie Gyllenhaal playing Edith Farnsworth and Ralph Fiennes playing Mies, was in the works.

22 Plano had a population of 2,154 in 1950 according to the Census of Population and Housing compared to Chicago, which measured 3,620,962 Census of Population and Housing, accessed December 2, 2019, census.gov. For a history of Plano see Kristy Lawrie Gravlin, Anne Sears, Jeanne Valentine, and the Plano Community Library District, *Images of America: Plano* (Charleston, SC: Arcadia Publishing, 2012).

23 See for example Alice T. Friedman, *Women and the Making of the Modern House: A Social and Architectural History* (New York: Abrams, 1998) and Nora Wendl, "Uncompromising Reasons for Going West: A Story of Sex and Real Estate, Reconsidered," *Thresholds* 43 (Spring 2015) and "Edith: An Architectural History," List Gallery, Swarthmore College, January 19-February 25, 2023.

24 Maritz Vandenberg, *Farnsworth House: Ludwig Mies van der Rohe* (London: Phaidon, 2003), p. 24. See the account given in "The Farnsworth Saga: 1946-2003" in Franz Schulze and Edward Windhorst, *Mies Van Der Rohe: A Critical Biography, New and Revised Edition* (Chicago: University of Chicago Press, 2014), pp. 248-73.

25 Dominic A. Pacyga and Ellen Skerrett, *Chicago, City of Neighborhoods: Histories & Tours* (Chicago: Loyola University Press, 1986).

26 For example: Everett Chamberlin, *Chicago and its Suburbs* (Chicago: T. A. Hungerford, 1874); Marian A. White, *Book of the North Shore: Homes, Gardens, Landscapes, Highways and Byways, Past and Present* (Chicago: J. Harrison White, 1910) followed by *Second Book of the North Shore: Homes, Gardens, Landscapes, Highways and Byways, Past and Present* (1911), and finally *Book of the Western Suburbs: Homes, Gardens, Landscapes, Highways and Byways, Past and Present* (1912). "Chicago and Suburbs" were included in the Works Progress Administration, *The WPA Guide to Illinois: The Prairie State* (1939; 2014); reissued with new introduction by Neil Harris and Michael Conzen, *The WPA Guide to Illinois: The Federal Writers Project Guide to 1930s Illinois* (New York: Pantheon, 1983).

27 Lewis A. Coffin, *American Country Houses of Today* (New York: Architectural Book Publishing, 1935) (reprinted as *American Country Houses of the Thirties with Photographs and Floor Plans* (Mineola, NY: Dover, 2007); Mark Alan Hewitt, *The Architect and the American Country House, 1890-1940* (Yale University Press, 1990).

28 Edgar Kaufmann Jr., *Fallingwater: A Frank Lloyd Wright Country House* (New York: Abbeville, 1986). Alice T. Friedman, *American Glamour and the Evolution of Modern Architecture* (New Haven: Yale University Press, 2010), in part. "Palm Springs Eternal: Richard Neutra's Kaufmann Desert House," pp.74-107.

29 Mary Anne Hunting, *Edward Durell Stone: Modernism's Populist Architect* (New York: Norton, 2013).

30 William D. Earls, *The Harvard Five in New Canaan: Midcentury Modern Houses by Marcel Breuer, Landis Gores, John Johansen, Philip Johnson, Eliot Noyes & Others* (New York: Norton, 2006); Jeffrey Matz, *Midcentury Houses Today: New Canaan, Connecticut* (New York: The Monacelli Press, 2014). Peter McMahon, *Cape Cod Modern: Midcentury Architecture and Community on the Outer Cape* (New York: Metropolis, 2014).

31 Joachim Driller, *Breuer Houses* (London: Phaidon, 2000); Bruce Gordon, *Eliot Noyes* (London: Phaidon, 2006); and, more recently, *James Crump, Breuer's Bohemia: The Architect, His Circle, and Midcentury Houses in New England* (New York: The Monacelli Press, 2021).

32 House Issue, *Architectural Forum* 95, no. 4 (October 1951): 155.

33 Peter Palumbo, "Farnsworth Impressions," *Inland Architect* 30, no. 2 (March/April 1986): 42-47. See also Maritz Vandenberg, *Farnsworth House* (London: Phaidon, 2003), in part. Foreword, pp. 4-5. See also Paul Goldberger & Lord Palumbo, in conversation at the Farnsworth House, April 2003, in Sotheby's International Realty, *The Farnsworth House, 1945-1951, Ludwig Mies van der Rohe, Sale 7957* (New York, 2003), pp. 22-24.

34 House Issue, p.160.

35 Dirk Lohan, Mies's grandson, has repeatedly shared with the author that Mies believed that painting his buildings white in Chicago would have been a losing battle with the polluted air that would have inevitably changed their color. On the other hand, the agrarian site of the Farnsworth was free from color-altering pollutants.

36 For detailed construction drawings see Dirk Lohan, *Farnsworth House, Plano 1945-1950* (Tokyo: ADA Edita, 2000); see also Neil Jackson, *The Modern Steel House* (London: Routledge, 2016), pp. 65-76.

37 Ludwig Mies van der Rohe, "Tribute," *College Art Journal* 6 (Autumn 1946): 41-42. Republished in H. Allen Brooks, ed., *Writings on Wright: Selected Comment on Frank Lloyd Wright* (Cambridge: MIT Press, 1961), pp. 129-30. See also: Frank Lloyd Wright, *Frank Lloyd Wright: Eine Studie zu Seiner Würdigung* (Berlin: E. Wasmuth, 1911): English translation (New York: Dover Publications, 1982). Anthony Alofsin, ed., *Frank Lloyd Wright: Europe and Beyond* (Berkeley: University of California Press, 1999).

38 James Ford and Katherine Morrow Ford, *The Modern House in America* (New York: Architectural Book Publishing, 1940), p. 14. (Re-issued as James Ford and Katherine Morrow Ford, *Classic Modern Houses of the Thirties: 64 Designs by Neutra, Gropius, Breuer, Stone, and Others* (New York: Dover, 1989); James Ford and Katherine Morrow Ford, *Design of Modern Interiors* (New York: Architectural Book Publishing, 1942), p. 14.

39 Katherine Morrow Ford and Thomas H. Creighton, *The American House Today: 85 Notable Examples Selected and Evaluated* (New York: Reinhold, 1951), p. 4.

40 "Modern Houses in America," *Architectural Forum* 71, no. 1 (July 1939): 1.

41 *"Modern Houses in America,"* pp. 1-2.

42 For announcement of the exhibition see: *Chicago Daily Tribune*, Sunday, June 12, 1932, p.63. See also: Terence Riley, *The International Style: Exhibition 15 and the Museum of Modern Art* (New York: Rizzoli, 1992). See Barry Bergdoll, "Layers of Polemic: MoMA's Founding International Exhibition Between Influence and Reality" in Alfred H. Barr Jr., Henry-Russell Hitchcock, Jr., Philip Johnson, and Lewis Mumford, *Modern Architects* (New York: Museum of Modern Art with Norton, 1932; reprint: Lisbon: Babel, 2011), pp. 23-30. Additionally, for other important MoMA exhibitions in Chicago see Terrence Riley and Edward Eigen, "Between the Museum and the Marketplace: Selling Good Design"; John Szarkowski, ed., *The Museum of Modern Art at Mid-Century at Home and Abroad* (New York: Museum of Modern Art, 1994), pp. 150-79.

43 Alfred H. Barr Jr., *Modern Architects*, 22: Henry Dubin is incorrectly referred to as "Harry." Joanna Merwood-Salisbury, "American Modern: The Chicago School and the International Style at New York's Museum of Modern Art," in *Chicagoisms: The City as Catalyst for Architectural Speculation*, eds. Alexander Eisenschmidt with Jonathan Mekinda (Zurich: Park Books, 2013), pp. 116-129.

44 Neil Levine, "Abstraction and Representation in Modern Architecture: The International Style and Frank Lloyd Wright," *AA Files* 57, no. 11 (Spring 1986): 3-21.

45 Dorothy Raley, *A Century of Progress Homes and Furnishings* (Chicago: M. A. Ring, 1934). See "Exposition Houses of Today and Tomorrow" in Lisa Schrenk, *Building a Century of Progress: The Architecture of Chicago's 1933-34 World Fair* (Minneapolis: University of Minnesota Press, 2007), pp. 157-86; Joseph J. Corn, *Yesterday's Tomorrows: Past Visions of the American Future* (Baltimore: Johns Hopkins Press, 1996).

46 Chicago-based architects in Johnson's exhibition were: Hamilton Beatty, Herbert C. Bebb, Howard T. Fisher, George Fred Keck, Hans Oberhammer,

Robert Paul Schweikher, Joseph L. Winberg, and Conrad & Teare.

47 Philip Johnson, *Young Architects in the Middle West: Exhibition 28* (New York: Museum of Modern Art, 1933) published in conjunction with an exhibition of the same title at the Museum of Modern Art, April 3-30, 1933.

48 William H. Jordy, "The International Style in the 1930s" in *"Symbolic Essence" and Other Writings on Modern Architecture and American Culture*, ed. Mardges Bacon (New Haven: Yale University Press, 2005), pp. 151-58. See also William H. Jordy, *American Buildings and Their Architects: The Impact of European Modernism in the Mid-Twentieth Century Volume 5* (Garden City, NY: Doubleday, 1970).

49 Henry-Russell Hitchcock Jr., "A House in Winnetka," *The Arts* 16, no. 6 (February 1930): 403.

50 Geoffrey Baker and Bruno Funaro, *Windows in Modern Architecture* (New York: Architectural Book Publishing, 1948).

51 Sandy Isenstadt, *The Modern American House: Spaciousness and Middle-Class Identity* (Cambridge: Cambridge University Press, 2006).

52 The houses included were both traditional and radical: Lumber Industries House (architect Ernest Grunsfeld Jr), Tropical Home (architect Robert Law Weed), Common Brick House (architect Andrew N. Rebori), House of Today (Corbett, Harrison & MacMurray architects), Stran-Steel House (O'Dell & Rowland Architects), House of Tomorrow (architect George Fred Keck), Design for Living (architect John C. B. Moore), Masonite House (Frazier & Raftery architects), Armco-Ferro Enamel House (architect Robert Smith Jr.).

53 *House & Garden*, March 1939, Section II, p. 40.

54 "Recent Work by the Office of Paul Schweikher and Theodore Warren Lamb, Associated Architects," *Architectural Forum* 71, no. 5 (November 1939): 350-66.

55 *Mies van der Rohe: McCormick House* (Elmhurst, IL: Elmhurst Art Museum, 2018), published in conjunction with the exhibition curated by Barry Bergdoll, *Mies's McCormick House Revealed: New Views* at Elmhurst Art Museum, June 10– August 26, 2018. The catalog includes an informative essay by Bergdoll.

56 Elizabeth A. T. Smith, *Blueprints for Modern Living: History and Legacy of the Case Study Houses* (Cambridge: MIT Press, 1989); Elizabeth A. T. Smith, *Case Study Houses* (Köln: Taschen, 2013).

57 Robert Boyce, *Keck & Keck* (Princeton, NJ: Princeton Architectural Press, 1993); Anthony Denzer, *The Solar House: Pioneering Sustainable Design* (New York: Rizzoli, 2013); Daniel A. Barber, *A House in the Sun: Modern Architecture and Solar Energy in the Cold War* (New York: Oxford University Press, 2016). Some important period publications include: Maron J. Simon, ed., *Your Solar House* (New York: Simon and Schuster, 1947) and Keck's "The Illinois State Solar House" designed for Libbey-Owens-Ford (1945) was featured in the Illinois section on pages 72-73.

58 For an overview of Schweikher's career and architectural production see John Zukowsky and Betty J. Blum, *Architecture in Context: The Avant-Garde in Chicago's Suburbs: Paul Schweikher and William Ferguson Deknatel* (Chicago: Graham Foundation for Advanced Studies in the Fine Arts and Art Institute of Chicago, 1984).

59 "House in Lake Forest, Ill.," *Architectural Forum* 72, no. 1 (January 1941), 44-46. In 1934, Schweikher established a partnership with Theodore "Ted" Warren Lamb; Elting joined in 1938 and the firm became Schweikher, Lamb, and Elting. Following Lamb's death in 1943 during the war, Schweikher & Elting was established in 1946 and disbanded almost a decade later when Schweikher was appointed Department Chair of Yale University's School of Architecture.

60 See Edward Robert Humrich, Interview with Maya Moran and Thomas Charles Roth, "The Architecture of Edward Robert Humrich," (MA thesis, University of Illinois at Chicago, 1993).

61 Jane King Hession, *Ralph Rapson: Sixty Years of Modern Design* (Afton, MN: Afton Historical Society Press, 1999), p. 56.

62 Werner Blaser, *After Mies: Mies van der Rohe, Teaching and Principles* (New York: Van Nostrand Reinhold, 1977); Alfred Swenson and Pao-Chi Chang, *Architectural Education at IIT, 1938-1978* (Chicago: Illinois Institute of Technology, 1980). Chicago's architectural landscape is also shaped by graduates of the University of Illinois School of Architecture in Urbana-Champaign and Chicago Circle.

63 As was demonstrated by Leonard Eaton's pioneering study, differences between clients made real impact on the design outcome. See Leonard K. Eaton, *Two Chicago Architects and Their Clients: Frank Lloyd Wright and Howard Van Doren Shaw* (Cambridge: MIT Press, 1969).

64 Chicago's Gold Coast was filled with urban houses of note ranging from the Helen Douglas and James Charnley House (1892) to the Elsa Seipp and Albert F. Madlener House (1902). These urban houses were in sharp contrast to the free-standing nineteenth-century Beaux-Arts "mansions" that occupied large parcels of land on N. Lake Shore Drive such as the Palmer Mansion by Cobb and Frost (1885) or the various mansions on Prairie Avenue including the Glessner House by Henry Hobson Richardson (1887) along with those of Chicago's mercantile elite such as Marshall Field, Philip Armour, and George M. Pullman. See John Graf, *Chicago Mansions* (Charleston, SC: Arcadia, 2004); William H. Tyre, *Chicago's Historic Prairie Avenue* (Charleston, SC: Arcadia, 2008); Wilbert Jones, Kathleen Willis-Morton, Maureen O'Brien, and Bob Dowey, *Chicago's Gold Coast* (Charleston, SC: Arcadia, 2014).

Patron of Modern Architecture: Excerpts from the Edith Farnsworth Memoirs

The previously unpublished handwritten memoirs transcribed and partially presented here are part of the "Edith Farnsworth Papers 1900–1977" collection located in the Modern Manuscripts and Archives, which also holds different materials pertaining to Dr. Edith B. Farnsworth, at Chicago's Newberry Library. Farnsworth wrote her memoirs during the last decade of her life, spent in a villa she purchased in Bagno a Ripoli, Italy, near Florence. She moved to Italy after retiring from her medical practice in the late 1960s, and after placing her famous glass-and-steel country house for sale.

Chapters Eleven and Twelve of the memoirs presented here were handwritten in a 6 x 8-inch Quaderno "Jumbo" (bright green, lined and unpaginated notebook manufactured by the historic Italian company Pigna).**1**

Chapter Thirteen of the memoirs presented here was also handwritten in a 6 x 8-inch Quaderno "Jumbo" (red). **2** Whereas Dr. Farnsworth dedicates all of Chapter Thirteen to discussion about the Fox River House, in the first part of Chapter Eleven and the second part of Chapter Twelve she discusses other aspects of her life and work.

The memoirs published here reveal a great deal about how Edith's life was forever changed by her decision to build the "Fox River House" (the informal name given to the house by Farnsworth, Mies, and collaborators before it would eventually become known as the Edith Farnsworth House). Farnsworth's memoirs encompass her search for property for a weekend house and purchase of the Plano site from Col. McCormick (lawyer, businessman, and publisher of the Chicago Tribune) to the fateful night she first met Mies and the early discussions concerning the design of the house. Farnsworth moves from expressing pride that "our project might well become the prototype of new and important elements in American architecture" to feeling disrespected and alienated by the process.

It is unclear if Farnsworth wanted to edit and publish these revealing memoirs. Given the intentional quality of her first-person writing, it seems a possibility, especially since she deeply valued writing and reading, having earned her undergraduate degree in English literature and composition from the University of Chicago before pursuing her medical degree at Northwestern University. After retiring to Italy, she edited and translated three bi-lingual collections of major Italian poets: *Salvatore Quasimodo: To Give and To Have, and Other Poems* (Chicago: H. Regnery Co., 1969), *Provisional Conclusions: A Selection of the Poetry of Eugenio Montale* (Chicago: H. Regnery Co., 1970), and *Albino Pierro, A Beautiful Story* (Milan: Vanni Scheiwiller, All'insegna del pesce d'oro, 1976). Given her knowledge of the publishing world, she would have been able to identify a publisher. The memoirs, even if unpublished, allowed Edith to reflect—*in her own words*—upon the Fox River House and how it had impacted her life.

In some instances, Farnsworth replaced words and either crossed out the previous ones or placed the alternative above; occasionally she also underlined words. These annotations are mostly maintained when they do not create confusion. Indentations have been left as they are in the original handwritten text. While she penned her memoirs on the recto (right) side of the notebook pages, in some instances she offered additional notes on the corresponding lines of the verso (opposite left-hand) pages that were meant presumably to supplement what was written in the main text. When the connection is clear these additions have been integrated. Although this is not a facsimile edition of her memoirs, the decision was made to publish a small sample of the actual notebook pages so to give the reader a sense of Dr. Edith Farnsworth's handwriting.

Nota Bene: A collection of Dr. Edith Farnsworth's professional and personal papers are located in the archives of Northwestern Memorial Hospital. Additional archival materials—related to Farnsworth's purchase of land near Plano from Col. McCormick (with the assistance of his secretary Genevieve L. Burke)—are held at Northwestern University, where Edith obtained her medical degree. See Sale to Dr. Edith Farnsworth, 1927–1947, 60, Box: 25. Chicago Tribune. Kirkland & Ellis Files (I), XI-175. Charles Deering McCormick Library of Special Collections & University Archives, Northwestern University Libraries.

Transcription by Michelangelo Sabatino with Serge Ambrose

1 "Edith Farnsworth Papers 1900–1977" collection, Modern Manuscripts and Archives at Chicago's Newberry Library, Box 1, Folder 26. Chapters Eleven and Twelve are available digitally, The Newberry Library Digital Collections.

2 "Edith Farnsworth Papers 1900–1977" collection, Modern Manuscripts and Archives at Chicago's Newberry Library, Box 2, Folder 27. The red Quaderno with Chapter Thirteen had not been digitized for online use during my research.

Quaderno "Jumbo" notebook containing Chapters Eleven and Twelve of Dr. Edith Farnsworth's memoirs, n.d.

Chapter Eleven

The strain of those early years was great, not only because of the weight of responsibility but because of the wild-cat calls for a physician, which came into every hospital. These included corpses washed up on the beach as well as all of the incidents to be expected in this life of a great city, and were apt to come from the wrong side of the tracks or from transients in hotels of various levels. Many of these were neither pleasant nor safe. On Sunday afternoon I used to stretch out on the sofa and listen to the N.Y. Philharmonic on the radio. Often I dropped to sleep during the program, and wakened to the gripping timbre of Msr. Sheen, as he worked his vineyards.[1] As Spring came on one year, I came to the conclusion that something would have to be done about those tired, dull Sundays.

A spot in the country which could be reached in an hour, from which important calls could be taken, patients could be hospitalized if advisable and, at the worst, I could get back to town. With the wife of one of the younger surgeons who had left with his unit, I explored the country about fifty miles west of Chicago one day and crossed the Fox River at Yorkville.[2] Taking the dirt River Road on the west side we came to an abandoned frame farmhouse from which the land sloped down to the river, and to the great views which bordered it. As we stood at the farm gate, a girl came down the road on a piebald pony. The house was unoccupied, she said, and the place was part of the Tribune Farms, and belonged to Col. McCormick.

We climbed the CantSag gate and walked down to the riverbank where we found the most inviting easy-chairs between the swelling roots of two immense black sugar maples whose shade was repeated and extended by the hackberries, the lindens and the walnut trees grouped about us.[3] In the water, close to the shore, a milk-white heron stood, motionless at the foot of his rippling image.

This was the first visit to the lovely Illinois River which was to offer me its moods and its reflections, its beauty and depredations, for some twenty-six years.

As Sue and I drove back to town, we talked about Col. McCormick and whether it might be difficult to induce him to part with that kiel-ned of his farm lands, and if he were to be sympathetic, what price would he want for it? As for the houses, Sue was a little more optimistic than I was: being a decorator by profession, she saw it remodeled, and generally "fixed up," whereas I saw only its rotting clapboards, timbers; its lack of light and water and its proximity to the dusty little River Road, and thought that the costs would run pretty high for a result which would hardly take it advantage of the possibilities of the site. I imagine that we both dreamed in the shade of the black sugar maple that night.

Negotiations with Mr. McCormick were dropped by one Sunday morning, and opened promptly and soon the local caretaker said, "You'll get it in the end and probably at your price, but it'll take him forever to put it in writing. You just come out whenever you feel like it and if you want to put in a few vegetables, there's no earthly reason why you shouldn't. I'll take mail for you, if you want me to, and you can always wash up at my house. I'd be glad to see you enjoy the place."

It was when I bought a Franklin stove and needed someone to install it in the farmhouse for me, that I met old George Skinner in the hardware store in Plano.[4]

1 Illinois native Monsignor Fulton Sheen of *The Catholic Hour* radio program.

2 The "wife" referenced is Sue Brill.

3 "Can't-Sag" was a steel-and-wood gate made by Rowe Manufacturing Co. of Galesburg, Illinois. "Every gate has from 6 to 8 backbones of steel—double bolted to every board at every joint. They can never sag—never warp or twist out of shape," *Farm Mechanics* 7, no. 1 (May 1922): 53.

4 Plano's main hardware store during those years was owned and operated by Harry Neubert and located on North Hugh Street. See Kristy Lawrie Gravlin, Anne Sears, Jeanne Valentine, and the Plano Community Library District, Images of Plano (Charleston: Arcadia Publishing), p. 24.

Mr. Skinner was a retired farmer who had nothing more to do than hoe his vegetable garden and trim the raspberry patch back of the old homestead on Hugh Street. He drove out with me forthwith and we succeeded in placing the stove and connecting up the pipe. After we had tried out the draft with an old newspaper and a few sticks of kindling wood, my new friend said that the house warming having been celebrated, a tree must be planted. "Kind of a pledge for the future," he said shyly. "The early settlers always planted a tree in the dooryard of a new house, and it's best that we do the same. It don't have to be big—I'll plant this pussy willow."

When I drove him back to Plano he invited me in for coffee and a doughnut, and from that day there was always a welcome with a hot cup, and help for whatever problems had arisen, such as a bit of ground to be dug, or fencing to be improvised to protect the vegetables from the rabbits. And when it was time to start back to town, there was often a "posy" or two or a little basket of raspberries. Through this gentle old man I came to feel the mid-west countryside with its broad snow streams and its six feet of black topsoil as I had come to love the rocky, exhausted, run-out hayfields of Eastern Maine through the wistful sites of Pomona and Flora.

During the several years which went by in correspondence with Mr. McCormick's secretary concerning the Fox River property, I took to the leafing through the books and bulletins on modern architecture which I came across on the shelves of bookstores and the coffee tables of my friends. I saw houses made of weathered boards hanging over cliffs and ravines or built out over water; I saw the white tiers and the cataracts of the Bear Run house of Wright, the novel deletions from the ground floor of the Savoye house of Le Corbusier. And I began to reflect on the modulus of "Le Corbu," upon architecture as an art, as a monument, a shelter, a machine for living. The solutions found by architects

and builders for the housing needs, public and private, of people of various cultures and climates, seemed to me fascinating and I marveled that I had been so slow to taking an interest in architectural forms and purposes. The interest once found, the erection of even a small little house in an out-of-the-way spot, began to seem an action calling for a certain sense of responsibility. As in every other situation, there must be a really fine solution for an inexpensive weekend retreat for a single person of my tastes and pre-occupations and, conversely it would be unbearably stupid to "put up" some contractor's cottage, which could only ruin the site and remain as a token of empirical mediocrity.

Then one evening I went to have dinner with Georgia and Ruth in their pleasant old-fashioned apartment in the Irving.[5] Also invited that evening was the massive stranger whom Georgia, with her peculiarly sweet smile, introduced, as I slipped off my coat: "This is Mies, darling."

I suppose he must have formed a few syllables as we had dinner, but if so, I do not remember them. My impression is that the three of us chatted among ourselves around the granite form of Mies. I related in detail, probably too much, the story of the finding of the property, the dickerings with Col. McCormick and the final acquisition of the nine-acre plot containing, aside from the rotting clapboards of the house and the farm buildings, the two ancient black sugar maples among the hackberries, the lindens and black walnuts, the rippling river and the milk-white heron.

All of this came to naught, conversationally speaking, and I concluded that Mies spoke almost no English; how much he understood remained problematical. We moved back to the sitting room after dinner and both Ruth and Georgia disappeared to wash the dishes.

"I am wondering whether there might be some young man in your office who

5 Georgia Lingafelt lived with her friend the widowed Mrs. [Edward H.] Ruth S. Lee in the Irving Apartments at 1018 N. State, Building H, Apt. 5 and ran The Georgia Lingafelt Books (rare, first editions, and imported books, with occasional art exhibitions). See 1950 Census, NARA; *The Library of International Relations Story Cove Children's Library – A Century of Progress* (Chicago: Library of International Relations, 1933), p. 29; "Georgia Lingafelt, A Book Dealer, 59," *The New York Times*, July 25, 1957, p. 23; *Intimate Landscapes: Photographs by Eliot Porter* (New York: E.P. Dutton, The Metropolitan Museum of Art, 1979), p. 135. Lingafelt also testified on behalf of Farnsworth at the trial. See "Index of Witnesses," p. 91 of this book. Concerning the unknown date of the dinner with Lingafelt, Lee, Farnsworth, and Mies: on Edith B. Farnsworth, M.D. letterhead dated February 27, 1946, she wrote to Mies about "[t]he project which I mentioned to you the other evening."; see image p. 44 of this book.

would be willing and disposed to design a small studio-weekend-house worthy of that lovely shore."

The response was that more dramatic for having been preceded by two hours of unbroken silence. "I would love to build any kind of a house for you." The effect was tremendous, like a storm, a flood or act of God. We planned a trip to Plano together, so that I could show him the property.

When I got home that night, I collected what books I had on modern architecture, the "International School" and the Bauhaus, and looked through them for references to Mies. There was mention of the German pavilion at the Barcelona Exposition of 1929 and of the Tugendhat House in Brno with its free-standing interior wall of onyx, as well as rather brief allusions to an architect who seemed to have a singular predilection for luxury materials.

At this point I am reminded of something which the Swiss painter, Paul Klee, once said to his pupils at the conclusion of a series of lectures. The book is no longer at hand I am quoting from memory writing about what I remember and not what the art historians have recorded—"after you have mastered the Formal Means, and the painting is before you, then you will need all possible patience for the public who will hang over your shoulder and say 'But that doesn't look anything like Uncle!'. For all of us, both public and artist, look at a painting and search therein for the known and trusted face."

So I searched the sundry texts that lay about the apartment, and saw in them an architect whose austerity had kept him from popularity and whose manner was determined by his insight. That was the face described to me by the few accounts of Mies which lay at hand.

Not many days later after the evening of our meeting in the pleasant, bookish little apartment in the old Irving, we set out for a day in the country, to inspect the property with a view to the ideal weekend house. It was either late autumn or late winter when I stopped at 200 East Pearson to call for Mies, and he came out wearing an enormous black overcoat of some kind of soft, fine wool, which reached well down toward his ankles. Installed beside me in the little Chevrolet he put up only feeble resistance to the advances of my white cocker who sprawled across his knees for the duration of the trip.

Finally we reached the dooryard of the farm house and I could open the car doors. The emergence of Mies and the cocker was spectacular, as it turned out that the latter had yielded most of his white coat in a soft frosting over the black wool of that splendid overcoat, and we had nothing on board with which to remove it.

We walked down the frozen slope, through the frozen meadow grass and dormant brush, and I worried for fear a European might be unable to see the beauty of the mid-west countryside at so unfavorable a season; but midway down, Mies stopped and looked all around him. "It is beautiful!" he said, his profile, suddenly alert and sensitive, and I didn't doubt the spontaneity of his exclamation.

We began to see each other from time to time and to make frequent Sunday excursions out to Plano, often including the boys from Mies' office and Mr. Bonnet.[6] The latter was a decorator who had known Mies in Europe and was a frequent visitor in the office. "Ah!, I love Mies" he would declare exuberantly, "I really love him!"

As the warm weather came on, we had to cut pathways through the weeds and meadow grass down to the shore where Mies had discovered a stump on which he could sit. The ankylosing arthritis of the right hip which crippled him in his later years was already advanced, and he was unable to sit directly on the ground. From the bank we studied various sites for the house and drove a few tentative stakes.

6 Felix Bonnet, also a German émigré, was employed by Mies in the office; "He did the typing, kept the books, generally managed things. …His family had owned a big interior decorating firm…" Myron Goldsmith, *Oral History of Myron Goldsmith/ Interviewed by Betty J. Blum, Compiled Under the Auspices of the Chicago Oral History Project, Department of Architecture, The Art Institute of Chicago,* 1990/2001 p. 42 https://artic.contentdm.oclc.org/digital/collection/caohp/id/3982. Bonnet also testified on behalf of Mies at the trial. See "Index of Witnesses," pp. 90–91 of this book.

"Mies, what building materials were you thinking of for the house?"

"I wouldn't think of the problem quite like that." I wouldn't think: "We'll build a brick house or a reinforced concrete house: I would think that here where everything is beautiful, and privacy is no issue, it would be a pity to erect an opaque wall between the outside and the inside. So I think we should build the house of steel and glass; in that way we'll let the outside in. If we were building in the city or in the suburbs, on the other hand, I would make it opaque from outside and bring in the light through a garden courtyard in the middle."

It was all great fun. Mies reminded me of a medieval peasant, and aspects of his nature which later proved themselves as cruel, during those years seemed simply clumsy. He never showed the trivial courtesies such as lighting cigarettes for woman guests—or the greater ones either, for that matter— and it never occurred to him to call a taxi or otherwise facilitate the safe return of any unescorted female visitor. She could just scurry through the dark streets however she saw fit.

After we had had a number of picnics together, and he had come to dinner with me several times, he suddenly said, "You can eat dinner at my house." I arrived for this innovation several days later and was disconcerted to find no evidence that a guest was expected that evening. The dining-room was occupied, as was the custom by an unused drawing table, and in the living room there was no card table to suggest the subsequent appearance of doilies, plates and glasses. But I did think I could hear low sounds of activity proceeding from the kitchen beyond the shadows. Mies got up from the black upholstered armchair at the end of the long marble table (let into the partition in a sort of double cantilever, as he had pointed out) and made for the pantry. "Can I be of help?" I called uncertainly, following along after him. Without answering

he thrust toward me a tray and took a similar one for himself. They were much like those used in cafeterias and each was set with an entire meal. Leading the way back to the living room Mies plumped his tray down on the end of the cantilevered marble table and sat down on the arm of his black easy-chair, his napkin somehow made fast to his suit. Not knowing what to do with mine, I sat down on the black sofa across the width of the room, with the tray on my lap; but I couldn't manage, and there seemed nothing else to do but place it on the table that held the lamp, and sit on the adjacent arm of the sofa. In that way, so collocated, we both faced west like two trout heading upstream, sustaining the exquisite discomforts of our positions from opposite ends of the room. No word was spoken—none could be—and nothing could be heard but an occasional fumble of silverware on China or teak and the soft sounds of food consumption, not to say digestion.

Mies made it in half the time it took for me to dawdle my way nervously through the cutting up and eating of a double lamb chop. When at last I gave up, he got to his feet abruptly, seized his tray and hurried out to the pantry while I picked up mine and fell in behind him.

Once more in our places, on the cushions rather than on the arms which had the shape and consistency of fence rails, we faced each other with watery smiles and began to talk about modules, about proportions, golden modules and metaphysical proportions. His glass now in place of the tray, on the end of the table, he sat there with half-closed eyes, in the black armchair his face as impassive as a landscape—and talked about his past life, from his childhood in Aachen to the present as head of the department of architecture at the Illinois Institute of Technology.

So I pictured Mies as a small boy attending the local trade school and earning a few pennies in his spare time by picking of disorders for which there is no answer in office practice. To deny the request is entirely uncomfortable and to give a moderate therapeutic dose is useless because the addict can tell exactly what amount he has received.

The strain of these
~~Our~~ early years ~~were~~ was great, not only because of the weight of responsibility, but because of the wild-cat calls for a physician, which came into ~~our~~ hospital. *corpses washed up on the beach or under* There included all of the incidents to be expected in the life of a great city, and were apt to come from the wrong side of the tracks ~~since~~ or from transients in hotels of various levels. Many of these were neither pleasant nor safe. On Sunday afternoons I used to stretch out on the sofa and listen to the N.Y. Philharmonic on the radio. Often I dropped to sleep during the program, and wakened to the gripping *timbre* ~~cadences~~ of Win. Sheen, as he worked his vineyards. As spring came on one year, I came to the conclusion that something would have to be done about those tired, dull Sundays.

A spot in the country which could be reached in an hour, from which important calls could be taken, patients could be hospitalized if advisable and, at the worst, I could get back to town. With *the wife* one of the younger surgeons who had left with *his* ~~the units~~, I explored the country, *about fifty miles* west of Chicago *one day* ~~where we~~ *and* crossed the Fox River at Yorkville. Taking the dirt River Road on the west side we came to an abandoned frame farmhouse ~~on our left~~, from which the land sloped down *and to the right this* to the river, which ~~was~~ bordered ~~with~~ *the*. As we stood at the farm gate, a girl came down the road on a piebald pony. The house was unoccupied, she said, and the place was part of the Tribune Farms, and belonged to Col. McCormick.

We climbed the *zigzag* ~~Cantsag~~ gate and *walked* ~~went~~ down to the river bank where we found the most ~~delightful~~ *inviting* easy-chairs between the swelling roots of two immense black sugar maples whose shade was repeated and *extended* ~~coupli~~ *the linden* fied by the hackberries, and the walnut trees grouped about us. *in the water* *mahogany* close to the shore, a heron

situation, there must be a really fine solution for an inexpensive weekend retreat house for a single person of my tastes and pre-occupations and, conversely, it would be unbearably stupid to "put up" some contractor's cottage which could only ruin the site and remain as a token of empirical mediocrity.

Then one evening I went to have dinner with Georgia and Ruth in their pleasant, old-fashioned apartment in the Irving. Also invited that evening was the massive strange man whom Georgia, with her peculiarly sweet smile, introduced, as I slipped off my coat; "This is Mies, darling."

I suppose he must have formed a few syllables as we had dinner, but my if so, I do not remember them. My impression is that the three of us chatted among ourselves around the granite form of Mies. I related in detail, probably too much, the story of the finding of the property, the dickerings with Col. McCormick and the final acquisition of the nine-acre

plot containing, aside from the rolling clapboards of the house and the farm buildings, the two ancient black sugar-maples among the hackberries, the lindens and black walnuts, the rippling river and the milk-white heron.

All of this came to naught, conversationally speaking, and I concluded that Mies spoke almost no English; how much he understood remained problematical. We moved back to the sitting-room after dinner and both Ruth and Georgia disappeared to wash the dishes.

"I am wondering whether there might be some young man in your office who would be willing and to design a small studio-weekend-house worthy of that lovely shore."

The response was the more dramatic having for being preceded by two hours of unbroken silence. "I would love to build any kind of a house for you." The effect was tremendous, like a storm, a flood or other act of God. We planned a trip to Plano together, so that I could show him the property.

Pages from Chapter Eleven of Dr. Edith Farnsworth's handwritten memoirs.

up nails where building was in progress. His father was a stone-cutter and the boy was taught to polish the inscription on tombstones. "The best part of the day came when the work was finished and we boys went to the factory and stood at the gates, waiting for the weavers' daughters to come out," he remarked with a reminiscent smile.

"Waiting for what, Mies?"

"Die weavers' daughter," he repeated, unperturbed. "To try to get a kiss from them. They were beautiful!"

The story of the weavers' daughters never lost its top place in the early Mies chronicles, and those of us who remained as familiar visitors during those six or eight years of the planning and erection of the Fox River house continued to urge him to tell us about them. There was another anecdote of the same period which also appealed to me, and this had to do with his boyhood in Aachen and the day the stone-cutter brought his son to the local "Kunstgewerbe Schule" to get him enrolled.[7] Father and son treaded helplessly around the corridors, ignorant of what door they should pass through. On all of them, Mies recalled, the word "Design" appeared in one context or another, and last he stopped his father to ask, "Who is this Mr. Design who lives in all the rooms of this school?"

But the monolithic Mies was not much given to nostalgic recollections of childhood, nor was there anything about him to suggest that he had ever been "brought up", or in fact modified by anyone. It was said later by Waltraut, the youngest of his three daughters, that Mies could never have driven a car because when the road turned he was so stubborn that he would have continued to go straight ahead. Lovely, unfortunate Waltraut.

Aside from Mr. Design, there was one reference made by Mies to his parents that slid open like a little trap-door and revealed a dark space; then the aperture closed without a sound and for years I forgot it was there. It happened late one evening: the cigar was burning down toward the wet, macerated end and the glass on the end of the table had been refilled many times.

"Did your parents continue to live in Aachen after you left home, Mies?"

"My parents? They didn't know much about me after I went to work in Behrens' office. Once I started to go back to see them in Aachen but I met some friends on the train and we were drinking and I forgot to get off at the station."

"So you got off at the next stop and went back"

"The next stop? No, I never went back."

"Never at all? You never saw them again?"

"Why should I?"

Perhaps Jim Speyer was there that evening and we slipped out together, leaving Mies still seated in the black armchair in a mist of cigar smoke.

There was a certain metaphysical vein which enhanced the standard topic of Mies himself. I suppose that it was pretty thoroughly bogus in the sense that it represented only an accoutrement to his professional personality and not a true inwardness inevitable in the character of the medieval peasant as I had chosen to see it; at any rate I read Guardini, as he urged, and tried to lend myself to the concept of liturgy as an element in the "hierarchy of values", or a mystic dimension of religion, or a setting up exercise in the hygiene of the soul — as almost anything which might enrich my own awareness, presumably by showing me how Mies had been enriched. And I dutifully contemplated Corbu's modules although I was never able to see any organic connection between the proportions of the human body and those of the Savoye or any other house, or what such a connection could have meant if it had existed. Could it have been the absolute which music with its comforting cadences had denied? A sort of mystic code of specifications for natural forms? In any case, I was interested to talk

7 Students at this type of Arts and Crafts school would receive "applied" training.

about, or at least to hear Mies talk about it, since nobody among the disciples was disposed to compete with those ponderous reminiscences whether of modules and dimensions, or of Behrens, van de Velde, van Doesburg, Lily Reich, the Mayor of Dessau, and the last days of the Bauhaus.

The story of the Mayor of Dessau was dark and opaque, less regularly retold than the chronicle of the hours spent on the benches in the outer office of I believe it was Goebels, waiting to plead for the survival of the Bauhaus.[8] The Goebels story was rehearsed so insistently that we were startled one late evening when Hugo said, "We got a new fact tonight. He gave us the width of the benches in the waiting room of Goebbels' office."[9] The story of the Mayor of Dessau was different and its telling always suggested an act of exorcism. It dealt essentially with kindness rendered by the Mayor to the personnel of the Bauhaus during the period from 1925 when still under the directorship of Gropius. the school was moved to Dessau from Weimar, and 1932 when it was permanently closed by the Nazis, and the Mayor was put on trial to answer for his friendliness. Mies was in Berlin at the time, trying to obtain permission to reopen the school there, and was called to Dessau to testify in the case of the Mayor. "I kept trying to think of what I could say to help him", Mies recalled. "There was one thing I could have said but I just couldn't remember it until I was on the train going back to Berlin. I could have kicked myself!" That anecdote turned up now and then, in moments of confidence, and for years I pitied him for so distressing a memory lapse and for the naggings of conscience which seemed, to torment him. Much later, however, I could not believe any longer in Mies as capable of any scruples whatever.

But at this stage in our relationship I took it for granted that our views on all such matters were the same. The impression was heightened by the discussions we had after Mies had read Schrödinger's

book "What is Life?"[10] I lent him that disciplined, lucid treatise by an eminent physicist, thinking that whatever might be his metaphysical vison, he could only admire a kind of heroic abstemiousness in Schrödinger's reduction of life to observable crystals, organic and inorganic. This turned out to be true, and on the occasion of our next evening with Mies, Jim and I found him limping heavily up and down the living room, obviously greatly agitated.

"Don't you approve of the Schrödinger book. Mies? You seem so upset."

"It is unspiritual. What about man and his hopes for immortality?" Does he think I can sit staring at the snowflakes on the window or the salt crystals on the dinner table and be satisfied? I want to know what I have to expect after death."

"Probably Schrödinger does too, but writing as a physicist and deleting the questions of the natural longings of human beings for a hereafter, he still offers to man the very considerable dignity of the observer of life. We don't have to just sit and get rained on—"

"That's not enough!"

"Why don't you write to him and find out whether he has some fringe comforts to suggest that he couldn't include in his book? He's at one of the Irish universities and he might well be pleased to hear from you. After all, he is at least as human as we are."

I was struck with the force of Mies' preoccupation with death and it lent a mystic context even to the project of the house by the river, and an indefinable dimension to the personality of Mies. I listened to the story of the monument designed by Mies for Karl Liebknecht and Rosa Luxemburg as a wall made of bricks accidentally fused in the kiln—and saw in it a kind of solidarity far transcending the political variety. This evening some thirty years later I come over the photograph of Mies evidently taken shortly before his death in 1972 in a London paper, the face of a man in the upper eighties, defiant and fearful and

[8] The Mayor of Dessau was Fritz Hesse (1918-1933). Joseph Goebbels was Nazi Party chief in Berlin, and in 1933 Hitler appointed him Minister for Public Enlightenment and Propaganda.

[9] Hugo Weber (1918-1971), Swiss-born American artist and educator.

[10] Erwin Schrödinger, *What is Life? The Physical Aspect of the Living Cell* (Cambridge, Eng.) The University Press; New York: The Macmillan Company, 1945). The book was written keeping in mind a general audience interested in science.

hard as Mies turned out to be, but also as it appeared in—and I recall the Schrödinger incident and the affectionate concern with which we tried to shield our medieval peasant from the intolerable apprehension of his own extinction.[11] At least that is what we thought we were doing although now as I contemplate that late portrait, I wonder whether the dread on those familiar features might rather have had to do with some more concrete unpropitiated regret. At any rate, Schrödinger served to bring an aroma of eternal verities into our notions of Mies and justify the cult which the disciples were feverishly elaborating

By 1947 there were sketches and a model of the house. The model was packed and shipped to New York for the Van der Rohe exhibit at the Museum of Modern Art. This event must have been planned by at least certain of his sponsors such as Philip Johnson, as a debut in the United States, and timed for a moment at which success might reasonably be counted upon. During the first eight or ten years of his residence in Chicago, Mies had offended some of the distinguished Chicago architects who had procured for him the chair in architecture at the Illinois Institute of Technology, the blank arrogance with which he, as a refugee from Nazi Germany, had accepted the courtesies of this most useful post. Then, the first few buildings designed by Mies for the campus did not please the graduates who wrote back to their alma mater in considerable numbers to describe in depth their dislike of structures which looked like factories or warehouses, and their protests that such warehouses should be chosen to house the great technological institute of the Mid-West. This naturally saddened the trustees and benefactors of the School who, themselves were not too sure of their adherence to the austerity of the rectangle as the absolute, sine qua non, of modern architecture. Likewise, the Promontory Apartments, the first residential building undertaken by

Mies, did not please either the tenants or the public: among other defects, its reinforced concrete soon began to show vertical streaks, seemingly of rusty water trickling from floor to floor. These were ineradicable and tended to disqualify the building as a prestigious apartment house as well as a subject to photograph for the exhibit at the Museum of Modern Art.

Finally, there was discontent among the undergraduates at the Institute whose families had made sacrifices to give their boys the opportunity to graduate from the Ill. Inst. of Tech and study under the great European architect. They maintained that they never saw Mies and that, so far as he was concerned, the curriculum consisted in the drawing of brick-bonds—not just a few bricks to indicate the system, but yards of them.

The disciples, however saw only un enlightenment and a back-country survival of the Victorian love of fake towers, battlements and pergolas in the messages of protest sent by the graduates of IIT and the stains on the concrete whiteness of the Promontory building seemed "just one of those things," and both factors encouraged me in the conviction that innovators in the arts or the sciences need not, and should not look to the general public for understanding and support. It was the obligation and privilege of innovators in other fields to supply the background for such advances. As for the students sitting in their schoolrooms drawing endless bricks, without ever a word from their Head or a glimpse of his ever-more-publicized features, here I thought that Mies was squarely in the wrong.

"Those boys come from farms and villages all over the country. Each one has some quality or talent, some scrap of something that has brought him here to you at considerable cost to his family. They all want to learn something from you. I do think you might at least pronounce a few words of welcome to the entering Freshman."

11 Mies died in 1969; however, initial searches in digitized London newspapers from 1969–72 has not yet led to a photograph of Mies. Diana Rowntree wrote of his life and work in *The Guardian*, August 19 1969, p. 6, which featured images of IIT's S. R. Crown Hall and Lake Shore Drive Apartments, with a mention of "the Farnsworth House"; Richard Roud's "The Legacy of Kings" *The Guardian*, July 29, 1970, p. 8 includes an image of his "New National Gallery," Berlin. During those years Mies and Lord Peter Palumbo were in the British press for the controversy surrounding Mansion House Square in London, a 19-story office building, originally commissioned in 1963 and never built. Jack Self, ed., *Mies in London* (London: REAL, 2017).

His reply was brief and coarse: "They can see me when I leave my room to go to the John!"

The art critics and the architects who attended the opening of the Museum exhibit found themselves dwarfed by the immense blow-ups of old photographs which covered the walls: the Barcelona Pavilion, the Tugendhat House with its onyx wall. The little Fox River house was set up on a table, and I was distressed that the handmade trees standing around it gave the observer no idea of the great lindens, the maples and the hackberries under which it was to stand. But it was the pivotal point of the exhibit, and I was happy as I boarded the train back to Chicago, reflecting that our project might well become the prototype of new and important elements in American architecture.

I do not remember what the New York critics wrote about the Van der Rohe exhibit. But there was one visitor who let fall a comment which found its way to Mies, not in minutes but in seconds. That visitor was Frank Lloyd Wright. The comment was pithy: "Negation is not enough."

Back in Chicago, a day or two later, we gathered at Mies's to consider what should be done about that comment. After long deliberation during which he sat in his black chair and puffed his cigar, inarticulate and huffy, we drafted a dignified complaint having a dim bearing upon negation. This was approved with one or two minor corrections, signed, addressed and mailed. The answer came promptly: "Sorry old chap," it said, "that my comment offended you. I apologize. But negation just isn't enough."

As we left, that evening, and went over to the nearest B+I for relaxation and scrambled eggs, we couldn't decide whether we had been umpiring a duel between giants or a squabble between two unbearably conceited old men...

Chapter Twelve

Not many months after the "retrospective" showing at the Museum, serious preparations began to be made for the execution of the house. After reviewing my financial prospects I went down to Mies's office one afternoon and wrote down on the edge of the drawing table before him the sum $40,000 and listed the assets it represented. "Now can we have the house?" I asked, half believing that the question was rhetorical in view of the extreme simplicity of the design.

"I should think so," Mies replied. "We haven't made any estimates yet, but it must be a cheap house—it's almost nothing. "Are you going to be happy building a small house out of conventional building materials, without any onyx?"

"I will build this house for you as I would build it for myself!"

In the big drafting room the boys sat at their tables, transfigured, "This is the most important house in the world," they crowed!"

In that way, on the edge of the thundering Chicago Loop, the Fox River House ceased to be an empty project and began its period of gestation; conventionally, the last basic slogan, doomed to dereliction because of its grandiose ambiguity, also got off the ground: Less is More.

At last, big machinery began to roll through the gate and excavations appeared in the lower meadow. There was a lot of talk about technical details such as the dimensions of the concrete footings which were to bear the weight of the columns, the length of the bay system, the method of heating and the material to be used for the floor. With some apprehension, I agreed to travertine for the latter. The utilities were all to be fed up from ground level to the house, welded to its columns, some six feet above the meadow, through an immense black iron cylinder which would somehow keep them warm. Modern technology had overcome the difficulties of insulation and we were to use exposed steel and single-pane glass.

As I passed some of these points on to members of my family and to friends who were outside the charmed circle I was met with growls and hoots. "You'll lose heat through all sides of your glass box! He could at least insulate the floors and ceilings. And you simply can't escape condensation on all your single pane glass and exposed steel! There's nothing he can say or that modern technology can do that's going to change that."

Those were trying moments for me, but loyalty to the "vertrautes Gesicht" prevailed. He must know what he's doing. And as Head of Architecture at IIT, there must be plenty of engineers who can assist if assistance is wanted," I responded.

Certain details, which could not be laid to "modern technology," bothered me even more. One of these was the absence of a second door to the house or of any window whatsoever. The second idea took my breath away, and I told Mies that I couldn't spend a night without an open window and would never except a house without at least one window. I felt almost as strongly about a second door. "I think I should have two ways of getting in or out," I complained. "In case of fire or other emergencies." "I'm not too happy about the 'glass box' motif, and I rebel at a glass trap."

Another contested point was the "open plan" of the interior, according to which a guest would have a bathroom, but no bedroom. He or she could sleep on a sofa or I would spread a mattress on the travertine floor. We would co-habit a sort of three-dimensional sketch, I in my "sleeping space," and he in his—unless sheer discomfort and depression should drive us together. In the end, I got two large windows, and no "back door" and no partitions. It was not hard to see Mies objections to a second door since this would have to be let into one of the big wall-panes and connected by a little flight of steps with the ground, and was bound to look like an automobile showroom. And a partition if introduced, would have to start at a column, in which case it would end by bisecting the fireplace or ending nowhere. So I subsided and we "let the outside in" and allowed our space to remain undisturbed, "caught between two horizontal planes." All useful things form follows function. So the simultaneousness realization of Mies' innovation in architecture, and mine in fluid and salt metabolism seemed to me just as it should be and absolutely thrilling.

Notwithstanding a few disagreements and tensions, the summer of 1949 was brilliant and exciting. For the true disciples, the bulldozers and shovels which scarred the flood meadows with deep purposeful pits and trenches meant the progressive realization of a youthful hope of dominion and grandeur. The big drafting room beside the brutal Chicago loop became a club-room, a sanctuary and a kibbutz, and the boys vied for the privilege of contributing to the realization of "the most important house in the world."

For me that summer was marvelous because it fulfilled my ideal that persons trained in different fields of the arts or the sciences should seek to understand the ideals and principles common to all fields of advancement and to lend their loyalty and support.

Chapter Thirteen

By the summer of 1950 the Fox River house had a roof, and the slabs of travertine waited in rows outside the brooding house. Students of all callings arrived in busloads to mill around open-mouthed and to drop a line into the river in the hope of carp. Architects came from various European countries and we brought one or two of them out from town with us about every weekend. Most of them were fulsome in their words of praise and wonderment at the miracle which was taking form in that rural spot; one or two of the German ones exclaimed, "Master!" and crawled across the terrace to the latter's feet where he sat on a low aluminum deck chair, impassively awaiting the throaty plaudits of the visitors, "Grossartig!," "Unglaublich!"

The blue canvas deck chair became the pivotal point in the travertine drama which drove the first nails of incredulity into my hither to well to order guarded tolerance. The slabs had been cut specially and selected before they left the yards of the marble firm, delivered at the farmhouse, they had been made visible to Mies who had assigned them to one of three categories; first quality, second quality, or rejects. This seemed appropriate and I took it for evidence of the architect's meticulous concern for the best use of his building materials.

When, however, the travertine ceremony was once again enacted, this time with Mies in the blue deck chair while a crew of men filed by, each man carrying a slab of stone like a precious painting before the eyes of a divine appraiser, until every slab had once more been viewed. I turned a corner in my regard for Mies. The absurdity became dramatic when it was discovered that there had been a misunderstanding about which pile belonged to which category and that there was no agreement between First Viewing and Second Viewing.

There were also irritations, that summer of 1950, for the workmen who complained that the young man from Mies's office who had been delegated as supervisor, interrupted their work with foolish questions. "He don't know anything about building and he expects us to teach him but that keeps us from getting anything done."

On this point I expostulated to Mies: "The workmen are complaining, and I get the impression that he is really raising our building costs through his inexperience."

Mies hesitated for a moment. "You go back to your nephritis where you belong and leave me to build your house without interference." It was a tough moment, and Mies and I were not far from a rift; but a house cannot very well be abandoned half-finished and a "vertrautes Gesicht" cannot be cancelled out for a squabble. So we softened our voices and parted friends.

Finally the travertine floors were complete, the furnace room was loaded with the boiler for the floor heating coils and two hot air furnaces as well as the overhead water tank, and the "core" was surrounded by a light wall in paneled wood veneer. It was at this point that I found that the utilities had been jammed together so ruthlessly that only the most emaciated of heating and plumbing men could hope to service the equipment lying to the east of the middle. As for the chimneys and dampers for the oil furnaces, they could only be reached by the plumber's oldest boy, a thin wiry child who could be poked back among the pipes and was just old enough to carry out orders. After one such session, the plumber dusted off his child and stood him on his feet. "You haven't chosen a name for this house yet, have you? My suggestion would be "My Miesconception."

At last the glass panes could be bolted in place, the fireplace could be tried out and a can of soup could be heated on a hot plate in the bathroom. The lighting of a fire on the hearth revealed a curious fact, namely, that the house was sealed so hermetically that the attempt of a flame to go up the chimney caused an interior negative pressure. This was surprisingly hard to correct.

One evening I went to a party in Hugo's studio, where I found a number of people from the Institute of Design most of whom I knew. The aura of the Bauhaus and Moholy-Nagy still surrounded the Institute in those days and the atmosphere was alight with trends from the old world and the new. Salvation was to be found in the enchanting titles and the linear reiterations of Paul Klee, in the cut-outs of the last Kandinsky, the two-dimensional mechanisms of Mondrian and, a little later, the large-scale product, the squirt gun where the brush was too fussy. The arty folk got plastered with cheap wine, and the paint was sprayed, dribbled, or applied with the heel, the elbow or the knee.

The sensitive and intellectual Hugo had a different problem and his hopes lay in automatic expression. Speed, not surface area, seemed to him the essential, and his tables were covered with ejaculations in India ink on paper napkins with which he hoped to elude the brain with all its paralyzing forms and tap a deeper source of animal force.

Mies came with me that evening of Hugo's studio party. Established in an equivalent of the blue canvas deck chair, with a drink in hand, he offered no comment whatever and his gelid silence discouraged even the drunkest from approaching him. In the other room, a stranger grasped my elbow. "How did you ever happen to involve yourself with Mies? You surely know that this is nothing but a very queer man with a queer name."

I was shocked and hurt on Mies' behalf, but before I had recovered enough to think of a reply, he had moved past me and disappeared among the other guests. When Hugo dropped by one evening a week or two later, I told him about the incident and asked him who the stranger was.

"He's a fellow I used to know when I worked around Arp's studio. He's an art historian, quite a smart fellow. He's visiting in Chicago and giving a few lectures at ID."

He hung his coat in the closet and, putting his immense and bulging briefcase on the floor he sat down on the sofa and pulled out a photostat page from Mallarmé and one from Apollinaire. The little silver poodle welcomed Hugo fondly and buried her head in his briefcase. "I have some cookies for her in there," he explained. Hugo was charming and I loved his occasional evening calls: he always telephoned first and arrived smelling of soap and Swiss snows, his odd little black fedora set straight on the top of his head and his long funereal overcoat well brushed. He never came empty-handed, and from the tattered briefcase came sparkling enthusiasms, perplexities, clippings from foreign reviews, disputed points of scholarship and, of course, hopes. The poodle curled up on the sofa beside him where he could pat her without disturbing our conversation, and we went on talking for hours. Once I wrote a sketch about Hugo which I presented to him on one of these occasions. In it, I put the soap, the sandpaper, the shy motions of his long limbs, the dueling Ego and Id and everything else that affectionate insight could know or divine. While he read it I went out in the kitchen to make him a drink. When I came back he got to his feet. "I protest" he said, a little embarrassed. "You left something out."

"Is that possible? Tell me, so that I can make amends!"

"You didn't say what I had in my pockets!"

Such was the Hugo of those still charmed days. That evening soon after the party and the cutting words of the stranger, I brought up the incident.

"I'm so accustomed to the premise that Mies is great that I was really shaken by the curt finality of those words. Of course I have been aware of his brutality for quite a while now, but I never seriously questioned his place and value in architecture. And yet I wonder if what I'm saying now is strictly true. Perhaps, in addition to a real and growing dislike for his arrogance and his monumental selfishness, I have been having some shadowy doubts concerning the sanctity of the rectangle. I mean as an absolute and not only one but the only one."

"That's bad," interposed Hugo lightly. Doesn't Mies himself say that culture spreads by proclamation? Well, you've heard the rectangle proclaimed emphatically enough, haven't you?

"And how! Of course, it isn't Mies who vocalizes the rectangle - he is the rectangle. Perhaps it's the vocalizing by the supporting cast which is getting hard to bear."

"Well, if one undertakes to proclaim one has to develop the means of emphasizing the proclamation. Emphasis is the main thing and the ordinary way to get it is through repetition, and here the supporting cast becomes important. And of course, modern advertising has a lot of resources."

"Hugo, did you ever hear anybody else express a similar viewpoint about Mies?

"A queer man with a queer name? Not precisely. But it wouldn't surprise me to hear that he has adverse critics in Europe. Anybody who achieves prominence has adverse, even hostile, critics, and I don't quite see why you should feel so upset about it. De-bunking has been a popular exercise for quite a time now."

"But your friend's message goes a good bit further than that."

"True. But don't forget that Germany of the Inflazionzeit must have been pretty nasty."

"It must have been a hot-house for all spies of opportunism."

"At any rate, so far as Mies and his rectangle are concerned, they have to be taken or left - the emperor wears the most superb cloak in the world or else he is naked. And it seems that neither the Trustees of IIT nor the architects of Chicago thought he was naked."

Not all the foreign architects who came to visit the glass house were German and not all the Germans prostrated themselves before the designer. Among others there were three particularly nice English ones who, though appreciative and cordial, managed to retain their calm. Chronologically the first of these was Mr. Malcolm Dark, who took the back seat as we drove out to Plano and from his slightly aloof position there, addressed Mies as "Mr. Mice." I was trying to accomplish a bit of economy in connection with the hardware that day. "I can't believe that the single door handle has to be made to order and to come from some far place. Sometimes I wonder whether the boys know how to shop for such details."

"Mr. Mies!" called the jolly Mr. Dark from the back seat, "Mr. Mice! She's begging for mercy!."

Mies offered no comment and we pulled in the gate in a mood of uncomfortable constraint. The glass panes were not in place yet and we had to watch carefully as we trailed around upon the lower of our two horizontal planes. This circumstance gave an opportunity to observe the manner of joining of the potential glass box to its columns. "My goodness, Mr. Mice" explained or irrepressible guest, "Are the channels welded to the columns?"

"Exactly!" replied Mies. The house is a glass box hanging from its supports."

"May I make so bold as to ask what the advantages are to that system? I'm afraid I never heard of welding such large surfaces together. It certainly looks very solid but I would think that the heat required might easily have warped either of the two, or both, joining members."

"I employ only expert welders."

"But Mr. Mice—please excuse me if

I persist— what are the advantages to be expected from this technique? I see, too, that it leaves the sawed-off ends, so to speak, of the columns exposed outside the glass circumference. And the same goes for the terrace? How original!"

"That was my concept," said Mies, evidently unsure of his position vis à vis our English visitor. It should be a glass box hanging from its supports."

At this moment the afternoon took on a different, a supernatural tint. The trees and meadows, as we saw them from our stone shelf, faded into a vision which we all saw and, in the sky, there floated a blush-pink celestial body like a pale pink moon, supremely large.

"Why Mr. Mice!" shouted Mr. Dark. "What in the world is going on?"

"For God's sake, how should I know? Eigenartig!"

We stared at one another and at the big pink heavenly body and at our altered world. "You don't imagine that we might have slipped out of orbit, do you, after so many years in the same one?" suggested Mr. Dark, now quite subdued.

We agreed that we had never seen anything like it and that the two horizontal planes of the unfinished building, floating over the meadows, were unearthly beautiful under a sun which glowed like a wild rose.

The explanation of the phenomenon, as it appeared in the paper the following morning, had to do with forest fires raging in Canada. But the mystery was unsolved as we got back into the automobile that Sunday afternoon.

The second of the three Englishmen was Fello Atkinson. The first snow had fallen during the night when I stopped for him at the Chicago Avenue YMCA and when we reached the river bank the rustlings and cracklings of autumn were muted by a light covering of crystalline white. Fello gathered up some dry wood and we lighted a fire and began to talk about the furnishing of the house.

"If you build a house with glass walls, not only to put a roof over your head but to procure certain aesthetic satisfactions, I think you should be careful not to lose those values through the furnishings and here where we look into the hearts of these great trees and across the meadows and the river, it would be a great mistake to set up the usual massive pieces of overstuffed furniture. And yet, if you want to use reed, wicker or something of that sort, the effect would not be humanly inviting and you would feel as if you were camping on travertine. Color, as well, turns out to present problems. It seems to be wanted, to take the chill off, and yet, however it is introduced, it turns out to be disastrous."

"I suspect that the difficulty has to do with an abstract quality which is perhaps the dominant ones. It will be interesting to see what means you will find to live happily in your weekend house. For it would be dreadful if you were not to be happy here," Fello poked up our brushwood fire and then went out to look for more wood.

On our way home we arranged that Fello was to come over that evening for a nightcap and that I would invite Mies to join us. "You would enjoy meeting him, wouldn't you?"

"I'd love to come over. As for meeting Mies, I can't honestly say that I care particularly."

Invited to come over for a nightcap— and the expression was never varied—Mies always agreed, I put the receiver down, took his hat and walked out the door. In five minutes, he was at his destination. And so it was, the evening when I got back from the country with Fello Atkinson.

Conversation moved heavily in spite of anything I could think of to get it off the ground, and by eleven Atkinson took his leave and offered to drop Mies at home on his way back to the Lawson Y. The next evening, however, he rang the doorbell unannounced and, taking the stairs two at a time, he threw himself down on the sofa.

"Look," he said, "I've been thinking a lot about the furnishing for the house and some of the other problems that we were talking about yesterday afternoon and I wanted to see you again before I leave Chicago. Am I disturbing you?"

"No, of course not. I'm terribly glad to see you."

"The thing I have on my mind is this; the history of architecture is badly served with quarrels between architects and their clients. I won't stop even to cite the best known of these rows between great architects and great clients which usually ended in the illustrious architect being forbidden to set foot on the grounds. These stories do no credit to architects and have done a great deal of damage to architecture. The situation seems even worse in recent years because we architects have broadened our pretensions and come to feel that we should not only design and execute the house itself, but furnish it as well."

"That presupposes, however, that the clients have no feelings of their own, no traditions, no taste and no personal requirements."

"That's about what it amounts to. Of course, you realize that all of us do not see it that way, but still it is a trend, one which is fortified, I'm afraid, by some of the innovations in architecture which combine so poorly with traditional furniture. And here we come back to your problems and your situation with respect to Mies which is the reason for my visit this evening. It should be possible for you to go ahead together until the project is complete, but I'm afraid you're not going to be able to. I kept thinking of it last night as you and he were sitting here on the sofa. He is a very stubborn man and you are far removed from the masochistic German woman he's accustomed to dealing with—I'm terribly afraid that it's going to turn out to be impossible for you keep on with him."

"That is certainly possible. I am sure that he would like to put several examples of the Barcelona chair, done in pink suede, beside that enormous glass coffee table, although the subject of furniture has never come up between us. I think the Barcelona chair is very handsome but it is fearfully heavy and utterly unsuitable for a small country house—the place would look like a Helena Rubinstein salon! There is already the local rumor that it's a tuberculosis sanitarium! The fact is that Mies has no taste and if you stop to think about it, that is not surprising. I would hate to be forced to break with him, but I would never consent to his ideas on furnishing. One's house is almost as personal as one's skin. I don't see how he could seriously think that I would go with him beyond the erection of the house itself."

"But I have no doubt that he does think just that. It shouldn't be this way, but I'm' afraid that this story is going to end badly."

"I suppose you have good reasons for your predictions, Fello, and I listen with a very heavy heart. It may well be that I have been mistaken in my impressions of Mies. Perhaps, as a man, he is not the clairvoyant primitive that I thought he was, but simply a colder and more cruel individual than anybody I have ever known. Perhaps it was never a friend and a collaborator, so to speak, that he wanted but a dupe and a victim. There are also the possibilities of a ruinous financial mess, in case our gloomy prognostications should really turn out to be well-founded." We finished our drinks and parted with a promise to write.

"I can be reached in New York at this address, and if I can be of any help, don't hesitate to let me know."

Not long after this, I wrote to Mies that I was unable to underwrite any further expenses in connection with the Fox River project. As I remember he did not acknowledge my communication either in writing or by word of mouth, and I felt that a refusal to authorize further expenses, should not involve a rupture of friendship between us and therefore made efforts to continue all of our cordial customs unchanged.

One evening a truly bizarre incident occurred—Mies was to have dinner with me at home, and when I opened the door, I found the table set in the bay window and Mies already established in his preferred corner of the lounge. I had hardly washed up and given him his Martini when the doorbell rang. Supposing that it was a telegram or something of the sort I released the front door without using the house phone and waited to see who or what it was. I was presently joined on the landing outside my door by a strikingly handsome young man in an immaculate white linen suit who gave his name as Snyder and preceded me in the door.[12] Whether he told me that he was a friend of someone I knew in New York or whether I thought the friend in New York had mentioned a lover of hers by that name and was ready to accept any handy explanation for the fortuitous presence in my living room of the young man in the white suit—I do not recall; in any case I could think of nothing more plausible to do than to present him to Mies and offer him a drink, which he accepted pleasantly as he made himself comfortable on the chaise lounge.

My tentative researches into the identity and background of Mr. Snyder had made no progress whatever when Laura appeared in the doorway and said decisively, "I'm sorry to interrupt you, Dr. Farnsworth, but dinner is ready."

We waited for the unidentified young man to spring to his feet, bid us good-night and leave, but he simply continued to sit.

"I'm awfully sorry that I can't urge you to join us for dinner, Mr. Snyder. Unfortunately, the meal was planned for one guest and doesn't lend itself to a third portion."

"That's quite all right — I understand perfectly, "responded the unsought guest,

still making not the slightest motion to get of the green chaise.

Laura appeared again in the door and Mies and I took our places at the table. By this time, I was uncomfortably aware that Mies had acknowledged by no word or sign the presence of a third person in the room.

"Perhaps you will excuse us if we proceed with dinner," I said, feeling definitely exasperated. "You can take the other chair, if you like."

He complied and, putting his elbows on the table and his chin in his hands, he surveyed us placidly and, it seemed insolently. Mies disposed of his tenderloin rapidly. Presently the stranger spoke: "I know all about you, Mr. Ludwig Mies van der Rohe"—were his astonishing words, pronounced with a kind of a feline sneer.

Without replying, Mies finished off his plate while I released my artillery: "I'd like to remind you, Mr. Snyder that you have surged into my house uninvited and insulted a guest of mine. This has gone far enough and I'm now asking you to leave."

But it was Mies who got up from the table, took his hat from the shelf in the coat closet and walked out, closing the door. Mr. Snyder went back to the end of the chaise and burst into tears. Laura appeared once again at the door, this time with a raised hatchet in her hand. "I'm not leaving until that young man's out of here", she announced.

"Snyder, I don't care whose friend you are, for God's sake, stop that idiotic bawling and go away!"

"I will, I'm terribly sorry."

Laura lowered the hatchet and bolted the door behind him. After a discrete interval I went to Mies with the idea of apologizing for the treatment he had received in my house. There too the doorbell rang, but Mies did not admit the caller, who was presumably Snyder. By that time, it occurred to me that it was I who had been mistreated and that Mies should have shown some regard for me since the incident evidently regarded him and not me.

12 First name unknown.

By the end of 1950 it seemed possible to spend a night in the house, and on New Year's Eve I brought out a couple of foam rubber mattresses and a number of other indispensable articles and prepared to inhabit the glass house for the first time. With the light of a bare 60-watt bulb on an extension cord I made up the foam rubber mattress on the floor, turned up the air furnaces and got something to eat. Spots and strokes of white paint remained here and there on the expanses of the glass walls and the sills were covered with ice. The silent meadows outside, white with old and hardened snow, reflected the bleak bulb within, as if the glass house itself, were an unshaded bulb of uncalculated watts lighting the winter plains. The telephone rang, shattering the solitary scene.

"Are you there alone in those cold meadows? I'm your neighbor from over the approach to the bridge. Won't you come and celebrate New Year's Eve with us? I'll send one of the boys to bring you over – I can't bear to think of you there all alone!"

At that time unknown to me, the voice was Leola's, the wife of Gar, the tavern keeper. It would have been easier to face the situation for which I was prepared: the new house, the seamy flood—meadows and the young moon over the black river. But I could hardly decline so warm an invitation; so, it was not long before two dark forms could be made out walking down from the farmhouse.

"We didn't know whether we could get down here in a car. Do you mind walking up?"

"Not a bit. You can make it in a car but it's a little hard to turn around. You did well not to try it."

Leola's cottage still wore its Christmas trim and all the lights were on when we knocked and entered. Leola herself was an immensely obese woman who played the organ and adored music. Gar had to work that evening, I was told, but there were five or six couples gathered around a long table, and I took one of several empty chairs. I remember nothing attractive about that evening except the haunting melancholy in the eyes of that tremendous woman who was married to Gar and loved music.

"I could have cried when I saw you was going to build down by the shore," she said. "You don't know how quick the river can rise. Often, I can't sleep at night for fear it's going to drown us all. Once it came up and flooded your barn so that the farmers could catch fish with a pitchfork."

"Really, Leola? What year was that?"

"Oh, it was a good many years ago, but still you never can tell when it'll rise again and we'll all be drowned."

Finally, the New Year came in, burdened with its future floods. I went home to my electric bulb escorted by one of the couples at the long table who lived just down the road.

It was an uneasy night, partly from the novel exposure provided by the un-curtained glass walls and partly from the fear of Mies's implacable intentions. Expenses in connection with the house had risen far beyond what I had expected or could well afford and the glacial bleakness of that winter night showed very clearly how much more would have to be spent before the place could be made even remotely habitable.

Perhaps it was not precisely the following morning—it might have been a few weeks later—that I went back to town to begin the week's work, deprived of any further doubt that my economic security had been seriously jeopardized by my architect and that my trust in Mies had been misplaced.

On hospital rounds I visited Room 35 which was occupied by a 59-year-old lawyer who had been hospitalized for treatment of a kidney disorder. As I entered the room, he stared at me from the bed. "You don't look very good yourself, this morning," he said. "Can't you sit down for a few minutes?"

After hearing the principal reasons for my debilitated health he sat up decisively.

"Well! how will you let me try to get you out of this mess?"

There being no other value left to save except my economic solvency, I agreed and in the ensuing weeks I learned in considerable detail the facts of my situation. "Do you realize that he hasn't obtained waivers of lien from the firms who supplied labor or materials and that any or all of them could claim that they weren't paid and take you to court? And from the records kept in that incredible office it's anybody's guess whether they were paid or not."

"Don't tell me any more awful things, Randy. I already have so much on my mind that I can't take any more. Put a period to the sentence—one that will stick—and then we'll see where we stand."

What passed between the two men I never knew as Randy, unkindly turned the "leather-hinged" journalist who covered the suit later brought against me by Mies, considered that the house was an incompetent botch and that I had been the gullible victim of exploitation by an opportunist in whose megalomania and pompousness had replaced the ordinary prerequisites, training and experience which I had had the right to expect of an architect. It is unlikely that he would have displayed, or wanted to display, much tact in his dealings with Mies; on the other hand, the latter had learned certain sordid lessons from the New World as well as from the German inflation of 1922–23, among which the percept that bad publicity was better than none. Probably contributing to the storm, one of the boys from Mies' office telephoned one day to tell me that the furniture for the house was to be delivered, namely, two Barcelona chairs, the glass coffee table and two of the chrome spring chairs. I answered that I had not ordered them and did not intend to use them. "You're not going to use them!" he repeated, stunned. "You can't mean it. They were ordered for you." Evidently. But not with

my knowledge, let alone, agreement. I'm sorry to have to clear up that point, Jerry. A pause followed before he said darkly. "You'll be sorry!"

A few weeks later I was served with a summons to appear in the Yorkville courthouse in connection with a suit for $30,000 brought against me by Ludwig Mies van der Rohe. "It doesn't seem possible," I said to the bailiff who served me with the document, "It certainly is a pity," he responded. "As long as I'm here, doctor, do you mind if I have a look around? I've heard so much about this house—it sure is unusual."

Mies had been poorly advised on the technique of his punitive action and the formula which began "as architect, contractor and agent," had to be revised several times in accordance with the regulations of the American Institute of Architects, before the final document, a Mechanic's Lien, was filed, claiming $30,000 in architect's fees for a house which, when first accepted as a material project, was not to cost more than $40,000, which I had, in the absence of any contract between us made the facts difficult to unravel, but after a time Randy filed counter suit. Strangely enough, it was not Mies's attack, but my defense suit which detonated the publicity and made it appear that I had suddenly and capriciously turned against him; and I soon found myself in a position to understudy Mr. Eric Hoffer as observer and analyst of mass movements. In my case the masses moved chiefly on Sundays, by busload or by private car, on horseback or on bicycles; their motivations must have been as described by Hoffer in that famous little book, The True Believer, and they thumbed their way tirelessly aboard my distress and my exposure behind glass walls, to whatever satisfactions they were seeking. Shirts fluttered from behind trees; cameras clicked, and heads encircled my "sleeping space" as I woke up in the morning. Qualified persons continued to ask permission to come and see the house, and for a year or so after the rupture with Mies, I thought that our personal relations should not affect my attitude toward those professionals who had a legitimate interest in the project. Into that rather restricted group fell the third nice Englishman, Mr. Michael Jaffe, and Mr. and Mrs. Richard Neutra.

The Neutras came when the forsythias were blooming. These were among the first gardening experiments to be tried indoors and half-a-dozen tubs of forsythias bushes were in luxuriant bloom when the Neutras came up the path to the terrace and saw them from the bare ground outside. The California architect had just recovered from a coronary occlusion and he moved slowly as he came up the travertine steps, giving me the impression of a frail man. His wife was charming and we fell to talking about the broken friendship between Mies and myself.

"I have built a good many residences," said Mr. Neutra, "but I cannot remember an instance in which I have left a client in the position in which you find yourself. This is a very sad story, to which the house stands as a monument. I do hope that finally you will find some degree of happiness here."

Their friendly and civilized presence was consoling and this evening as I come across the name of Richard Neutra in the little Garzanti Dictionary of Art I am glad to see that in spite of the coronary occlusion of 1950, he lived until 1970.

Mr. Michael Jaffe came late one Sunday afternoon and I liked him well enough to share a chicken with him for supper. By that time, I had a proper woodpile, and the firelight brought out the shadows of swelling buds on the black maple at this end of the terrace. We talked about Cyril Connolly and his "Unquiet Grave" and the collapse of the review, Horizon. "Do you remember the terrible story of the oil slick in the Baltic, wasn't it that, that trapped the seagulls so that they couldn't get off the surface, and the boys who stoned them from the shore?

I think it was in the last issue of Horizon."

"That became the most famous story of post-war writing. The oil-slick was of such dimensions that it could only have come from a torpedoed sunken tanker, so the anecdote was full of tragic overtones. No one of my generation will ever forget it."

As of that evening, passed in the company of a stranger who shared not only the chicken, but Connolly with his pervading/sive angst and his fascinating anecdote, the swelling buds and the stoned and dying birds—the glass house took on life and became my own home. Michael found his way back to town rather late that evening and went back to England a few days later, leaving flowers and a note.

A year or two ago I found an article in one of the Italian dailies which reported the tracking down and authenticating of a Titian painting long disappeared and located at last in Scotland by Prof. Michael Jaffe of Cambridge University. So, he is still at his work and perhaps some day I shall be trying to tell him how it was that the Fox River house was converted from a propaganda issue into a home.

The court hearings went on forever, futile, nasty and infinitely tedious, in the old courthouse in Yorkville. "Remember that a lawsuit is only a method of settling a quarrel, by no means to be confused with a way of finding out the truth." This was Randy's instruction as the session opened and I took the witness stand.

As a witness I was disappointing to my defense. The reduction to a legal brief of my relationship with Mies looked completely hopeless to me, and I was unable to furnish dates for the few points which could have had some validity in a court of law. Moreover, a sense of profound isolation brought to my mind those multitudes who have tried to defend themselves, their values, their honor and freedom, their lives, in some court, regular or irregular—and plunged me into depression. The only light note was introduced by a whopping bumble bee which drifted into the court room from the lilacs outside and caused the attorneys on both sides of the table to erase their professional smiles and spring to their feet batting the air violently. The presiding judge displayed notable resourcefulness with respect to the bee and after chasing it around the room for a while, cornered it and put it outside with a heavy-duty broom, so that the legal squad could take their places again and mop their brows, while I took up the thread of my useless reminiscences and one of the opposing attorneys announced his intention to register an objection to any statement I would make. At the end of the session, I took the East-West freeway back to town and to work, half-sick with distress.

One Saturday in early June I packed a few groceries in the usual thermos can and embarked for the weekend in the country. Hugo's little friend, the silver poodle, had had puppies and they too were packed in a little basket and put on the floor of the car, out of the sun. A violent thunderstorm overtook us on the way, and the river shore glimmered with spectral drops as I mounted the travertine terrace carrying the three puppies and the rest of the paraphernalia. Shall I make a bed for Lucy out here where there is a bit of a breeze, or inside, I wondered as I fitted the key in the lock and opened the door.

Inside, however, I found the floor covered with water. The wood veneer of the core showed a high water mark an inch or two above the floor, and the shantung folds which enclosed the entire house hung, stained and soaked, from their aluminum tracks overhead. Thunderstruck, I took of my shoes and waded around the core to check the possibility of a leak in the plumbing; but there was none, and it soon became clear that the water came from above, not below, and not from one point but from the entire periphery of the roof. When the heating and plumbing man arrived, we set up the ladder and went up on to the roof which I examined then for the first time. It was a flat tarpaper and gravel covering with a slight pitch directed not toward peripheral gutters but to a pipe downspout leading down through the core to the ground below the house. Around the outer edge the tarpaper had been cut off where it reached the border of ornamental steel and in the absence of flashing, had responded to a half-year of weathering by bubbling and retracting. We found a defect broad enough to admit a finger, which extended all around the structure and had provided for the destruction of the hundreds of yards of shantung which curtained off the interior.

Coached by Harry Callahan, I was a discrete photographer at that time and I spent a roll of film on flounces of tarpaper, on the border of ornamental steel which had supplanted the normal flashing, on the plumber's forefinger inserted in the crack and the ruler which showed the breadth and depth of the defect.[15] All the negatives were masterly and, helped by one of the teachers of photography, from the Institute of Design, one evening was enough to provide me with a small album of photographs to present to the court at the next of its interminable sessions. This contribution excited general admiration, I was told by Randy, but it seemed nobody could believe his eyes, and a court session was called to meet on the roof, in the course of which it was made clear that the roofing company accepted no responsibility for damages contingent upon its mode of construction, since they had refused to guarantee a roof so constructed and had acted under order of the architect. All hands, made it up the ladder and down again, I was told, including even Mies who had been present at all, or most, of the hearings.

The fate of a witness, let alone a litigant, in a court of law depends largely upon the identification which he is able to set up in the minds of the personnel therein, not only of the judge and the attorneys, but the bailiffs, the court secretary, even the janitors. In this connection by all odds the most convincing witness was Georgia in whose apartment in the old Irving, Mies and I had met for the

15 Detroit-born photographer who lived in Chicago and taught at the Institute of Design (1946–61) before moving to Rhode Island to establish a photography program at RISD. David Travis and Elizabeth Siegel, eds. *Taken by Design: Photographs from the Institute of Design, 1937–1971* (Chicago: University of Chicago Press, 2002).

first time. Georgia was one of the fine old book women in the Chicago of the pre-Master period and the friendship between us was deep and affectionate. As my misadventure took on even more weight and threatened greater danger, she evidently suffered from regret, and remorse that she had ever brought us together, for she volunteered to testify to the extremely modest character of the Fox River project as it was originally conceived. I was not in the room to hear the testimony, but it was described to me as amazingly effective for its clarity, its simplicity and sincerity.

It was Mies himself who took the hardest punishment on the witness stand, not only because of his language limitations but because of his total ignorance of everything that everybody present thought any architect should know. You should have heard him!" reported Randy. "You can't imagine what an exhibition of ignorance he put on! He didn't know anything about steel, its properties or its standard dimensions, nor about construction, or highschool physics or just plain common sense. All he knows is that guff about his concept and in the Kendall County Courthouse that doesn't go down. I tell you, we had him sweating blood—he was heard to say afterwards that he would never start another lawsuit."

For six mortal weeks those grotesque hearings continued and until at last, the records had grown to such proportions that there would be no further doubt that nobody would ever read them.

The actions were finally settled out of court many months later, for a division of court costs. I never heard the particulars of the agreement; with infinite thanks to Randy, I made out a check for two thousand dollars, well knowing that that amount would hardly have paid for the court secretary, let alone the rest of the costs.

Some time following the litigation, the American Institute of Architects murmured some kind of official admonition which was immediately sweetened, presumably by other elements in the organization, by a medal in recognition of valor as a designer. The Museum of Modern Art intimated that it was a pity that an architect should have to crush his friend and client but that in the creation of so great a work of art, the crusher could not hope to prevail against the generations to come.

The big glossy reviews polished up their terms and phrases with such patience that the simpler of the minds that came to have a look, expected to find the glass box light enough to stay afloat on air or water moored to its columns and enclosing its mystic space while the more advanced found "implacable calm" and "incredible meticulousness," as they were supposed to. So "culture spreads by proclamation," and one got the impression that if the house had had the form of a banana rampant instead of a rectangle couchant, the proclamation would have been just as imperative.

So, also, a mass movement begins to coalesce, and all those standing by who bear rancor because they are not other human beings or perhaps even bear nothing else than rancor, sign up for the ride, and whether the destination is positive in the sense that the desired feelings of prestige and snob support are attained by innocuous means or negative insofar as attained through damage to those who are not hooking the same ride, still it is the ride that counts. All aboard!

It was hard to bear the insolence, the boorishness, of the hundreds of persons who invaded the solitude of my shore and my home, and I never could see why it should have to be born. It was maddening and heart-breaking to find the wild flowers and ground covers so laboriously brought in to hide the scars of building, battered and crushed by the boots beneath the noses pressed against the glass. The only possible victory seemed to be the survival on some degree of my original idea. But the alienation which I feel today must have had its beginning on that shady river bank all too soon abandoned by the herons which flew away to seek their lost seclusion farther upstream.

Edith Farnsworth, passport renewal portrait, c. 1976.

Ex-owner of Mies-created Farnsworth House dies

DR. EDITH BROOKS Farnsworth, 71, a former Chicago physician for whom Mies van der Rohe designed his world-famous Farnsworth House near Plano in Kendall County in 1950, died Dec. 4 at her villa near Florence, Italy, it was learned Tuesday.

Dr. Farnsworth spent 27 years on the staff of Passavant Memorial Hospital in Chicago and had lived at Antella, just outside Florence, since her retirement several years ago.

The Mies van der Rohe-designed house she formerly owned is a white-painted steel and glass box resting on eight supporting columns. It was built in 1950 on land she acquired seven years earlier from Col. Robert R. McCormick, the late editor and publisher of The Tribune.

A GRADUATE OF THE University of Chicago in literature, Dr. Farnsworth spent extensive periods in France, Germany, Italy, and Austria, studying music and the languages of those countries.

Returning to the United States, she became interested in medicine, enrolled in the Northwestern Medical School, and received her degree in 1939.

After her retirement, she devoted her time to translating into English the works of Eugenio Montale, Salvatore Quasimodo, and other Italian poets.

IN 1967 SHE DONATED a collection of Chinese bronzes and ceramics and Chinese sculpture to the Art Institute of Chicago.

She is survived by a sister, Mrs. Marion Carpenter of Far Hills, N. J.

Dr. Farnsworth's ashes will be returned to Chicago for interment.

Dr. Edith Brooks Farnsworth's obituary, December 14, 1977, *Chicago Tribune*, p. 56. Peculiarly, the headline calls attention to her "Mies-created" house rather than to her own extraordinary accomplishments.

Ludwig Mies van der Rohe on the Edith Farnsworth House

The extraordinary consolidation of Mies's national and international reputation in the 1950s and '60s–in no small part due to the reception of the Farnsworth House–led to a number of high-profile interviews for print media, radio, and television. In some of these interviews, the Farnsworth House inevitably came up as part of a broader discussion about his work. Gathered here are excerpts focused on the Edith Farnsworth House that are part of longer extracts published in *Mies in His Own Words: Complete Writings, Speeches, and Interviews* edited by Vittorio Pizzigoni and Michelangelo Sabatino, (Berlin: DOM Publishers, 2024).

John Peter, Conversation Regarding the Future of Architecture, Part 1 (1955)

What do you think of the use of color in architecture?

In our IIT campus I painted the steel black. At Farnsworth House I painted it white because it was in the green. I could have used any color.

And you've even been known to chrome the structure, as you did with the Barcelona Pavilion.

Oh, certainly, yes. I would do that. I love natural materials or metallic things, you know. I very seldom have used colored walls, for instance. I would really like to give it to Picasso or to Klee. In fact, I ordered from Klee a large picture, two pictures, one side white and the other black. I said: "I don't care what you paint on it."

So if it were a problem of color, you would give it to a master.

Oh, certainly, yes. I would do that.

Christian Norberg-Schulz, A Talk with Mies van der Rohe (1958)

One is surprised that you collect [Paul] Klee pictures; one thinks that does not fit your building.

I hope to make my buildings neutral frames in which man and artworks can carry on their own lives. To do that, one needs a respectful attitude toward things.

If you view your buildings as neutral frames, what role does nature play with respect to the buildings?

Nature, too, shall live its own life. We must beware not to disrupt it with the color of our houses and interior fittings. Yet we should attempt to bring nature, houses, and human beings together into a higher unity. If you view nature through the glass walls of the Farnsworth House, it gains a more profound significance than if viewed from outside. This way, more is said about nature; it becomes a part of a larger whole.

I have noticed that you rarely make a normal corner in your buildings but you let one wall be the corner and separate it from the other wall.

The reason for that is that a normal corner formation appears massive, something that is difficult to combine with a variable ground plan. The free ground plan is a new concept and has its own "grammar," just like a language. Many believe that the variable ground plan implies total freedom. That is a misunderstanding. It demands just as much discipline and intelligence from the architect as the conventional ground plan; it demands, for example, that enclosed elements, and they are always needed, be separated from the outside walls, as in Farnsworth House. Only that way can a free space be obtained.

H. T. Cadbury-Brown, An Address of Appreciation (1959)

Now there is a big jump in time to 1950, the [Edith] Farnsworth House. It is also a big jump in space–from Berlin and Germany to the Middle West.

The floor was travertine, the same all the way through. The kitchen, the bathrooms, and even the utility room were all the same. We thought this would be cheaper.

The professor was asked whether the client was not difficult.

At the beginning, no, but later she was. We got into trouble about the curtains. This is very interesting. I had a great experience with this house. Before you live in a glass house, you do not know how colorful nature is. It changes every day. We had this flooring all the way through, and the wood was very light-colored. I decided to make raw-silk curtains, in a natural color. She said, "Not over my dead body." She had had a piece of advice from somebody; she wanted a very strong yellow color. That material cost us about $7 per 1/2 yard. Our silk curtains cost us $2 per 1/2 yard. That decided her. She did not die, but she was furious.

The professor was asked whether he had ever had any difficulty collecting his fees.

Only with this building. It cost $50,000, and the fee was about $5000 or $6000.

He was asked whether the client liked it now.

I have not the slightest idea. I like it still.

Graeme Shankland, BBC Third Programme Interview (1956)

The most perfect small house Mies has built is Farnsworth House. It is a classic example of the open plan: a single space glazed on all four sides, free of partitions, and with only a service core with bathrooms, a kitchen, and mechanical equipment rising to the ceiling in the center. Was this not an aesthetic idea imposed on a reluctant client? I told Mies that the Italian critic Bruno Zevi said this was not a house at all but a museum.

Mies van der Rohe with contractor Carl Freund (left) and others at the construction site of Edith Farnsworth House, photograph by Hedrich Blessing, fall 1951.

No, that is not a fact. It was a house for a single person. That made the problem more simple. Later, I made a house in glass with five bedrooms and five bathrooms, and even a room for the help. That is really a difficult problem. From my point of view, the open plan, when it is possible, makes you work really much harder. Well, Farnsworth House is, I think, not really understood. I have seen it. I was in the house morning to evening. I didn't know how colorful nature really is. But you have to take care to use neutral colors on the inside because you have the colors outside. This absolutely changed...and I must say it's beautiful.

You had raw silk curtains, I think, in the same house...
Yes, and a very neutral primavera wood, and the house's entire floor was Roman travertine—kitchen, bathrooms, altogether, and the terrace too.

And that was why, I think, you painted the columns white, as you told us...
Yes, that was in the countryside, you know, against the green. I think, white...It does not always have to be black. But I like black too. Black particularly for cities. Even in our tall glass buildings, where you are in an apartment and you have these huge glass walls. You see the sky and even the city changing every hour. I think that is really new in our concept.

Conversation at the Architectural League (c. 1958–59)
I'm not talking only about the Seagram Building. For instance, Farnsworth House is a case where you didn't have anything surrounding you on four sides and yet you [used] exactly the same theory. I just wanted to know whether you considered that block faithfully honest?
Did you see it?

Yes, regardless...
Did you see it? Did you see the trees around there?

That's just adding something after it's done, I feel, to make up for...
No, the trees have been there for 100 years, or 150 years...

Yes, but to depend entirely upon the trees instead of the resources of the architect...of that nature. I just wanted to know...
Well, you are talking about the orientation of the building. We moved the building close to the trees so it would get as much shade as possible in the summer.

Well, let me phrase it differently...if there weren't any trees, would you still design on all four...
It may be. See, we had the building on our drafting board. We didn't have many drafting boards. They made a model out of these things. That is from [steel], and that is glass,

but [here] we just cantilevered the roof, so that the building is in the shadow. There are many ways you can do that. But in a tall building you cannot do it. You know, you can just hang your eyelashes out there, and so on...

George Danforth Interviews Mies, Heritage Program WTTW Television (1960)
Then in the residential sector in this country, in about 1950, you did this house in the Fox River Valley, to the west of Chicago.
Yes. That is a steel building, you know. Plain steel, the clearest construction you can think of.

It's a very pristine example.
Yes, and that's its importance, in my opinion. You cannot make it better.

You raised the floor level above the ground.
Because once in a while the river goes a little over the bank.

I see. It overflows.
It overflows, and we wanted to have [the floor level] high enough so that nothing would happen to the inside.

Lisa Dechêne, The Will of the Epoch Revealed in Construction (c. 1968)
The Tower of Babel demythologized, so to speak. Nothing at all about a ritual of civilization, or am I wrong?
Yes, you probably know of the court cases I went through with Mrs. [sic] Farnsworth. Because all that played a role in the argumentation. Farnsworth House, which I designed for the eminent doctor, was an almost completely hollow space. It stood on stilts so as to emphasize its floating, fantastical equilibrium. It was like a crystal. And I thought I had translated, so to speak—not irrationally but with the help of proportion—the emancipation of mankind from the power of gravity into the form of a building. But Mrs. [sic] Farnsworth accused me of having realized an ice-cold and very male, typically masculine obsession in which people could not live, and certainly not as a woman. And she sued me for damages, in all seriousness. And I had to prove—and here the word probably occurred for the first time—that I had not built a Tower of Babel for Mrs. [sic] Farnsworth. Well, there was a settlement eventually. And Mrs. [sic] Farnsworth sold the house, quite advantageously, to a designer of machines. And he was comfortable in it.

Translation from German by John Nicolson. Originally a radio interview, a transcript was later published in *Deutsche Volkszeitung*. The use of "Mrs." Farnsworth is consistent with the use of *Frau*, upon request for unmarried women, in official settings in 1955 (per Bundessinnenminister Gerhard Schröder). By 1971, a few years after the interview, *Frau* would be used exclusively in official documents and address on the basis of equality.

Ludwig Mies van der Rohe on the Edith Farnsworth House

Edith Farnsworth House Oral Histories

In conversation with Peter and Hayat Palumbo

A compiled and edited transcript of three conversations recorded via Zoom on September 24, October 1, and October 4, 2021.

Michelangelo Sabatino Let us start this conversation with you, Peter, by exploring the beginning of your arts education.

Peter Palumbo I went to school [between 1948–54] and ended up at Eton; my housemaster Oliver van Oss had an encyclopedic knowledge of the arts. He said, "Never, never talk to me about art. Talk to me about the arts, because one discipline informs another." And so, when we came to the actual study time, which was one hour every Sunday, the class was done with photographs and descriptions of the artist, his life, and his work. We did Jackson Pollock and it was shortly thereafter, he showed us photographs of the Farnsworth House. When we saw the photographs, I thought to myself, "I've never seen anything as beautiful as this—or as historic." I mean, it was like the contemporary version of the Temple of Paestum, or somewhere like that, springing up out of the meadow. Purchasing the Farnsworth House really came out of the blue. When I was [in Chicago], it was just being listed for sale.

1 Peter Garth Palumbo, photograph by Cecil Beaton, July 24, 1979.

MS I believe the first comprehensive restoration was initiated shortly after you purchased it in 1972 and a major one in 1996 and 1997 following the catastrophic flood damage.

PP Well, that really began when I put a deposit on the house in 1968. It's not commonly known what deplorable condition the house was in when I acquired it. Dr. Farnsworth, whom I personally got on with very well, was known to be a difficult person and, I believe, she had done everything she knew that would upset Mies. It was very difficult to hear her loathing of him. I mean, when we first met in 1968, she started up—and I put it to rest, but that was nearly two decades later. I said, "Dr. Farnsworth, we should understand one another from the start. Mies is a hero of mine so let's just leave it at that." And she didn't bring it up again because she wanted to sell the house.

MS Do you think she disrespected the house out of spite for Mies or simply because she brought her own personality to the place over time?

PP I think both. She was a very intelligent woman, but if you look at the court transcripts, these characteristics really shine through. Later on (in the trial), she didn't have any real legal representation—she chose to represent herself and she was very forceful about it. By that time, she was out for revenge, with trumped-up charges and a smear campaign—sort of a megalomaniac, I think.

MS So, shortly after you purchased the Edith Farnsworth House, you began to restore it and to improve the landscape.

PP When I came, Edith Farnsworth never had much of a landscape—let alone a swimming pool or tennis court or anything of that kind. Of course, it was very rural and quiet back in those days, which it's not now.

MS The Edith Farnsworth House is now one of four twentieth-century houses owned by the National Trust for Historic Preservation, the other three being Frank Lloyd Wright's Pope-Leighey House in Alexandria, Virginia; Marcel Breuer's House at Pocantico, New York; and Philip Johnson's Glass House in New Canaan, Connecticut. Did you spend any time in the Glass House?

PP Yes, I used to go for lunch there on Sunday when I worked at the Metropolitan Museum of Art for a year and my boss, who was head curator of the Drawings Department, Old Master Drawings, was a friend of Philip's. I suppose we must've gone about a half-dozen times, up to Connecticut for lunch. They were hilarious occasions—and interesting ones, too.

2

3

2 Portrait of Peter Palumbo and his father Rudolph, Buckhurst Park, Berkshire, United Kingdom, attributed to Milton H. Greene, c. late 1960s.

3 Lord Peter and Lady Hayat Palumbo at their Le Corbusier-designed Maisons Jaoul, Paris, published in *Harper's Bazaar,* January 1993, and *Country Life,* June 3, 1993.

4 Lord Peter Palumbo in the woods surrounding Edith Farnsworth House, photograph by Hayat Palumbo, c. late 1980s.

5 Lord Peter and Lady Hayat Palumbo at Arts Council of Great Britain gala dinner, Banqueting House, London, 1989.

4

5

That year really opened my eyes to other art forms which I hadn't fully appreciated. I saw in Johnson's underground gallery, these amazing modern paintings, and it really opened my eyes. And Philip was such a wonderfully witty and wicked host.

MS So, when you visited Johnson's Glass House, you already owned the Edith Farnsworth House?

PP Yes, I bought it a few years before. I went out to see the Farnsworth House in 1962, I think, when I went to see Mies in Chicago for the first time. And then in 1968, when I was going to meet Mies for lunch on a July weekend in Chicago, I was sitting having breakfast in the Drake Hotel, and as I flipped through the *Chicago Tribune* classified section, there was the notice: Farnsworth House for Sale, and a telephone number. So, I telephoned right away. She was there, picked up the telephone, and I explained who I was. And she said, "Well, why don't you come to lunch?" So, I said, "I'd love to."

So that's how it happened. It was a very hot July day, and I wore my best blue suit. When I got to the house, I virtually bought it that afternoon because it was a dream come true—I mean, talk about serendipity and being in the right place at the right time. Here I was in Chicago on maybe the first day it was publicly advertised. And of course, Mies died the following year, so I was glad to have made the commitment when I did.

MS So you made a commitment to purchase the Farnsworth House in 1968 by way of a deposit, and finally held title in 1972?

PP Well, just to clarify that. She said, "I can't sell it to you now, but I can sell it to you in four years' time." This was for various financial reasons. She said, "I'm moving to Italy, and I'm going to translate the works of Montale from Italian to English." And so, I said, "Well, let's draw up a contract now, and I'll pay a deposit; and in 1972, I'll buy it." Well, it wasn't quite as simple as that because we had a thing in Britain in those days called the dollar premium, which was a sort of [open] market. So, when I finally bought it in 1972, I paid $120,000 for the house, plus the dollar premium of 22 percent.

MS And at the time, in 1972, did that seem expensive?

PP I thought it was rather cheap, to tell you the truth. But then, looking around the property, there was no fencing anywhere. It was open to the roads. The house was in a terrible state, there was water coming through the roof. You know, it really had been let go—not beyond redemption but getting towards that.

But until 1979, the exchange controls were in place. So, during those first seven years, anything I wanted to do had to go through the Bank of England. If I wanted to plant a tree, or paint the ceiling, or stop the roof from leaking, I had to get estimates and submit.

MS But already you were laying the groundwork for a brighter future at the Farnsworth House. And I'm assuming you also felt a sense of relief and duty to have taken this masterpiece out of its imminent demise?

PP Yes, that's right. Before I bought the house, I wrote to my great friend Lanning Roper, who was one of the two great modern landscape architects in London at that time. He was the most wonderful man and a brilliant natural designer, but he couldn't draft in the way most landscape architects did. He had done work for me before, and I said, "Look, I've just done this crazy thing of buying a house in America, but I want to be absolutely sure; I want your promise that we will garden together there one week in the spring and one week in the fall each year." So, I had him to do the landscape design work.

MS Did your collaboration with Lanning Roper at Farnsworth look to any precedents? For example, Johnson's Glass House is also in a natural setting that was transformed over time.

PP Well, they were different as one was tethered to the ground, and the other was floating in the air. But what first struck me about Phillip's house was that he had the most beautiful eighteenth-century painting on an easel, and it really was a remarkably beautiful contrast. The painting is by the French painter [Nicolas] Poussin, a landscape. And I thought to myself, what a wonderful juxtaposition. That moment taught me that you could put a Chippendale chair and a Mies van der Rohe Barcelona chair together—and they can have a very happy relationship because they are both at the top of their game. They are friends, and they

6

6 Lord Peter Palumbo's memory-filled desk at the Edith Farnsworth House recreated for *Every Line is a Decision: The Life and Legacies of Peter Palumbo,* March 2023.

talk to one another—they converse as equals. That juxtaposition of the very old and the very new was fascinating to me.

MS But when it came to furnishing the Farnsworth House, you and Dirk Lohan chose primarily Mies van der Rohe designs. So why didn't you bring in antiques at Farnsworth?

PP Well, I did—a few. I had collected some beautiful antique glassware and had some Egyptian pottery on the glass table. And I had some T'ang pottery, Chinese, on the black glass table I had bought from the Barcelona Pavilion of 1929. It had been part of the original furniture there, and I had it at Farnsworth for many years.

MS Let's go back to what, if anything, you learned from Johnson's Glass House. You mentioned seeing his art collection on display in his underground gallery. So, when you decided to bring art to the Farnsworth House, did Philip perhaps influence you in that way? I am thinking about your commissioning Andy Goldsworthy and the Henry Moore sculpture, just to name a few. You must have understood that the art you brought to Farnsworth was to be experienced within a rural setting? How did you think of bringing art and countryside together?

PP Well, Lanning and I did the placing of them. Whether we succeeded, I don't know, but certainly, they added interest to the landscape. We also planted a lot of trees at Farnsworth, over six hundred of them. And we dotted the sculpture about, placing pieces as you came round a corner so you would come upon something wonderful and unexpected. It was never meant to be a museum. The pieces and the settings were simply guided by my own feelings.

MS And which was your first major acquisition of outdoor sculpture?

PP Oh, well, the first major acquisition was the Goldsworthy. I think that was the first such commission he ever received.

MS Goldsworthy's "Flood Stones" had this amazing quality of combining the artist's vision with the natural materials of the site. Did Goldsworthy spend time at Farnsworth?

PP Oh, yes—absolutely. He had sort of burst onto the London scene. And we, at the Arts Council which I was involved with at the time, gave him an exhibition, and I got to know him then. I brought him to America, and he did two or three different schemes... but eventually he did a cairn of stones found in the

fields around the area, which was sited along the riverbank. And he scored the stones to record, as far back as records went, the heights of the various floods—and floodwater in the spring circled around the thing. But it was sort of abandoned when we had the monumental flood in 1996, and the cairn disappeared under three feet of water. And so, I had it taken to Kentuck Knob.

MS Over the course of your lifetime, you have lived in a remarkable array of houses and apartments, both historic and modern: Buckhurst Park, Bagnor Manor, your current London townhome, an apartment at the Waldorf Astoria, another at 860 Lakeshore Drive, several islands off the coast of Scotland—not to mention iconic houses by Mies, Wright, and Le Corbusier. Is there a common thread that unites your fascination for interesting buildings and places?

PP Well, I suppose the design itself would have been one big consideration: the beauty of the place, the quality of the home itself, and its location.

MS So, one common thread is beauty, but another might be described as a special sense of place that appeals to you. It also sounds as though the opportunity to protect these beautiful properties has inspired your decision-making.

PP I do believe in preservation yes, but I don't think people always recognize that it's an ongoing commitment.

Scott Mehaffey: Hayat, we've had a long conversation with Peter about preservation and stewardship, but we want to talk with both of you about living in these special places, stewarding them over time, and developing them for public access. We talked about the challenges of preserving historic homes, but we didn't talk about living in them—and living with the collections of course, that have been part of your life in these places. Hayat, you were quoted in a *New York Times* article some years ago, as saying, "Sometimes I long for the freedom of having nothing." And yet all of your historic houses have a lot of things! So, I wonder if you could talk about that.

Hayat Palumbo Well, that longing hasn't left me, but I don't think I can actually do it, at this point. That's my Middle Eastern side, the idea of living like a nomad, you "up sticks and go" with nothing but whatever is on your back. Not that I've ever lived like that but there's a longing—it's wishful thinking and you know, it's a hopeful thing to remember there's more to life than materiality.

7 Frank Lloyd Wright, Kentuck Knob (I. N. and Bernardine Hagan House), 1956, Chalk Hill, Pennsylvania, c. 1983.

7

SM Sure, but can you speak to the joys and the burdens of creating a wholistic vision for a place—a feeling that extends beyond architecture and feels engaging and immersive.

HP Remember wherever you live, you need to have the things you live with—out of choice or necessity. I mean, it's not as though you can just walk in and walk out—you've got to live there. So, it's very difficult to keep everything pristine, but you know, beauty takes discipline.

SM True. You and Peter have collected art and objects of beauty that enrich these homes and your everyday life—can you talk about that?

HP I think architects see their home designs as shapes on the outside and volumes on the inside, but it's very different for the people who live there. I think there's an inherent need to personalize our living spaces, and I think it comes from that instinctive need for safety and familiarity—as well as beauty.

SM But you're collectors of sorts, and I've seen that you've taken things from Farnsworth to Kentuck Knob and back to England—so some of your favorite things tend to follow you, no matter where you are.

HP When you love someone you want to be with them, and when you love something, it's the same. We like some things more than others, so we've taken them around with us.

MS Hayat, Peter purchased Farnsworth before you married, but you were already married when you purchased the Maisons Jaoul and Kentuck Knob. Is that correct?

HP Peter already had Kentuck Knob, but it was just being restored so I had a hand in that—but Kentuck is not a house you can easily furnish. And the volumes inside Maisons Jaoul are pretty weird. The sitting room is a little den and the library is another little hole...well anyway, it was a difficult house to make functional. They're all lovely homes, but in different

8

9

8 Portrait of Rudolph Palumbo painted by Oscar Kokoschka, 1962, on display at The Walbrook Club, London (originally the location of the Palumbo's business office).

9 Lord Peter and Hayat Palumbo at snake rail fence and Anthony Caro, *Emma Dance* (1977–78) in background, Kentuck Knob, Chalk Hill, Pennsylvania, c. 1990.

ways. Jaoul has a very urban setting, so it was lovely in a different sort of way. The other two, Farnsworth and Kentuck, were so rural.

SM And so, you started opening these homes to visitors in the mid-1990s, I think?

HP Well, Peter was already doing that at Farnsworth, you know, for special groups, the Art Institute and so on. Same at Kentuck.

SM So, you have a lot of history and experience with the way these historic properties are stewarded and interpreted, and I wonder if you could think how that might have changed over time—how your thinking has evolved, and maybe how the public's interests have evolved in visiting these places.

HP Well, early on, visitors to Kentuck would come from Fallingwater and it is one thing when you live there and have guests, but another when you aren't there and want to show it to people. One year, I realized that we only spent three weeks there, and I said to Peter, "Isn't it a little selfish to have this wonderful house locked up with so many people wanting to see it? So, we talked to our lawyers, and they were both dead set against it. But I prevailed, and it was so successful—particularly Kentuck Knob because it's much easier to access than Farnsworth—Fallingwater is so close, so we already had a lot of people knocking on the door. The lawyers were shocked by the number of visitors: clearly the demand was there. Properties like this are not inexpensive to run properly, as you well know.

I think people like a house that feels lived in. This brings more life to it—it's not just an inanimate object. We feel it's important to keep these old houses alive and used. You must experience the same thing at Farnsworth—visitors who don't know much about Mies or about architecture in general, but they are curious, and they want to learn. You also get a lot of foreigners. Sometimes they travel all the way just to see that house, which is amazing. We had a lot of interesting visitors at Farnsworth.

SM I wonder if we could talk a bit about that. Peter mentioned that Jay and Cindy Pritzker were sometimes lunch guests, and I know Myron Goldsmith, Peter Carter, and many important architects visited you—and artists, of course. Peter, you mentioned Andy Goldsworthy—did he stay in the house when he was working on ideas for Farnsworth?

PP He stayed in the Eldridge House—our house in Plano.

HP We would have guests stay in the Farnsworth House. Norman Foster stayed there with his son. Claes and Coosje Oldenburg stayed there...a lot of artists came to Farnsworth.

PP Ellsworth Kelly and Jack Shear stayed there.

HP Yes, and Jim and Nancy Dine. At the time, we had a lot of artist friends.

PP And John Cage came for the weekend.

SM So, you would stay up at Eldridge House and allow them to spend the night in Farnsworth House?

HP Yes, Peter was so keen on sharing his house, his love, that he didn't think twice. We also entertained a lot at Farnsworth before it was opened to the public. After we began to offer tours, we would spend the day there—the pool was there, and the children were young. We used the grounds and kept an eye on the house, and we watched the visitors to see what they were interested in. I noticed at both properties, Farnsworth and Kentuck, people were not really interested in the art and the sculptures. Maybe people didn't like walking very much, because it was too hot

10

10 Andy Goldworthy, *Floodstones Cairn*, 1993-2003, Feltos Sand & Gravel Co quarry at Aurora (IL), as reinstalled at Kentuck Knob, 2020.

in the summer or too muddy, or too far or whatever. You know, there was not that much of an added value to maintaining the sculpture collection because visitors really didn't show an interest.

SM Do many of the visitors at Kentuck Knob take advantage of the sculpture collection?

HP Some do. They like the Goldsworthy or a few things they've heard about, but I wouldn't say that sculpture is the first reason to visit or even to stay longer.

PP Some like the sections of the Berlin Wall. They're very evocative for the generations who know about that but now maybe the interest is fading.

MS There seems to be on your part a sense of duty to share, but also an understanding that these historic properties are complex, and their curation and maintenance take considerable effort.

HP But then you get proud of it in a way, you really do. It's lovely that people admire it, and maybe we've done something right. It's nice to share, not to be selfish, and just keep it to ourselves. It was nothing more than these very straightforward feelings, to share these special places with the public, and they're grateful they had the opportunity to see it— and they're also paying for that opportunity, which is humbling.

MS Back to your point about personalizing these homes, I would also add something about the way we perceive them through photography. It's interesting that over the last twenty years, with the mass diffusion of the digital camera by way of mobile phones, many have embraced photography and shared their photos on social media. Whereas previously, Farnsworth appeared only in carefully composed photographs by luminaries such as Hedrich Blessing or Hiroshi Sugimoto, now there are so many images out there taken by a wide variety of individuals. It's very interesting to see how these people, both amateur and professional, interpret the built environment over time—capturing it in different light, seasons, and circumstances.

HP Well, some of the work of those big-name photographers has become mythical, which, you know, sort of validates the importance of these houses. But the others show these houses can be appreciated by anyone—but also that they have shared something beautiful with a big-name photographer whose work they admire, that they shared an experience, a common link.

MS The excitement of being able to see and experience buildings for themselves leads enthusiasts to go to great effort to visit.

HP Like a beautiful woman, they are photographing this beauty not only to capture her image but also to try and understand her essence, you know? Farnsworth is a very photogenic house that way.

MS Agreed—and what I've appreciated during this conversation with both of you, Peter and Hayat, is the love for the houses you have owned, along with the challenging moments associated with their stewardship.

HP Nothing can survive without care, whether it's a house, a work of art, or a person. And when that house is already an acknowledged work of art, the pressure and expectations are that much greater. It's a real commitment and a sense of responsibility.

On Lady Hayat (née Mrowa) Palumbo see: Youssef M. Ibrahim, "Al Hayat: The Noah's Ark of Arabic Newspapers," *The New York Times,* January 15, 1997, p. 6; Gay Gassmann, "Parties, Fashion & Charities: Lady Hayat Palumbo's Incredible Life Story," *Vogue Arabia*, November 29, 2020, https://en.vogue.me/culture/lady-hayat-palumbo-incredible-life-story/.

For a biographical overview of Lord Peter Palumbo see his official website: http://lordpeterpalumbo.com/index.html.

11 Regis House with new elevation superimposed onto existing streetscape, developed by Rudolph Palumbo, published in *The Story of the Site of Regis House*, London, 1931.

12 *Eton Days* (London, 1976) by Oliver van Oss, Peter Palumbo's influential housemaster at Eton College, who first introduced him to Mies van der Rohe and the Farnsworth House.

13 Courtyard with carport, Kentuck Knob, fall 2020.

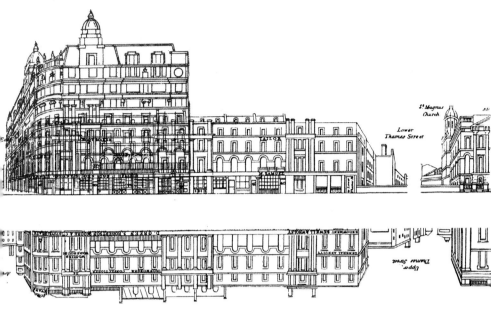

Elevation of the buildings on both sides of King William Street, about which has been superimposed that of the western front of Regis House.

Photographs by Nicholas Barlow **ETON DAYS** Text by Oliver Van Oss

12

13

Edith Farnsworth House Oral Histories

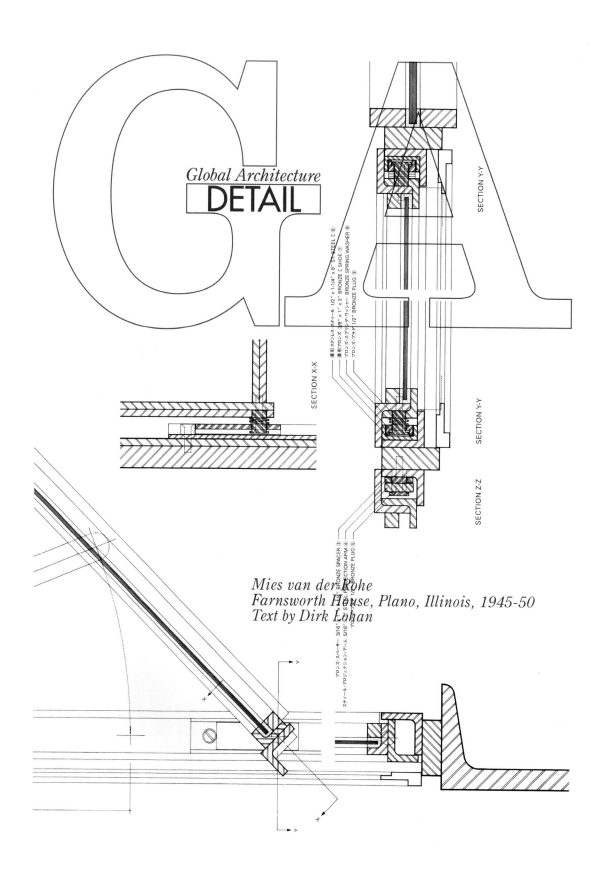

Global Architecture
DETAIL

SECTION Y-Y

SECTION X-X

SECTION Y-Y

SECTION Z-Z

Mies van der Rohe
Farnsworth House, Plano, Illinois, 1945-50
Text by Dirk Lohan

In conversation with Dirk Lohan

An edited transcript of a conversation held and recorded on June 29, 2021 at the Edith Farnsworth House.

Part I

Scott Mehaffey You've said in previous interviews that you grew up with the 1951 Hedrich Blessing photos of the Farnsworth House pinned up in your bedroom in Germany, along with some other photos that your grandfather sent from America. So tell us about your first impressions.

Dirk Lohan This house was airy—it seemed to be floating in air, so I was very impressed. And I decided ultimately to become an architect. I enrolled at IIT in the fall of 1957, and after just a few weeks at IIT, I said, I've got to see the Farnsworth House, and invited one or two friends to go with me. So, we drove out here, and we looked through the fence at the house. And as we were looking, we noticed a person getting up from a chair, going to a table and picking up something. And then we saw it was Edith Farnsworth raising binoculars to look at us. We didn't have the guts to ask if we could come in to see her house because the binoculars were like a gun being pointed at you.

SM We've heard similar stories from other architecture students at that time.

DL So that was my first visit, and I did not meet Edith Farnsworth then, and I never actually did. Sometime later in the 1960s, she put the house on the market and moved to Italy. I thought, my God, I wish I had the money—and I tried to persuade Mies, my grandfather, to purchase it, but he wouldn't touch it.

SM Too many bad memories.

DL Maybe. But before that, we, meaning Mies's architectural office, were commissioned by Peter Palumbo to design a headquarters building for Lloyds Bank on some property that he owned in the City of London in the Mansion House district. Peter came to visit us and because he had never been to Chicago, I took him on a trip around the city in Mies's car, which was a large Lincoln convertible—black and white. And during our ride, he asked me, "What would Mies say if I asked him to design a vacation house for me on an island in Scotland where I have some property?" I said, "Well, at Mies's age"—he was 80 or 81 years

old—"that may not be the highest priority in his life. But the best private home, a vacation home, that he ever designed, and a famous one, is the Farnsworth house." And he said, "Yes, I heard about that house. We should go there!"

So, I drove him out to Plano, and we entered the property and walked up to the house. Because it's all glass, you could see enough of what the house is like inside. Peter fell in love with it and went back to England—but eventually, he ended up buying the house.

SM Records show that he closed on the property in July of 1971. But you didn't start renovations until 1972.

DL At first, he asked me if I would look after the house and make the necessary repairs or suggest improvements—and also purchase for him some furniture, or have it made, which I then did. But one of the things I discovered when I was out there in the winter and started a fire...the wind blew in right along the floor over to the fireplace and would swirl up the glowing ashes. There was no hearth—just the flat travertine floor, where you put the logs and you lit them. My dear grandfather didn't know how to design a proper fireplace. So, we added a piece of solid travertine, carved out with a dish for the logs.

SM So that change was made very soon after possession—like 1972.

DL Yes, my office helped assess what should be done. There were waterproofing issues, window cracks, rust...but Peter was always fabulous—he did what was needed.

SM Did Mies ever talk about the house in his later years, or was it still sort of irritating for him?

DL I didn't ask him touchy questions like, "What was the reason for the fight with Edith Farnsworth?" At that time, in the late '60s, Franz Schulze was already doing research for his biography on Mies, and I was the person in the office who gave him information and documents. And so, I learned a lot about the history of Mies's life and his coming to America and his early work here. But I swore to myself, I would not become a Mies historian. But I am one now, because I'm one of the very few people that knew him during his lifetime.

SM Yes, *The Lost, Last Words of Mies van der Rohe: The Lohan Tapes from 1969* have just been just published as a book—but there were other tapes that were lost. Did you ever talk with Mies on those missing tapes about the Farnsworth House?

DL I don't recall what was missing. Just before he died, I had a heure fixe once a week, with him in his

1 *Mies van der Rohe Farnsworth House, Plano, Illinois, 1945-1950 (Detail 1)*, text by Dirk Lohan with a new comprehensive set of architectural drawings based on the originals. Tokyo, A. D. A. Edita, 1976.

2 Peter Palumbo cutting the cake with Dirk Lohan and Hayat Palumbo at an open house to celebrate an extensive restoration following the 1996 flood, spring 1997.

3 Peter Palumbo and Dirk Lohan, with a rare black glass top table designed by Mies for the Barcelona Pavilion, and Jim Dine, *Flo-Master Hearts* (1969) on the music stand, late 1980s.

apartment, and his cook would make us dinner. I learned so much about him and his stories about Berlin and coming to America. So, I asked to take a tape recorder and said, "We'll just put it on the table and let it run...and we'll talk as if nothing is there." He agreed, but we never got to the end...he died before I could. But these tapes I gave to the Museum of Modern Art, and only last year, they came out in book form.

SM At this point, you've pretty much given everything that pertains to the Farnsworth House to MoMA.
DL Yes. I also separated his architectural projects and other drawings, from his personal correspondence and the letters he received, and those went to the Library of Congress.

SM If you look at the book *Mies in America*, it's interesting to see that the design of Farnsworth House started and stopped from 1945 to 1949, and Mies developed many similar-looking projects during that time—the recently constructed building at Indiana University being one of them. Was Mies proud of the Farnsworth House, despite all the controversies?
DL Oh, no doubt about it. This concept of doing a house in nature was in his head early on—I don't know when it started. He had a perhaps somewhat unique ability to dream up and think through design concepts long before he even had a client—like Crown Hall. I am absolutely sure he was thinking about something like that many years before.

SM The Farnsworth House was a design/build project because Mies couldn't find a general contractor who would take the project on, and so his office served as the general contractor. But this gave him the freedom to work out many details that would later reappear in 860-880 Lake Shore Drive and in Crown Hall. So, this house was a real turning point for his American career. I wonder if Edith knew that—if she felt she was really Mies's patron more than a client, and may have had a chip on her shoulder about it?
DL I've often asked myself this question as well. We weren't there, and I don't know. But it is sad that it got to the point where there was a lawsuit. And you know, of course, there was no contract.

SM That's right. So, your real involvement with Farnsworth began in the early 1970s when Peter first restored the house—through the second restoration in the late 1990s, after the floods. And throughout the 1980s and '90s, Lord Palumbo was adding sculpture, creating the landscape, and occasionally opening the property for the Art Institute or a charity tour.
DL Yes—and gradually it developed in his mind to make it into a museum, let's say.

SM I believe he had a hangar at the Aurora Airport where he stored collections of antique cars and Native American artifacts and so forth—with the intention of adding a museum building to the Farnsworth site. So, he had a grand vision for Farnsworth, I think. And then he tried to sell the property to the State of Illinois as a house museum and sculpture park.
DL Well, I think he came gradually to the conclusion that this isn't a practical house for his family—and also, in the '90s, there was a major flood in the house that was quite expensive and time-consuming to restore.

SM And to his credit, he was very patient with the State of Illinois. It took several years of back and forth until finally, Lisa Madigan said that given the State's financial crisis, we're never going to be able to justify purchasing this. So then came the dramatic Sotheby's auction and after the National Trust acquired it, you were involved with opening it to the public in 2004, I think?
DL To some degree, yes.

SM So now, twenty years later, you're a founding member of the Farnsworth House Stewardship Council. I wonder if you could talk about our expanding vision and what it means for future stewards of the Farnsworth House?
DL Well, I've always felt a certain responsibility for making sure this house is protected and preserved. And we are having wide-ranging discussions about the branding of this place, the use of the land and not only the house, and its needed repairs and improvements. We're discussing the landscape and establishing a more parklike feeling where people enjoy taking walks, maybe a picnic or a small cafe. It's a new and different feeling and the property is a very important aspect of the Farnsworth House experience, in my opinion.

SM Yes, nature is integral to the design and ultimately, the preservation of this house—wouldn't you agree?
DL It's a very special place that deserves to be protected, and to remain as a symbol and icon of the twentieth century. Mies was certainly the kind of thoughtful architect who strived all his life to express the essence of that century. And I think this is probably the one place that tells it all.

Dirk Lohan and Cheryl Kent, eds., *Dirk Lohan: Buildings and Projects of Lohan Associates, 1978–1993* (Tübingen/Berlin: Wasmuth, 1993).

Part II

Michelangelo Sabatino Since Scott asked you about your experience with Farnsworth, I want to have you reflect on your time here in Chicago, your education, and also about the changing nature of stewardship and preservation. So, let's start with the last point first: the Farnsworth House is currently at the center of a collective effort to tell more inclusive stories about buildings, the land on which they sit, and the people who made them possible. In what ways do you think more inclusive narratives about architectural icons will help win new audiences and ensure long-term preservation and stewardship?

Dirk Lohan Well, there's no doubt that the Farnsworth House is a very good example of the kind of question you raise because the house, I think, has been through an early phase of strictly architectural appreciation, but now we're talking much more about the bigger picture. Who was Edith Farnsworth and why did she ask Mies for this unique house? How was this house used by a single woman doctor from Chicago during the 1950s and '60s—and what did it mean to her? As we now know, her relationship with Mies deteriorated to the point where they sued each other so apparently, there were some deep misunderstandings. Each of them, I think, had a different expectation but perhaps by sheer force of personality, Mies achieved what he expected. Maybe she was disappointed that she had less of a role in the creation of this work of art than she had hoped for. We have just finished an exhibition of the house as it was actually furnished and used by Edith Farnsworth. It's remarkable that in all these years since it was opened to the public, nobody had ever given thought to—or had any vision of what it was like.

MS And through that exhibition, we find connections to incredible furniture designers like Franco Albini, and the Good Design exhibitions that MoMA and the Art Institute were promoting. So, it demonstrates a more complex history of influences and connections—which brings me back to Mies. You know that Mies had a great admiration for Frank Lloyd Wright but what is it about Wright's work that intrigued him?

DL Well, Wright has an interesting history in German architecture because the first major publication of his work occurred in Berlin, the Wasmuth papers. When Wright left America and went to Berlin to arrange the publication of his work, it became quite well known and Mies was one of the people who saw this portfolio. If you look at it through German eyes, it was revolutionarily different. At first sight, the way the roofs are arranged, and overhang and cover the exteriors, terraces and so on—that was certainly very Frank Lloyd Wright and very American. But what Mies, I think, took from what he saw, is the spatial flow of rooms from one to another. The Robie House is a great example of this and is related in some ways to the Farnsworth House.

MS Also by way of the central hearth, would you say? In Robie, Wright gave the hearth incredible importance, and in Farnsworth, Mies also made the hearth its central feature and point of congregation.

DL Which was not typically found in German houses. Fireplaces were functional but not predominant.

MS So, this is Mies looking to Wright. What about the aspect of nature?

DL That's the other aspect—the relationship to nature. Frank Lloyd Wright's houses all seem to extend out and draw in the outside world. Most European homes of that era are more fortresslike, and they were often done in stone. Frank Lloyd Wright's American homes are based more on the tradition of wood construction—not solid masonry.

MS But there's another difference. You mentioned Wright's generous overhangs. With the exception of the Bacardi building which Mies did in reinforced concrete, he tended to keep the roof tight with no overhangs. But the visual engagement with the surroundings was always very strong—as it was for Wright. Would you agree with that?

DL Yes, but if I may point out that the latitude of Chicago is somewhere between Rome and Naples, and the sun is much more predominant here—influencing Wright's overhangs. While in northern Germany, you are at the same latitude as the southern end of Hudson Bay and Canada. So, protection from the sun was not as important in those years when people actually wanted the sun, especially in cooler climates. Although that is now changing.

MS This reminds me of the famous journey Mies took up to Wisconsin, to see Wright's Johnson Wax and Taliesin. There are several accounts of that visit, but do you recall him talking about Robie or any other Wright buildings?

DL I cannot recall if I had a discussion with him about any specific Frank Lloyd Wright building, but he said to me that Frank Lloyd Wright was a significant architect of great creative powers.

MS And after Mies spent so many decades here, do you think he understood Wright's "Americanness?" Do you think Mies began to understand his engagement with the Midwest, climatically, territorially...do

4 Mies and Dirk Lohan entering a meeting at the Graham Foundation, Chicago, c. 1965.

5 Mies at Lohan's parents' residence during his first visit to Munich, Germany following World War II, photograph by Dirk Lohan, 1952.

6 Mies in his 200 E. Pearson Street apartment shortly before his death on August 17, 1969, photograph by Dirk Lohan.

5

6

7

7 Memorial for Ludwig Mies van der Rohe held in center core of S. R. Crown Hall, IIT campus, 1969. Dirk Lohan, Phyllis Lambert, and Philip Johnson are visible in the front row.

8 Memorial for Ludwig Mies van der Rohe, IIT campus, with performance by famed cellist János Starker, 1969.

8

you think that he actually changed? A cluster of his most important works: Farnsworth, 860-880 [Lake Shore Drive], Crown Hall, and so many others, are here in the Midwest. So, there's Berlin on the one hand and Chicago on the other. He was already 51 when he arrived, but he spent thirty years of his life here, so was there any transformation?

DL Well, to answer that, I'd like to say that he lived in Berlin the same number of years that he lived in Chicago. Exactly. And the amount of work he did in Berlin is almost negligible—meaning he had almost no real impact in Berlin. With his early work, there were these villas done in a more traditional style, but then after World War I, he became a modernist and he did the Friedrichstrasse—the high-rise concepts—but those were not realized, nor were several other bigger buildings. He built the pavilion in Barcelona, he built Tugendhat in Czechoslovakia, but nothing significant in Berlin. In Chicago it's just the opposite: he built one building after another rather quickly. So, in my opinion, when I compare the oeuvre, up to his departure from Germany, and his time here in Chicago, there is a noticeable difference. And there is also the complete reliance on steel and glass. He concentrated on technological architecture, as he had convinced himself that the use of modern or advanced technology in those years was the essence of the time that he lived in. His older buildings in Berlin are really from another time—the nineteenth century.

MS So, Mies's impact was, we could say, global, right? But Chicago gave him an opportunity to build again and again, which is really interesting because when you see architects today that have offices all over the world, they don't seem to concentrate anywhere too long—whereas Mies had this amazing opportunity to experiment, from Promontory all the way through to the IIT campus. So, my question is, did his deep understanding of how you build in America and specifically in Chicago, help him achieve the heights of architecture that he did? Even though his buildings were copied by many others around the world, he had an intense relationship with this city. Did that have any direct impact on his creative process?

DL Oh, I'm sure it did. But I really believe there's another aspect to Mies that most people don't think so much about. He was a philosopher in his own way. He read very serious books. And that began in his life because the first client he ever had was Alois Riehl, a professor of philosophy in Berlin, who gave him some books and paid for Mies to travel to Italy to see Florence and Rome. And these experiences helped open his mind.

MS So, he was German-born, he came to Chicago at 51 years old, but by the time he [completed] the Farnsworth house, he had been here for more than ten years. Here in the land that birthed Frank Lloyd Wright, he was asked by an American client to design a weekend home, so what was he thinking? Was he trying to make a transition to become an American architect, or did he by that time, perceive himself as someone who would never really belong—so he would create his own architecture?

DL I think it was more the latter. I don't think you could say he was a typical German architect, but he was not a typical American architect either. And that's what I meant by him being a philosopher: he read, and he educated himself and his mind. And he always asked himself, what is important in this place, what is important in life, and what is important in the twentieth century? And he developed certain answers by himself or through the books of the philosophers he read. Those are, in my opinion, what guided him and his thinking. And then of course, when you think about it, he was trained practically, as an apprentice in stonework, bricklaying, stucco, plastering, etc. That's what he learned. In other words, he didn't learn this kind of architecture—he made it up. He developed this in his own head. Really, the detailing of these steel and glass structures, and how they should be put together, was an invention.

MS That's a powerful thing. I have just one more question. You are really the oldest living testament to this house. And this house and its architect have been an outsized presence in your life for nearly seventy years. To what extent has Farnsworth's presence enhanced your life here in Chicago since making the city your adoptive home?

DL Well, those pictures by Hedrich Blessing that Mies sent to Germany also included 860 and 880 Lake Shore Drive, and there was an image of a room looking out the window, and you could see twenty floors below the cars and the edge of the lake. I remember how that fascinated me—to think that people could live that high over a street, surrounded by glass and overlooking everything. I live there now because my subconscious dictated that to me, but I can tell you that my wife and I are totally in love with the views and the relationship to nature. And this house does the same thing and even more so. The way Mies opened the walls of buildings and saw the potential of floor-to-ceiling glass—as though nothing is there. It's still incredible.

The Edith Farnsworth House: Lives, 1972–2024

Edith Farnsworth House,
uninhabited, reflection
of black sugar maple and
Fox River upon a damaged
glass pane, late 1960s.

Peter Palumbo during his visit to Edith Farnsworth House on the day he offered to purchase it, photograph by Edith Farnsworth, summer 1968.

Elizabeth Ernst portrait, commissioned by *The New York Times*, of Lord Peter Palumbo on a Mies-designed Barcelona day bed, 1983.

Baird & Warner For Sale sign, "House by Mies van der Rohe," c. 1970.

RESIDENTIAL   No.   DESCRIPTION

Address River Road & Fox River Drive
Plano, Ill., Kendall County Lot Size 60 Acres   RESIDENCE
                                         Separated
Style and Const. Mies Van der Rohe Zoned Farm Garage 2 Car
The only house designed and built by Ludwig Mies Van der Rohe.

No. Rooms: ......, 1st Fl. ...... Rms. ...... Baths; 2nd Fl. ...... Rms. ...... Baths;
28x78 ft. - Concrete Slab & ceiling - Steel columns and all glass -
partition - 5' - thru the middle - Travertine Floors.
Kitchen .... Thermal   LR
                                                              Glass
Range   Yes   Refrig.   Yes   Screens   Yes   Storm Sash   DR

Total Baths   2   Bathroom Walls Finished Kind of Tub B.I. Showers xx   KIT

Bldg. Age   20   Basement   No.   BR

Heat Radiant - Oil   Electric   220 V xxx
                     H.W. Heater Electric Elect: 110 V   BR
      Est.
Taxes 196. $1600 Possession Immediate Mtge. Info.   BR

Schools 1½ Miles - Plano,Ill.   Churches   Plano, Ill.

Other Information: Worldwide known as an Architectural Jewel -- Only House
in U.S.A. by Ludwig Van der Rohe. Recognized for its influence   Reason for Selling
on recent domestic architecture.
                              EXCLUSIVE

Office BAIRD & WARNER, INC.   Phone 236-1855   PRICE

Address 10 S. LaSalle St.,Chicago Sales Person G. Gauntt $249,000.00

Above information is subject to verification or change without notice, and no liability for errors or omission is assumed. This is not a prospectus

APR 21 1970

Realtor listing of Edith Farnsworth House for $249,000 "Worldwide known as an Architectural Jewel," Baird & Warner, dated April 21, 1970. Palumbo recounts in the interview conducted in 2021 that he paid $120,000 (p. 169 in this book).

The uninhabited house in state of neglect after Edith Farnsworth moved to Italy in 1967, screened porch still in place on left and Florence Knoll table and Angelo Lelli Triennale floor lamp visible on the right, late 1960s.

Fox River Drive north of the house during flooding, May 17, 1974.

The Edith Farnsworth House

In Community Service Since 1872

Kendall County News

Locally Owned and Edited

SINGLE COPY
10c
$3.50 per year
by mail

101st YEAR   PLANO, ILLINOIS 60545   THURSDAY, APRIL 26, 1973   NO. 1

FOX RIVER FLOODS OVER

Saturday Storm Hits Area Hard

The famous Farnsworth house on the Fox River was surrounded by flood waters Sunday as an aftermath of the heavy storm Saturday night.

The middle photo is the flood scene at the boy scout camp. Note the abandoned car on the left, almost completely submerged.

Millhurst Road was closed to traffic as the river and the creek swelled to flood stage. A car had to be towed out when it got stalled in the road earlier Sunday.

Reports had it that over two inches of rain fell. Heavier rains have been reported without causing flood conditions, however, the rain came down in a short period of time and the ground is so saturated with water it could not absorb any more. Rain took the place of snow during most of the winter and this spring has been exceptionally wet. NEWS Photos

The first flood under Peter Palumbo's ownership makes the front page, "Fox River Floods Over," *Kendall County News*, April 26, 1973.

Edith Farnsworth House,
view from southwest, pho-
tograph by Jack E. Boucher
(HABS), winter 1971.

Edith Farnsworth House,
view from southeast, pho-
tograph by Jack E. Boucher
(HABS), winter 1971.

197

Edith Farnsworth House,
north elevation, photo-
graph by Jack E. Boucher
(HABS), winter 1971.

Edith Farnsworth House boat house designed by London-based architect Donald Armstrong Smith, late 1980s. Palumbo purchased two nineteenth-century mahogany skiffs with brass fittings for leisure boating.

Drawings for Dirk Lohan-designed dining table based on the one Mies designed for his 200 E. Pearson St. apartment. The writing desk was also designed by Lohan. It was inspired by a similar one designed by Mies and Lilly Reich for the Tugendhat Villa (shelves for books were added in 1978). Both the new dining table and writing desk (as well as the new bed and boot box) were designed for Peter Palumbo and fabricated with quartered teak veneer with Swedish oil finish and polished stainless-steel legs, 1972.

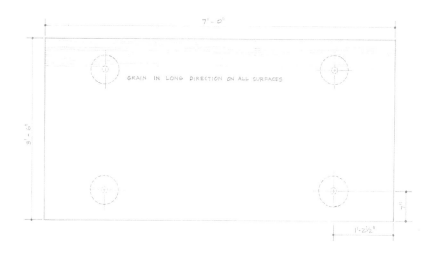

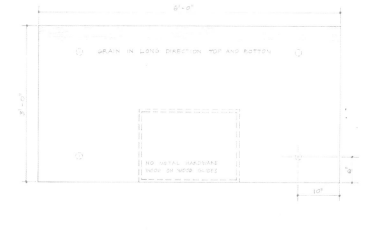

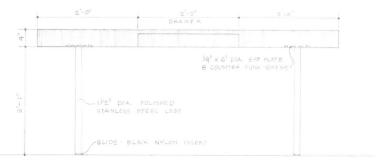

TABLE
QUARTERED TEAK VENEER, SOLID CORE
SWEDISH OIL FINISH

WRITING DESK
QUARTERED TEAK VENEER
SWEDISH OIL FINISH

The Edith Farnsworth House

Dining table setting for
Palumbo-era entertaining
with Mies-designed MR 10
chairs, summer 1990.

Peter Palumbo's "curated"
desk with personal objects
and framed photographs
including himself with
Prime Minister Margaret
Thatcher and Diana, Prin-
cess of Wales, a portrait
of his father, Rudolph, and
other mementos, 1997.

Dan Flavin, *Monument for V. Tatlin* (1969), purchased by Peter Palumbo and installed at the Edith Farnsworth House, c. 1973.

Edith Farnsworth House reinstalled with original Palumbo-era furniture and artworks on the occasion of *Every Line is a Decision: The Life and Legacies of Peter Palumbo*, March 2023.

The Palumbo-era teak
wardrobe, 1997.

Edith Farnsworth House
with Palumbo-era
furniture, including a MR
adjustable chaise lounge,
and George Rickey's *Large
Vertical Arms* visible outdoors to the left, 1997.

205

Landscape architect
Lanning Roper at the Edith
Farnsworth House, late
1970s.

View of Edith Farnsworth House with daffodils, a detail of the landscape design developed by Peter Palumbo and Lanning Roper beginning in the 1970s, c. 1990.

The tennis court that was installed in the late 1980s following the marriage of Peter and Hayat Palumbo, part of a plan to make fuller use of the Farnsworth House through new amenities, c. 1990.

Swimming pool designed by Adrian Gale, an English architect who worked for Mies, with Peter Palumbo on lounge chair in the background, c. 1990.

Opposite right
Rebuilding of frame for panels of primavera core following the 1996 flood.

Opposite left and below
Peter Palumbo on-site with workers following 1996 flood.

Damage from the major flood of July 1996 with sleeping-area furniture (Lohan-designed bed and Mies-designed Brno Chair with tubular steel frame) swept into the northeast corner.

View of sleeping area with floodwater level visible on curtains and dismantled bathroom plumbing fixtures, 1996.

Phillip King, *Smoke Risen* (1979).

Salvaged section of the reinforced concrete Berlin Wall, (with graffiti "Create Life!"), relocated to Kentuck Knob.

Michael Warren, *De-Creation Five* (1978–79).

Anthony Caro, *Bailey* (1971).

Anthony Caro, *Shadow* (1970).

Peter Palumbo and Wendy Taylor in front of her *Square Piece* (1990), a site-specific work commissioned by Palumbo, now located at Mystic Rock at Nemacolin, Farmington, Pennsylvania.

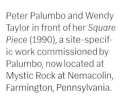

Private gathering at Edith Farnsworth House with Zaha Hadid and Patrick Schumacher on Barcelona day bed, Robin and Chandra Goldsmith in background, Spring 1997.

Zaha Hadid next to pool at Edith Farnsworth House with Palumbo-era plantings including blue squills and daffodils, photograph by Hayat Palumbo, 1996.

Hayat Palumbo's needlepoint pillow of the Farnsworth House, c. 2005.

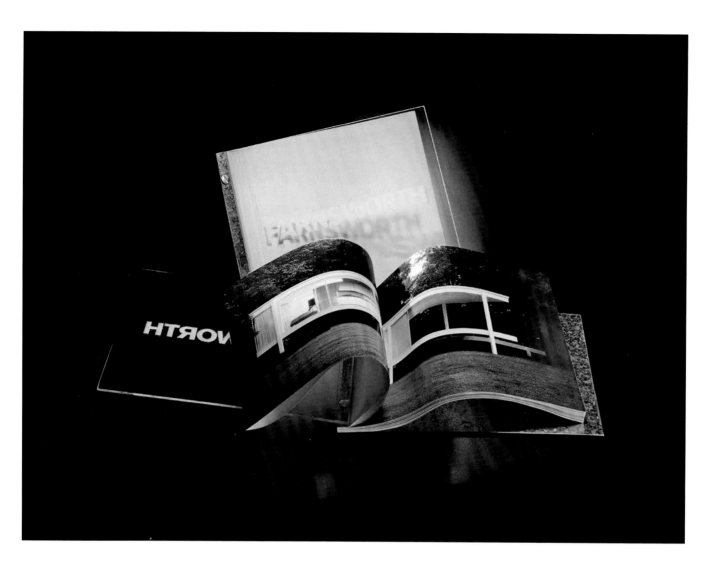

The Sotheby's catalog for the auction of the Farnsworth House, metal spine and Plexiglass cover, opened to photograph by George Lambros.

Model of Edith Farnsworth
House and vitrine fabricated for auction of the house
at Sotheby's New York on
December 12, 2003.

Opening day ribbon-cutting celebrating the Farnsworth House under new ownership/administration by Landmarks Illinois and National Trust for Historic Preservation, May 1, 2004.

Ribbon-cutting ceremony with key individuals involved in the transfer of ownership, left to right: Joe Antunovich (Antunovich Associates, Inc.), David Bahlman (Landmarks Illinois), Richard Moe (National Trust for Historic Preservation), Dirk Lohan, and William Hart (National Trust for Historic Preservation), May 1, 2004.

Sign installed on Fox River Road advertising opening and new status of Farnsworth House, 2004.

Former president of Land-
marks Illinois David Bahlman, under whose watch
the Farnsworth House was
purchased in 2003, rowing
a boat to check for damage
during flooding in 2004.
Photograph by Jim Peters
(who succeeded Bahlman
as president of Landmarks
Illinois).

Barnsworth Gallery, designed and built by IIT Associate Professor Frank Flury with College of Archtiecture students, completed in 2012. The Palumbo-era, metal-clad visitor center was redesigned for the 2004 opening by Antunovich Associates, Inc.

The Edith Farnsworth House

223

Executive Director Whitney French and Brad Pitt with commercial film crew for EDWIN, a Japanese denim apparel company, August 13, 2007.

Virgil Abloh, Illinois native and IIT-College of Architecture-trained fashion designer at the Edith Farnsworth House, shortly after being named artistic director of Louis Vuitton's Mens Ready-to-Wear in 2018, featured in *Kaleidoscope Magazine*, Fall-Winter 2018/2019 issue.

Annie Leibovitz visits
Edith Farnsworth House to
photograph it for her book
Pilgrimage, March 2011.

Edith Farnsworth House
at dusk, photograph by
George Lambros, 1996.

227

Condensation, photograph by Lee F. Mindel, *Architectural Digest*, July 2013.

The Edith Farnsworth House

Arina Dähnick, *Farnsworth House* 16, photograph from *The MIES Project*, 2018.

Bik Van der Pol, *Are you really sure that a floor can't also be a ceiling?*, installation at MACRO – Museum of Contemporary Art, Rome, 2010.

Sarah Morris, *Points on a Line*, 35mm/HD Digital film, 2010.

233

Luftwerk in collaboration with Iker Gil, *Geometry of Light*, installation, Chicago Architecture Biennial partner program, October 11–13, 2019.

The Edith Farnsworth House

Primavera core and living area with reproduction furniture and wardrobe, recreated for *Edith Farnsworth Reconsidered*, spring 2020. Note violin and sheet music stand.

Edith Farnsworth House with reproduction Bruno Mathsson Model 36 lounge chairs for the exhibition *Edith Farnsworth Reconsidered*, spring 2020.

Palumbo-era teak bed designed by Dirk Lohan (1972) and new teak wardrobe (1997, the Farnsworth-era original was destroyed in the 1996 flood) reinstalled for *Every Line is a Decision: The Life and Legacies of Peter Palumbo*, March 2023.

West bathroom installed with Palumbo's collection of original art and accessories, *Every Line is a Decision: The Life and Legacies of Peter Palumbo*, March 2023.

Book spread of Edith Farnsworth House with black sugar maple with fall color, from *Thank You Songs* (CoComelon, 2020).

"F is for Farnsworth House. A marvel to this day," *The ABCs of Architecture* by John and Chloe Doessel (House Logos, 2022).

Cultural programming at Edith Farnsworth House: canoeing in the Fox River, 2020; staged reading of June Finfer's play *The Glass House*, September 13, 2020 (originally performed at the Clurman Theatre, New York, with Harris Yulen as Mies, Madd River Productions, May–June 2010); open-air yoga, June 2016.

241

Edith Farnsworth House in winter, black sugar maple removed and awaiting re-planting of new tree, 2021.

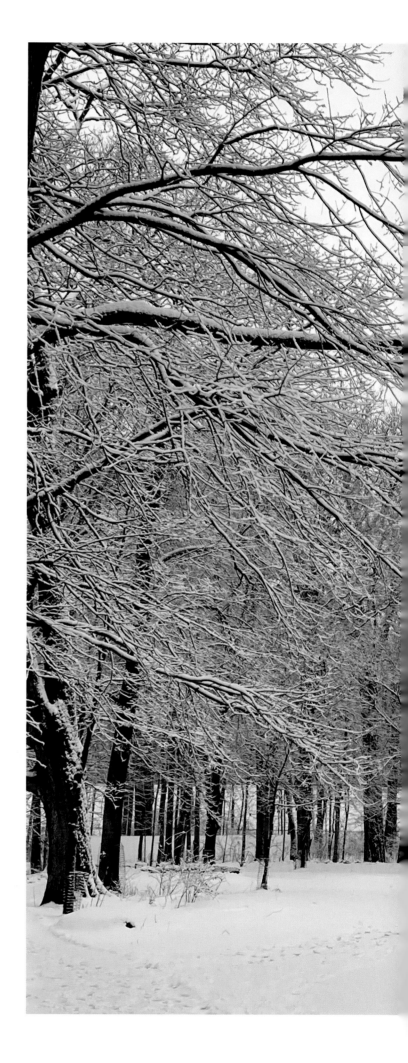

Edith Farnsworth House
and lawn in summer, 2014.

Lives of the Edith Farnsworth House: Preservation, Advocacy, and Stewardship

Michelangelo Sabatino

After more than fifty years of a "public" life fueled in large part by the circulation of photography, the Edith Farnsworth House finally opened to the general public on May 1, 2004, after it was sold for $7.5 million on December 12, 2003, during a dramatically competitive auction held by Sotheby's New York.1 Although the Edith Farnsworth House has been owned and managed by the Washington-based National Trust for Historic Preservation (NTHP) since January 1, 2010, the effort that "rescued" and "saved" it from "imminent threat" of private ownership and the alarming possibility that it might be deconstructed and reassembled outside of Chicago, was truly collaborative. Chicago-based Landmarks Illinois (Landmarks Preservation Council of Illinois) jump-started the advocacy process several years before Palumbo sold the property.2 In 2003, the council intensified its focus by placing the site on its "Most Endangered" list in order to draw attention to its imminent sale.3 [Figs. 1a–1c] A combined, concerted effort led by Landmarks Illinois, the ad hoc nonprofit Friends of the Farnsworth House, and the National Trust for Historic Preservation made this outcome possible.4

To be sure, keeping the iconic Edith Farnsworth House in Chicago, a city that prides itself in the preservation, advocacy, and stewardship of its architectural heritage, was a significant victory that also came with a set of challenges. Today, as in the past when the house was owned first by Dr. Edith Farnsworth and then by Lord Peter and Hayat Palumbo, the single greatest threat looming over this building and site, like a Sword of Damocles, is flooding. Thus, the day-to-day reality of historic sites such as the Edith Farnsworth House, require much more strategic planning and resources, than beguiling photographs alone can provide.

Even as her relationship with Mies and the house moved from enthusiastic commissioning client to disappointed owner, Dr. Edith Farnsworth endeavored to keep her weekend country getaway relatively private despite constant attempts by architectural "enthusiasts" at invading her space of leisure. Her attitude toward the house and site as a place of retreat was significantly more informal than the curated "showcase" atmosphere for visitors created by Peter and Hayat Palumbo. For example, Edith's decision to leave a meadow on the north side of the house, as well as the "organic" furnishings she selected, all point to this dimension.5 The idyllic country quality (and sense of privacy) that drew Edith to the site was further compromised by the construction of the new Fox River Bridge, starting in 1967, when Kendall County acquired the western portion of the site through eminent domain. Once the bridge was completed, automobiles and their drivers were even closer to observe the house. The establishment during those very same years of the Silver Springs State Fish and Wildlife Area on the land immediately across the Fox River from the Farnsworth House brought additional visitors. As Dirk Lohan recounts in an interview published in this book (see pp. 176–83), Dr. Farnsworth became increasingly concerned about unannounced visitors. Lohan, whose personal and professional history is deeply intertwined with the house since arriving to Chicago from Germany and since Lord Palumbo purchased it, had this to say:

> I enrolled at IIT in the fall of 1957, and after just a few weeks at IIT, I said, I've got to see the Farnsworth House, and invited one or two friends to go with me. So, we drove out here and we looked through the fence at the house. And as we were looking, we noticed a person getting up from a chair, going to a table and picking up something. And then we saw it was Edith Farnsworth raising binoculars to look at us. We didn't have the guts to ask if we could come in to see her house because the binoculars were like a gun being pointed at you.

Over the thirty years that Lord Peter Palumbo owned the house, he and Lady Hayat Palumbo opened it regularly to a host of select visitors from Chicago and all over the

1a–1c Newspaper clippings, *New York Times* and *Chicago Sun-Times*.

world. They eventually purchased a late-nineteenth-century Italianate house, also in Plano, so as to expand their hospitality beyond the Farnsworth House. In response to a constant crush of visitor demand and with the intention of generating some revenue to help offset significant maintenance costs associated with the site, the Palumbos opened a visitor center in the spring of 1997.[6] This understated steel structure with a pitched roof echoed the utilitarian buildings found in the agrarian setting of the Fox River Valley.[7]

In conjunction with the opening of the visitor center in 1997, Palumbo launched the Sculpture Walk, a project he began in the late 1970s, in consultation with Lanning Roper. Palumbo wanted to extend the experience of the Farnsworth House with outdoor sculptures, both acquired and commissioned; the first phase of this project was centered mainly around the house, then eventually expanded toward the east during the 1980s and '90s. The Sculpture Walk began at the visitor center with the sightseer gradually descending toward the Fox River crossing the Rob Roy Creek bridge before eventually arriving at the house and then returning west to complete the loop. Sightseers would first encounter two commissioned site-specific works Andy Goldsworthy's *Floodstones Cairn* (1993–2003) and Wendy Taylor's *Square Piece* (1990) along the banks of the Fox River and complete the walk with *British Call Boxes* by Giles Gilbert Scott (1936), before returning to the visitor center. Although the sculptures installed by Palumbo were removed in anticipation of the sale of the house, today works by artists-in-residence like David Wallace Haskin's *Image Continuous* (2021) pay homage to Palumbo's desire to bring nature into dialogue with art and architecture.

Lord Palumbo, a property developer and patron of the arts who read Law at Worcester College, Oxford, was equal parts owner and curator of the Edith Farnsworth House.[8] It is perhaps not a coincidence that the Sotheby's sale treated the property more as an art object than as mere real estate.[9] As Palumbo recounts in the interview published in this book (pp. 166–75), he was particularly indebted to his Lower Master at Eton College, Oliver van Oss, for having first introduced him to the Farnsworth House and for having fostered his appreciation for, and knowledge of, arts of all ages.[10] It was likely Palumbo's father, Rudolph Palumbo (1901–1987), who also transmitted to his son a fascination for architecture, through his work as developer in rebuilding a devasted post-World-War-II London. In addition to developing buildings like the Regis House office building on King William Street in London, E.C. 4 (1931), Rudolph Palumbo valued the arts and the associated prestige, as attests the commissioning of his portrait by Oscar Kokoschka (1962).[11] Ultimately, it was the project for Mies's unbuilt Mansion House Square in London that brought Mies in close contact with both Rudolph and Peter Palumbo.[12]

Although not an architect himself, Palumbo's curatorial oversight of the Farnsworth House shared an affinity with Philip Johnson, who used his Glass House in New Canaan as a canvas on which to project his image as collector and curator. Over time Johnson added various buildings to the site while keeping the furnishings and art of his Glass House relatively consistent. Although Palumbo kept the furniture consistent (Mies and Dirk Lohan designs), as attests the photographs of the house over time, he was constantly introducing art and design objects from a range of periods, both inside and outside. By selecting objects that would enhance the experience of the house and site, Palumbo brought his deep knowledge and remarkable taste to bear on the Farnsworth House. Palumbo's appreciation for beauty extended beyond art and design to include natural artifacts; for example, he displayed a piece of elm tree bark showing the effects of Dutch elm disease, as well as a coco-de-mer that he discovered during his travels. Palumbo not only brought art to the Farnsworth House, he also regularly invited creatives so they could produce new art. This is especially true when he invited photographers, both local and international, to visit and produce new photographic interpretations of the Farnsworth House, ranging from Chicago-based Iñigo Manglano-Ovalle and George Lambros, to distinguished Japanese photographer Yukio Futagawa. A particularly revelatory and personal episode in Palumbo's love for curating is seen with his teak desk (designed by Dirk Lohan); along its perimeter Palumbo typically placed a number of carefully selected portraits and objects to fill his environment while he was going about writing. His desk at Farnsworth serves as a self-portrait of an individual who deeply values art and dialogue with those who sustain it. It is not a coincidence that correspondence with his extensive network of colleagues and acquaintances was one of Palumbo's most frequent activities at his desk.

Shortly before marrying Hayat (née Mrowa) in 1986, Peter purchased Frank Lloyd Wright's Kentuck Knob (I. N. and Bernardine Hagan House, 1956) in the Laurel Highlands of Pennsylvania, located only a brief drive from Fallingwater.[13] Shortly after marrying, he purchased Le Corbusier's Maisons Jaoul (1956) in the Paris suburb of Neuilly-sur-Seine.[14] Today, Palumbo's family still own and operate Kentuck Knob, where he has also moved a number of artworks originally installed at the Farnsworth House. Despite purchasing houses designed by Mies, Le Corbusier, and Wright, Palumbo never considered himself as a collector of modern houses: "I just fell in love—three times….They all came out of the blue—pure serendipity."[15] On the occasion of the centennial of Mies's birth in 1986, Palumbo wrote about the Edith Farnsworth House:

I believe that houses and structure are not simply inanimate objects, but have a "soul" of their own, and the Farnsworth House is no exception. Before owning the

2 *Inland Architect: The Midwestern Magazine of the Building Arts*, Mies Centennial issue, March–April 1986.

3 "'Glass House' on display," *Plano Record*, August 13, 2009.

4 Docent John Palmatier with Edith Farnsworth House official logo and geographic coordinates (41° 38'5.96" N; 88° 32' 8.6" W) tattooed on his right arm, August 2022.

2

MIES VAN DER ROHE

Illinois in the spring of 2004. Thanks to the considerable efforts of Joe Antunovich of Antunovich Associates, the visitor center first built by Palumbo was updated and enhanced in preparation for the grand opening. As part of an effort to welcome primarily the local community that was both intrigued and perplexed at why the site was attracting so many visitors since opening to the general public in 2004, a free-to-all open house was held on August 9, 2009. The *Plano Record* reported an estimate of 2,000 people attending.**17** **[Fig. 3]** In an effort to encourage repeat visits to the house and site over time and in response to the need for a space to temporarily house the large wardrobe damaged by a flood, the Barnsworth Gallery was commissioned in 2008. Designed and built by IIT Professor Frank Flury and his students, this award-winning cylindrical building was sited next to the visitor's center and completed in 2012.**18**

4

house, I had always imagined that steel and glass, by their constitutions, could not possess this quality—unlike brick, for example, which is a softer, more porous material that seems to absorb as well as emanate a particular atmosphere. But steel and glass are equally responsive to the mood of the moment. The Farnsworth House is equable by inclination and nature. It never frowns. It is sometimes sad, but rarely forlorn. Most often it smiles and chuckles, especially when it is host to children's laughter and shout of delight. It seems to eschew pretension and to welcome informality.**16** **[Fig. 2]**

Even with the Palumbos's efforts to welcome visitors, both personal acquaintances and strangers, the allure of the Farnworth House created considerable pent-up desire from the broader public to see and experience it first-hand, especially once it opened under the management of Landmarks

Since the Edith Farnsworth House was permanently opened to the general public in 2004, site guides have been instrumental in enhancing the visitor experience. Two long-time guides, Joan Knutson and John Palmatier, have accumulated a series of observations after having witnessed the behavior of many visitors over the years. For example, Knutson, the employee with the longest track record, recounted how: "On one tour one of the ladies had her camera in front of her face during the entire tour. I do not believe she actually saw the house or experienced the space at all."**19** Palmatier, on the other hand, has engaged with the Farnsworth House at a more emotional level in the sense that he wants to share his fascination with the house: **[Fig. 4]**

I came on a tour of the House many years ago and it seems that I just never left. The House, unknowingly, lures you to relax, forget troubles, and dissolve into it. I never tire of sharing this unique space with her many guests. The borderless expanse of her walls, dissolves you into the surrounding countryside. The House and nature are seamlessly converged in one harmonious space.

Although people can spend a lifetime studying this retreat, I never tire of experiencing their reactions once they can inhabit the actual space. I am grateful that I have gotten to spend my Sundays, for the last sixteen years, sharing my love of the house with our many visitors. This deep experience with the space, lead me to get a tattoo of the Edith Farnsworth House Logo and later an addition of the house's coordinates. [Before that] I [never] believed that there was...anything that would ever drive me to permanently alter my appearance. Well, the experience with the space was that "thing."[20]

The ways in which the multilayered history of the Edith Farnsworth House has been told through its guides and the narrative they have been asked to follow have significantly changed since Knutson and Palmatier began their tenure at the site. Up until recently, the tour script of the Edith Farnsworth House went unchanged—mostly because the focus was on Mies van der Rohe and the architectural attributes of the house. With the arrival of Executive Director Scott Mehaffey in 2018, the guides provided more site information and were asked to always begin with a few questions so they could better understand the interests of the visitors and customize their narrative accordingly. This approach was geared toward tailoring the narrative to respond to the interests of local, regional, national and international visitors. In 2020–21, a completely new tour script focused mainly on Edith Farnsworth was introduced; Alex Beam's book detailing the interpersonal dynamic and legal fallout between Farnsworth and Mies, *Broken Glass*, had been published in 2020,[21] and the *Edith Farnsworth Reconsidered* installation showed the house appointed with replicas of her 1950s-era furnishings. At this point detailed information about the original furnishings for those who were interested was shared in order to accommodate interior design students and professionals as well as architecture students. The grounds were recently opened to self-guided exterior-only tours starting in 2020, with an online exhibition guide accessible via QR codes placed near the entrance to the house as well as in the visitor center. Guides were equipped with iPads containing files of period photographs used to address visitor questions.

The transition from Lord Peter and Hayat Palumbo's ownership to the public realm in 2004 overseen by Landmarks Illinois and the National Trust for Historic Preservation, took some adjustment. Over time, a number of leaders have brought their different backgrounds and experience to bear on the preservation, advocacy, and stewardship of the Edith Farnsworth House. Before the first executive director Whitney French (2006–12) was hired, Jodi Black served in the capacity as manager/director (2004–06). Maurice Parrish (2013–17), was the first executive director to be hired directly by the National Trust after Landmarks

Illinois relinquished management of the site in 2010. Significantly, Parrish, who was trained as an architect and came with extensive museum experience, was the very first Black executive director of a National Trust historic site. Scott Mehaffey (2018–present) is the first executive director to have trained as a landscape architect. **[Fig. 5]** Today, the Edith Farnsworth House is one of twenty-seven historic sites in the National Trust for Historic Preservation portfolio. In addition to the Edith Farnsworth House, other significant modern houses owned by the National Trust include Philip Johnson's Glass House (1949; New Canaan, Connecticut) and Frank Lloyd Wright's Pope-Leighey House (1941; Alexandria, Virginia).[22] While the Marcel Breuer Exhibition House (1949; Kykuit, Pocantico Hills, New York) is owned by the National Trust, it is co-operated with the Rockefeller Brothers Fund (The Pocantico Center).[23] The addition of these three midcentury houses reflects a process of diversification of the temporal reach of the National Trust's portfolio of historic sites.

At the time Palumbo listed his beloved Farnsworth House for sale, he was quoted in the *Chicago Sun Times*: "It has been my intent...to find a buyer for the Farnsworth House who would be as devoted to its preservation as I have been for the last thirty years."[24] Although the $7.5 million price tag garnered at auction for the house was steeper than most wished to pay for it, the reality is that Palumbo invested resources, time, and much care during his decades-long oversight of the iconic house and site. In the interview conducted for this book (pp. 166–75), he revealed his first impressions of the house shortly after he purchased it and his preservation efforts began:

> But we should go back to the first restoration, in 1972—which really began when I put a deposit on the house in 1968. It's not commonly known what a deplorable condition the house was in when I acquired it. Dr.

5 Tour with Edith Farnsworth House executive director Maurice Parrish (far left, front row) summer 2017.

5

6 The effects of the major Fox River flood of 1996.

7 Edith Farnsworth House, Survey No. IL-1105, Historic American Buildings Survey (HABS), National Park Service, Summer 2009.

6

Farnsworth, whom I personally got on with very well but was known to be a difficult person, for example, by doing everything she knew that would upset Mies: attaching shelves to the primavera core and planting climbing roses along the front of the house, enclosing the west open end of the house with netting to protect herself from mosquitoes, etcetera. And so, in a certain sense she had painted herself in a corner when it came to selling the house. It was very difficult to hear her loathing of Mies. When we first met in 1968, she fired the first salvo, which I was able to deflect. If there was love to begin with, or even admiration, it was hatred at the end. When I first looked over the house with her, nothing worked. For her, it was a goldfish bowl and a constant cause of frustration.

Through his scrupulous care of the Farnsworth House, Palumbo gained a deep appreciation and understanding of the need for expertise in preservation of modern architecture; when he purchased Wright's Kentuck Knob and Le Corbusier's Maisons Jaoul he demanded the same meticulous care.[25]

A turning point in Palumbo's own understanding of the harrowing financial consequences of flooding occurred following the 1996 catastrophic flood that did serious damage to the house; although he spared no expense in engaging architect Dirk Lohan to repair and rebuild it, it was clear that this ongoing vulnerability, inherent in the very DNA of the Edith Farnsworth House, could undermine the long-term sustainability of the site. The flooding over the years had increased in proportion to an

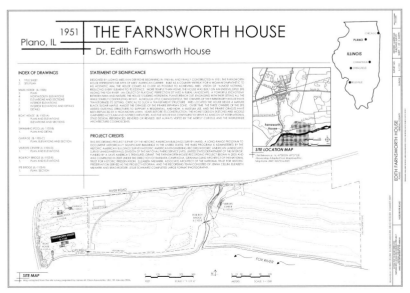

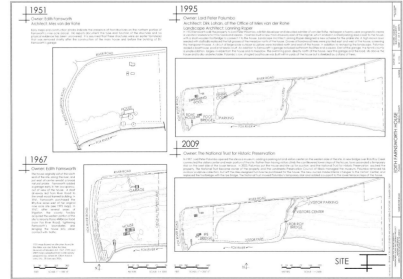

7

251

increase in impervious surface area within the watershed, and stormwater drainage being channeled directly into the Fox River. Quoted in an *Architectural Digest* article published to celebrate the extensive restoration following the '96 flood, Lohan stated, "I'm very concerned that the flooding could happen again, and I'm sure Lord Palumbo is too."26 Unfortunately, should another flooding occur today, one cannot count on the deep pockets of the likes of Palumbo. [Fig. 6] Studies like those done by the National Park Service program, Historic American Buildings Survey (HABS), mapped the changes to the overall site and are useful to study potential long-term changes.27 [Fig. 7] While various solutions have been put forward, including one based on a hydraulic lift system developed by the National Trust for Historic Preservation with Silman Structural Engineering in 2014, the costs associated with this type of project remain high.28 This type of approach also calls into question notions of authenticity in terms of the building, even as the landscape points to the ongoing need for study of the site.29 [Fig. 8] To be sure, the pursuit of authenticity is particularly challenging with the Edith Farnsworth House. Over the years most of the original single-pane plate glass has been replaced with tempered glass that was not available at the time. Modern architecture was supposed to be always "new" and yet time (and weathering) inevitably takes a toll. Recall the replacement in 2021 of all existing travertine on the lower terrace and both sets of stairs (Wiss, Janney, Elstner Associates (WEJ) and Zera Construction), the Edith Farnsworth House demonstrates that it is a living building with all of the challenges the passage of time entails.

More than just a country weekend house, the Edith Farnsworth House and its sprawling agrarian site has required a significantly more complex approach to preservation, advocacy, and stewardship. A turning point in the preservation of twentieth-century houses (and opening them to the general public) in Chicago occurred in 1957, when the leaders of the Chicago Theological Seminary decided to proceed with the demolition of Frank Lloyd Wright's Robie House (1910) in Hyde Park in order to build a married students' dormitory in its place.30 Were it not for the vocal protests of Wright himself (who was eighty-seven at the time) along with a local and international community of architects, historians, and preservationists, the house—recognized as a masterpiece of American (and Prairie) residential design—would no longer be standing. During the very same years that the Robie House was being saved from the wrecking ball, the iconic Villa Savoye (1931) on the outskirts of Paris lay nearly in ruins.31 Today, the Robie House is part of a growing local network of house museums that are part of a consortium founded in 2011—*At Home in Chicago*.32 More importantly, in 2019, Robie House was ascribed, along with other Wright sites, to the UNESCO World Heritage List.33

Several of Chicago-area modern houses are in the public realm and have been converted into house museums open to the general public: in addition to the Edith Farnsworth House, there are the Schweikher House (1938, and later, Studio, 1949) in Schaumburg, and the Stevenson II House designed by Perkins, Wheeler & Will in Libertyville (1936), which now serves as the Adlai Stevenson Center on Democracy. It is worth noting that another Mies-designed house in the Chicagoland area—the Isabella Gardner and Robert Hall McCormick III House—was sold to the Elmhurst Fine Arts and Civic Center Foundation and eventually moved to its current location in Wilder Park in 1994, reopened in 1997 as part of the Elmhurst Art Museum with an attached addition by De Stefano + Partners.34

As access to modern houses in Chicago and beyond expands and programming has adapted to encourage visitors from a wide range of cultural and socioeconomic backgrounds, these sites have continued to enter into the popular imagination. Whether one prefers LEGO Architecture's Farnsworth House released in 2011 or more recently the "low-tech" wood version by Marcus Bree (Little Building Co.), which gives great prominence to the site's original black sugar maple tree, opportunities for serious fun abound. As a testament to changing narratives, the Edith Farnsworth House's visitor center has moved away from selling t-shirts with writing "It's all about Mies," to ones with Dr. Edith's portrait sporting hipster shades, underlined with the adjective, "Fearless." Cultural programming too has been extensive at the Edith Farnsworth House during these past years. Alongside a number of in-situ art installations, documented elsewhere in this book, thanks to the Chicago Architecture Biennial, the Edith Farnsworth House has continued to attract creatives of all sorts. For example, as an extension of Gerard & Kelly's *Modern Living* series the duo created a choreographic score to be performed specifically at the Edith Farnsworth House (2017). [Figs. 9-12]

The different layers of ownership and oversight discussed in this chapter and throughout the book—Dr. Edith Farnsworth, Lord Peter and Hayat Palumbo, Landmarks Illinois and the National Trust for Historic Preservation—reveal the remarkably different "lives" of the Edith Farnsworth House over time. To ignore this complexity would undermine the richness of a collective story that needs to be told again and again by a range of diverse individuals and stakeholders. Only by bringing together different yet complementary approaches to architectural history, preservation, advocacy, and stewardship can we hope to extend the life of beguiling yet fragile modern icons like the Edith Farnsworth House.

8 Robert Silman Associates Structural Engineers, axonometric view of house with proposed hydraulic lift system, 2014.

9 Gerard & Kelly, *Modern Living*; site-specific performance, Chicago Architecture Biennial, September 16, 2017.

10 "Farnsworth House" architectural model kit with black sugar maple by Marcus Bree, Little Buildings Co, 2020.

11 "It's all about Mies" T-shirt formerly sold in the Edith Farnsworth House visitor center, c. 2015.

12 "Fearless" T-shirt currently sold in the Edith Farnsworth House visitor center, 2020.

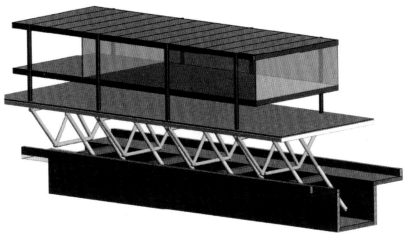

8

9

10

11

12

Notes

1 See Sam Lubell, "Preservationists Rally to Save Mies's Farnsworth House," *Architectural Record* 191, no. 12 (December 2003): 32; Carol Vogel, "Landmark Mies House Goes to Preservationists," *The New York Times*, Dec. 13, 2003, Section B, p. 7; Lynne Duke, "National Trust Wins Bid for Mies Treasure," *The Washington Post*, Dec. 13, 2003; Stevenson Swanson (with Blair Kamin), "Farnsworth House saved. Last-minute donations rescue Mies masterpiece at auction," *Chicago Tribune*, Sunday, Dec. 13, 2003, pp. 1, 24.

2 The Preservation & Conservation Easement established in 2003 set up a system of checks-and-balances that helps guide change at the Edith Farnsworth House. The Executive Director or the Preservation Architect present to Landmarks Illinois's Easement Committee a few times each year, depending on the projects being planned and discussed.

3 "Thanks to the support of several generous donors, the organizations were able to secure an additional $5.5 million to become the successful bidders and ultimately establish it as a house museum." https://www.landmarks.org/farnsworth-house/. According to Memorandum of Understanding and Supplement Agreement, Dec. 4, 2003 (only 8 days before the auction), the NTHP was to retain title and Landmarks Illinois was to retain the easement. Additional support came from international, national, and local donors ranging from AIA National to Alphawood Foundation Chicago.

4 Ongoing conversations between Lord Palumbo and Governor George Ryan led to an agreement for the State of Illinois to purchase the house for $7 million in 2001. However, in 2003, Attorney General Lisa Madigan blocked the sale claiming budgetary limitations; following this decision and due to a series of health and financial challenges, Palumbo decided to put the house immediately for sale. Key players at the time were: David Bahlman (1945–2023), president, of Landmarks Illinois (Landmarks Preservation Council of Illinois/LPCI) and its board chairman Joe Antunovich, and Richard Moe, president of the National Trust for Historic Preservation. John Bryan (1936–2018), former chairman of the Sara Lee Corporation and arts philanthropist, served as chairman of the non-for-profit Friends of the Farnsworth House. He worked closely with Richard Gray (1928-2018), art dealer, collector, and benefactor, throughout the process. Gray, who had significant experience at auctions, served as official bidder on behalf of the group. See Nancy Moffett, "Gov urges potential buyers not to remove Farnsworth House," *Chicago Sun Times*, December 12, 2003, p. 32. Lynn Becker, "On the Block. Will Illinois let Mies's spectacular Farnsworth House slip through its fingers?" *Chicago Reader* 33, no. 5 (October 30, 2003).

5 Despite the extensive planting of trees throughout the site by Palumbo, the transformation of the meadow into "lawn" (and the removal of a tree located in close proximity to the north facade of the house) undermined the informal agrarian setting of the house that was very much visible in the early photographs. During Farnsworth's ownership, the contrast between the unruly meadow and pristine house could not have been greater.

6 The visits were concentrated mainly on the weekends and tour leaders were hired. The Farnsworth House site required constant oversight. Independent of maintaining the architectural qualities of the house, Palumbo invested considerably in such "improvements" as air conditioning, as well as transitioning the oil furnace to an electric heat pump. Thomas Blanchard, Palumbo's full-time property manager for almost three decades, oversaw these "behind the scenes" projects during his tenure. Special thanks to Tom for sharing his knowledge and experience with me.

7 At this time, Palumbo set up a for-profit house museum corporation for all three of his modern houses: Farnsworth House, Kentuck Knob, and Maisons Jaoul. He eventually would keep only Kentuck Knob.

8 lordpeterpalumbo.com/index.html

9 The Guest House Philip Johnson designed for Blanchette Rockefeller in 1949 had also been auctioned at Sotheby's and sold for $3.5 million. See Rita Reif, "Philip Johnson Town House Brings $3.5 Million at Auction," *New York Times* (May 7, 1989), Section 1, p. 38. The sale of the Farnsworth House was overseen at Sotheby's by Chicago-born Jodi Pollack (Chairman, Co-Worldwide Head of 20th Century Design, New York).

10 Oliver van Oss, *Eton Days* (London: Lund Humphries Publishers Ltd, 1976). Van Oss's approach would serve Palumbo well during his stint as Chairman of the Arts Council of Britain in which he exercised qualities of "quiet tenacity and patient diplomacy." See Andrew Sinclair, *Arts and Culture: The History of the 50 Years of the Arts Council of Great Britain* (London: Sinclair-Stevenson, 1995), p. 318.

11 Quintin Waddington, *The Story of the Site of Regis House* (London: Rudolph Palumbo, Regis House, 1931). See also Wolfgang Fischer, *Homage to Kokoschka* (March-April 1966) (London: Marlborough Fine Art Limited, 1966), p. 30. The painting now hangs over the mantel of The Walbrook Club in London.

12 Jack Self and Yulia Rudenko, *Mies in London* (London: REAL, 2017).

13 Bernardine Hagan, *Kentuck Knob: Frank Lloyd Wright's House for I. N. and Bernardine Hagan* (Pittsburgh: The Local History Company, 2005). Marylynn Uricchio, "Kentuck Knob: The Other Frank Lloyd Wright," *Pittsburg Quarterly* (Fall 2015).

14 Caroline Maniaque Benton, *Le Corbusier and the Maisons Jaoul* (New York: Princeton Architectural Press, 2009).

15 Edwin Heathcote, "Meet the people who collect modernist houses," *Financial Times*, June 21, 2021, ft.com/content/0900efe8-606f-4482-848a-952fbb94fc48. Paula Deitz, "Keeper of 3 Architectural Icons of the 20th Century. Collecting houses by Le Corbusier, Mies and Wright," *The New York Times* (December 28, 1989), Section C, p. 1.

16 Peter Palumbo, "Farnsworth Impressions," *Inland Architect* 30, no. 2 (March/April 1986):45–46.

17 "'Glass House' on display," *Plano Record*, August, 13, 2009, p. 1. Special thanks to Jeanne Valentine for her assistance.

18 Pamela Dittmer McKuen, "Barn Again: For Farnsworth Site, Studio Echoes Vernacular Farm Structures," *Chicago Architect* (July-August 2012), p. 16.

19 Joan Knutson has been an Edith Farnsworth House Guide since 1997 (with a few years of hiatus).

20 John Palmatier has been an Edith Farnsworth House Guide since 2007.

21 Alex Beam's readable *Broken Glass: Mies van der Rohe, Edith Farnsworth, and the Fight Over a Modernist Masterpiece* (New York: Random House, 2020)repeats well-worn rumors.

22 David Whitney, *Philip Johnson: The Glass House* (New York: Pantheon Books, 1993); Terry B. Morton, *The Pope-Leighey House: National Trust for Historic Preservation* (Washington, DC: Preservation Press, 1983); Steven M. Reiss, *Frank Lloyd Wright's Pope-Leighey House* (Charlottesville: University of Virginia Press, 2014).

23 This "country home for the commuter" was designed by Marcel Breuer in 1948 as part of the exhibition *The House in the Museum Garden* held at the Museum of Modern Art from April 12-October 30, 1949. See Barry Bergdoll, ed., *Home Delivery: Fabricating the Modern Dwelling* (New York: Museum of Modern Art, 2008).

24 Shamus Toomey, "Farnsworth House will stay put. Preservationists pay $7.5 million for one-room Mies work," *Chicago Sun Times*, December 13, 2003.

25 At Kentuck Knob, Palumbo engaged Bob Taylor, the original job architect for Wright, to oversee the restoration. At the Maisons Jaoul he did the same: "We found the houses in terrible condition. But I purchased and restored them happily because the job architect [Jacques Michel], who had overseen the construction of the houses for Corb was was still alive. And so, I put him in charge of restoration and he persuaded the original workmen [led by artisan Salvatore Bertocchi] to come out of retirement for one more time, put on their *bleu de travail*, their working clothes, and undertake work, in consultation with Colin St. John "Sandy" Wilson, a close friend of mine, and a great admirer of Corb. It was actually a rather moving moment because when my wife and I paid a second visit to Paris a few weeks later, there they were in a line on the approach to the house, in their *bleu de travail*, to introduce themselves. [...] They had all retired but for this one project, they would return in memory of the Master!" For the full interview with Lord Peter and Lady Palumbo go to the Edith Farnsworth House website, https://edithfarnsworthhouse.org/education-at-the-edith-farnsworth-house/.

26 Roland Flamini, "The Farnsworth House Restored: Mies van der Rohe's Illinois Icon Survives the Flood," *Architectural Digest*, February 1999, "Before and After" pp. 66, 70, 72, 74, 76, 78.

27 Survey No. IL-1105. Summer 2009 (Delineated by Jenna Cellini, Elizabeth Milnarik, Brad Roeder); Edith Farnsworth House, 14520 River Road, Plano, Kendall County.

28 Jenna Cellini Bresler, "Mitigating the Flooding Threat at Mies van der Rohe's Farnsworth House in Plano, Illinois" *APT Bulletin, The Journal of Preservation Technology* 48, no. 2-3(2017): 13-19. Special Issue on Modernism.

29 See Julia Bachrach Consulting with Teska Associates, Inc., *Edith Farnsworth House, Cultural Landscape Report* (June 9, 2022) and Rebecca S. Graff, PhD, RPA, *Edith Farnsworth House Site Report: An Investigation into the Archaeology of the Fox River Valley* (2022).

30 Daniel M. Bluestone, "Wright Saving Wright: Preserving the Robie House, 1957," in *Rethinking Wright: History, Reception, Preservation*, eds. Neil Levine and Richard Longstreth (Charlottesville: University of Virginia Press, 2023), pp. 179-212.

31 Edward Diestelkamp, "Modern Houses Open to the Public in Europe and America," in The Modern House Revisited (theme issue), *Journal of Twentieth Century Society* 2 (1996): 86-94.

32 Daniel Joseph Whittaker, "Chicago House Museums: An Examination of Motives, Origins, and Transformations of the Institution" (PhD diss., IIT College of Architecture, 2018), for Robie see in part. Ch. 7. A group of more than twenty former residences—large and small—have banded together to form *At Home in Chicago*. See chicagohousemuseums.org.

33 See "The 20th-Century Architecture of Frank Lloyd Wright," accessed Oct. 30, 2023, whc.unesco.org/en/list/1496/.

34 See Barry Bergdoll, *Mies van der Rohe: McCormick House* (Elmhurst: Elmhurst Art Museum, 2018).

Reflecting on Two Glass Houses

Hilary Lewis

1

Although many people may think of the homes managed by the National Trust for Historic Preservation as those of the premodern era, in fact, two of the greatest modern homes in the US are maintained and open to the public due to the Trust: the Edith Farnsworth House in Plano, Illinois and the Glass House in New Canaan, Connecticut. How these two entered this esteemed collection are very different tales, reflecting the histories of their original owners. Both properties factor strongly into my own life and career, in part due to my current role with the National Trust. But I am hardly alone; so many architects, designers, artists, and aficionados feel strong connections to both of these distinct, yet deeply linked, residences.

My first visit to the Glass House was more than thirty years ago, when I was beginning my work with Philip Johnson, which would eventually lead to our book, *Philip Johnson: The Architect in His Own Words*, which was published in 1994. My coauthor, John O'Connor, and I had already begun work with Johnson at his offices in Manhattan, and in one of our early interviews with the architect, he asked about our understanding of some specific aspect of the house. In our silence, Johnson queried, "But you've been?" Sheepishly, I admitted we had not yet been to the house, something only possible if Johnson himself had invited us. He seemed at once annoyed but amused by the comment. "Then you must go now,"

he stated. My visit to the house was scheduled in the next few days when both Johnson and his partner David Whitney would be in New York. I would have the place to myself. John would visit at a later date.

I arrived by taxi and was dropped at the base of the drive directly at the heart of the complex between the glass and brick pavilions; I seemed to be the only person on the property. Cautiously, I entered the Glass House and continued to look for someone to arrive and show me where it was appropriate to be. Finally, I rang the Johnson office from the Trimline phone next to his bed. In those days, mobile phones were not common, and David Whitney had not yet bought the Bang & Olufsen phone to replace the old Trimline. Johnson's assistant calmly told me to wait; a few minutes later a man arrived riding a lawnmower. This was the groundskeeper who lived on-site and generously informed me I had the run of the place. Mr. Johnson and Mr. Whitney were not at home, and it was fine for me to go about as I pleased.

The magic of that first day was extraordinary, especially since I knew the occupants, but up to that time I had only experienced this significant place via images and classrooms; I had to compare the experience of being there with what had already been built up in mind, an experience that is probably analogous for any of our visitors entering the property for the first time. For me, the change of grade of the landscape and its lushness may have been one of the greatest surprises. I would learn from Johnson just how inextricable the landscape was from his architectural creation. To enter each of the buildings in silence and with no pressure from the clock was a true luxury.

That was my first direct encounter with the Glass House; I would not see the Farnsworth House in person until the year of its opening to the public, a dozen years later, in 2004. I was stunned by how the space flows through its horizontal form and the elegance of its proportions, which make that glass house so special. The work of the hand of Mies reads differently than that of his many imitators. Johnson always acknowledged this and even his articulateness was strained when attempting to explain Mies's greatness.

While the story of the Farnsworth House is extensively explored elsewhere in this volume, it may only be necessary to underscore that this temple-like expression of modernism at midcentury only remained in the hands of its original owner, Dr. Edith Farnsworth, for twenty years after its completion. Contract to title lasted from 1968–72 when she sold it to Lord Peter Palumbo, who would change the home's furnishings and landscape, as well as engage in necessary preservation. More than

thirty years later, the house was auctioned by Lord Palumbo and acquired by a consortium including the National Trust. Thanks to the diligence and dedication of many who believed that it should be preserved and seen by the public, the house was publicly opened in 2004.

2

The background of the Glass House is quite different, although its form grew out of a very close connection with the original design of the Farnsworth House. Its design nonetheless represents some deeply divergent architectural attitudes, as well as a very serious commitment

3

4

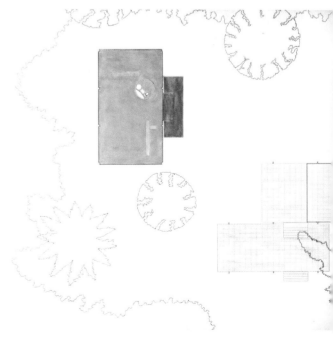

to art and preservation by its designer and owner, who were one and the same: Philip Johnson. Johnson, a central figure in the history of American architecture of the twentieth century, never considered selling his home and, indeed, over the years acquired more land, eventually expanding the property to nearly ten times the size of the original five-acre site that he had purchased in 1946.

Like his art collection and other possessions, Johnson made sure that his home would be donated philanthropically, and those arrangements were settled with the Trust nearly twenty years before his death in 2005. The other major recipient of his generosity was The Museum of Modern Art (MoMA) in New York, which had been receiving art from Johnson's collection since his earliest days at the institution in 1930. Today, Johnson is considered one of the most significant donors to the museum.

Therefore, it's hardly surprising that, according to Johnson, he seriously considered donating the house itself to MoMA. As he reported it, the museum told him that it was not in a position to manage such a property, and Johnson turned instead to the National Trust, inking an arrangement to leave the full property, major artworks, rights to his intellectual property, and a financial endowment in 1986. The intent was that all would be received by the Trust upon his passing, allowing his partner, David Whitney, a life estate on the portion of the property where Whitney maintained his own house. Surely, in the mid-1980s, the Trust would have expected that at 80 years old, Johnson would most probably be leaving the site to the institution in the near future. However, Johnson would live for nearly another two decades, giving the Trust much more time to take possession. Both he and Whitney would die in 2005 and the site, after some adjustments by the Trust, would open to the public in 2007.

It is worth noting that the Edith Farnsworth House and the Glass House were both intended not only as part-time residences but also as domestic spaces for nontraditional households. In neither case were spouses nor children part of the expected program. In Johnson's case, he would live with David Whitney from 1960 until the end of both their lives, but his home was built to be his alone as a break from city life, just as Dr. Farnsworth's was her commission for a country home for her own enjoyment.

Both these houses became available to the public within a few years of each other at the start of the twenty-first century. Their mutual link goes even further back. When Ludwig Mies van der Rohe first developed the design for the Farnsworth House, he presented this in the form of sketches and a model as part of the Johnson-curated retrospective of Mies's work that MoMA exhibited in 1947. The house was not yet built and would not be completed for another four years. But Johnson considered this design as part of his own thinking for the house he wanted for the property he had just acquired in 1946 in New Canaan, Connecticut. (Mies's grandson Dirk Lohan would later comment on the link between the two houses in an especially playful artwork, *The Prodigies of Modernism*, 2010.) Johnson would work on designs during 1947–48, and the Glass House and its second wing, the Brick House, would be ready for his occupancy in 1949. Johnson would furnish the glass pavilion with the same Mies-designed furniture he had owned since 1930, when he first commissioned Mies to design an apartment interior for him in New York.

As Johnson would describe it, he also borrowed from the architectural ideas of Mies van der Rohe of the 1920s, when Mies had developed his "court-house" concept and had explored the idea of using glass for walls, which Johnson then adapted to the landscape of Southern New England at midcentury. Embracing in the Glass House far more symmetry and classical proportion (based on the golden mean) than Mies did for the Farnsworth, Johnson placed his house flat on the ground with a modest few stairs leading up to the home's centrally placed doorway. (In fact, all four facades have a door at their centers). Mies's work floated five feet above the floodplain, while the Glass House was "a clunky thing," according to Johnson, who insisted this was precisely what he wanted. "It's a house, an American house," he explained. In Connecticut, Johnson adjusted Mies's solitary house to a two-winged complex of the Glass House plus Brick House–a direct reference to Mies's double-winged court-houses and a clever move that allowed Johnson to hide the mechanicals of the Glass House within the opaque walls of the Brick House and connect the two structures via an underground system beneath a grassy court between them.

This reference to an earlier history, in this case the 1920s, was hardly rare for Johnson, who was fond of saying, "You cannot not know history." He nearly

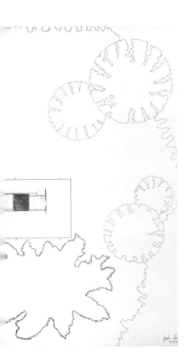

Reflecting on Two Glass Houses

Acknowledgments

First and foremost, heartfelt thanks are due to Scott Mehaffey, Executive Director/Curator of the Edith Farnsworth House Historic Site/National Trust for Historic Preservation, for his tireless support of this book during the research and writing process. Trained as a landscape architect, Scott's deep knowledge of the house and site, have made it possible to promote a deeper understanding of the relationship between architecture and nature. Additional National Trust staff members such as Arianna Kiriakos, Joan Knutson, Carolyn Lioce, and John Palmatier, also contributed in various capacities. Special thanks to Alan Rapp at Monacelli for his multifaceted contributions and support throughout the process. Together with production director Michael Vagnetti, they have worked very hard to ensure the publication of this book to coincide with the twentieth anniversary of the Edith Farnsworth House's opening to the general public in 2004. Chris Grimley, principal of the design studio SIGNALS, brought his creativity to bear on the design of a book that is meant to present a multi-layered history of a house (and its inhabitants) that forever changed modern architecture. The objective from the get-go was to expand architectural history to include a discussion about the relationship of architecture and preservation to culture. Chris and Monacelli were especially responsive to our desire to produce a visually rich book with heterogenous materials whose contents would attract both specialized and general audience readership. My editor Nancy Mangum McCaslin deserves special thanks for embracing multiple editorial roles and sharing her research.

Several figures who were uniquely positioned to extend the living legacy of the Edith Farnsworth House, starting with Lord and Lady Peter and Hayat Palumbo, former owners of the Farnsworth House, were very generous with their time, and we are privileged to have their stories told in their own words, as part of the book. In addition to several online video meetings, Lord and Lady Palumbo were particularly gracious hosts at Kentuck Knob, located in the Laurel Highlands region of Southwest Pennsylvania. Excerpts of interviews conducted with all of them, focused on the history of the Edith Farnsworth House as well as stewardship and preservation initiatives, are published in this book. Complete transcripts of the interviews are available on the Edith Farnsworth House/National Trust for Historic Preservation website. Thanks to Philip Palumbo, Peter and Hayat's son, who has also been helpful throughout the research process. Thanks to Tom Blanchard, the Palumbos' longtime site manager, for sharing insights with me that he gained over time.

Dirk Lohan, a Chicago-based architect who worked over the years to preserve the house, and a grandson of Ludwig Mies van der Rohe, has been a knowledgeable and unwavering supporter of the Edith Farnsworth House as well as the architectural legacy of his grandfather. Dirk had generously shared his expertise and insights about Mies with me even before I began writing this book. I first met Dirk shortly after arriving to Chicago to serve as Professor and Director of the PhD Program in IIT's College of Architecture. His support and collaboration continued during my recent tenure as Interim Dean of the College of Architecture. I will always cherish Dirk's support and friendship over the years, and I dedicate this book to him.

Contributing authors Ron Henderson, Hilary Lewis, and Dietrich Neumann have greatly enhanced the book's scope with their expertise. Over the years, numerous individuals have written about Mies in general and about the Edith Farnsworth House more specifically. From Franz Schulze (with Edward Windhorst) to Alice T. Friedman and, more recently, Nora Wendl, researchers have continued to rethink the history of a remarkable patron, her remarkable architect, and house. Many architects, artists, and architectural photographers have revealed different dimensions of the house and site over time. This diverse group of creatives from different generations spread across the globe, some of whom I interacted directly and others simply with their works, deserve a collective works, deserve a collective thank you for keeping the Edith Farnsworth House alive through their work.

Alison Hinderliter, Manuscripts and Archives Librarian of the Newberry Library, where the Edith Farnsworth Papers are located, provided valuable assistance in facilitating the publication of excerpts of Edith's memoirs in this book. In 1991 and 2019, Fairbank Carpenter, the son of Edith's sister Marion, donated his aunt's papers to the Newberry Library. Today, his children continue to support the publication of materials that reveal Edith Farnsworth's multifaceted personality and her important role as a medical researcher and patron of modern architecture. Serge Ambrose worked very hard to transcribe Edith's handwriting as well as assisting in many different ways throughout the research and writing of the book. Bill Zbaren, a friend and passionate photographer, generously shared his photographs taken on the occasion of the *Edith Farnsworth Reconsidered* exhibition, curated by Nora Wendl and Scott Mehaffey in 2020. A series of unprocessed Farnsworth-related materials were recently discovered in the offices of Goettsch Partners (former Lohan Caprile Goettsch Architects). Thanks to Len Korosky of Goettsch Partners for granting me access to these materials before being donated to MoMA. Benn Joseph, Head, and Gary Strawn, Librarian, Collection Services, McCormick Library of Special Collections & University Archives of Northwestern University Libraries assisted with materials related to Farnsworth's purchase of land from Col. McCormick. Archivisit Susan Sacharski at the archives of Northwestern Memorial Hospital, which holds Dr. Edith Farnsworth's professional and personal papers, was also helpful.

Financial support for this book was provided by the John Vinci Distinguished Research Fellowship, as well as by Dean Reed Kroloff of the IIT College of Architecture. The National Trust for Historic Preservation also contributed financial support to this publication. Early in the process, Katherine Malone-France, former Chief Preservation Officer of the National Trust for Historic preservation, expressed her support for a book that would reveal the different "lives" of the Edith Farnsworth House, especially the part of the story that focused on the transition from private ownership to devising strategies for opening and re-programing for a general as well as specialized public. Former National Trust employees such as Frank Sanchis (former Vice President of Historic Sites) and William A. Dupont (former Chief Architect), gave freely of their time to discuss stewardship and preservation of modern architecture sites. Mark Stoner, Senior Director of Preservation Architecture (Graham Gund Architect) also shared insights about ongoing challenges regarding the Edith Farnsworth House. Former Landmarks Illinois Presidents Jim Peters and the late David Bahlman also shared their memories surrounding the sale of the Edith Farnsworth House. Special thanks to current President and CEO Bonnie McDonald for her support of this book and to former staff member Jodi Black. Special thanks to Joseph M. Antunovich (Antunovich Associates) for sharing his experience as Board Chair during the purchase of the house from Palumbo/Sotheby's. Former Executive Directors of the Farnsworth House, Maurice Parrish and Whitney French, also shared their experiences with me. Chicago-based Rebecca S. Graff gave me insight into her archaeological research about the Fox River Valley, and Julia Bachrach shared her cultural landscape report with me. Special thanks are due to Omar Eaton-Martinez, the National Trust's Senior Vice President of Historic Sites, for his ongoing support of the Edith Farnsworth House.

This book is dedicated to all of those individuals who have worked in many different capacities to research and preserve the house and site for future generations, and above all to those who have helped put the person and legacy of Edith back into the Edith Farnsworth House. This book is also dedicated to the memory of my dear friend Jean-Louis Cohen. Shortly before he left us this past summer, we spent a memorable day together discussing Mies-designed buildings (and more) here in Chicago.

Contributors

Michelangelo Sabatino is Professor and Director of the PhD Program in Architecture at the College of Architecture of Illinois Institute of Technology (IIT). Trained as an architect, preservationist, and historian, he earned a Laurea in Architecture at the Università IUAV di Venezia and a PhD from the Department of Fine Art, University of Toronto. His monograph *Pride in Modesty: Modernist Architecture and the Vernacular Tradition in Italy* (University of Toronto Press, 2010) won critical acclaim and multiple awards, including the Society of Architectural Historians' Alice Davis Hitchcock Award. He is the author, coauthor, and coeditor of numerous books, including *Canada: Modern Architectures in History* (Reaktion Books, 2016), *Avant-Garde in the Cornfields: Architecture, Landscape, and Preservation in New Harmony* (University of Minnesota Press, 2019), *Modern in the Middle: Chicago Houses 1929–1975* (Monacelli, 2019), *Making Houston Modern: The Life and Art of Howard Barnstone* (University of Texas Press 2020), *Carlo Mollino: Architect & Storyteller* (Park Books, 2021), *Mies in His Own Words: Writings, Speeches, and Interviews 1922–1969* (DOM Publishers, 2024), and *Building, Breaking, and Rebuilding: The IIT Campus and Chicago's South Side* (2024).

Scott Mehaffey has served as Executive Director and Curator of the Edith Farnsworth House, a National Trust Historic Site, since 2018. He holds a Bachelor of Landscape Architecture from the University of Illinois and a Master of Science in Organizational Leadership from Dominican University. He is a Fellow of the American Society of Landscape Architects. Scott was formerly the Landscape Coordinator for the City of Chicago, following more than a decade as Landscape Architect for The Morton Arboretum. While an adjunct professor in the College of Architecture at Illinois Institute of Technology, Scott taught courses on the Prairie School and midcentury modern design. In his private practice, Scott provides instruction in cultural landscape preservation for design professionals and property owners and managers.

Hilary Lewis is the inaugural Chief Curator and Creative Director at the Glass House, a site of the National Trust for Historic Preservation and former home of the architect Philip Johnson. An architectural historian, curator, and critic, she is coauthor of two books on the architect: *Philip Johnson: The Architect in His Own Words* (Rizzoli, 1994) and *The Architecture of Philip Johnson* (Bulfinch/Time Warner Book Group, 2002).

Dietrich Neumann is a professor of the history of Modern Architecture and Urban Studies at Brown University. Trained as an architect in Munich and London, he received his PhD from Munich University. His publications have dealt with the history of skyscrapers, movie set design, architectural illumination, building materials, the Milanese architect Mario Palanti, and Ludwig Mies van der Rohe. He has held fellowships at the Canadian Center for Architecture, the Institute for Advanced Study at Princeton, at the American Academies in Berlin and Rome and won the Founder's and Philip Johnson Awards from the Society of Architectural Historians for two of his publications. He served as president of the society 2008–10 and was named a fellow in 2018. At Brown University he has served as Director of Urban Studies and Director of the John Nicholas Brown Center for Public Humanities. He is the author of *An Accidental Masterpiece: Mies van der Rohe's Barcelona Pavilion* (Birkhauser, 2020) and *Mies van der Rohe: An Architect in His Time* (Yale University Press, 2024).

Ron Henderson is a landscape architect and educator. He is Professor of Landscape Architecture + Urbanism at Illinois Institute of Technology and founding principal of LIRIO Landscape Architecture. He previously held appointments at Harvard University, Pennsylvania State University, Tsinghua University, and Rhode Island School of Design. At IIT, he is founding faculty for The Alphawood Arboretum, advises on campus planning and landscapes, directs The Driverless City Project, and has ongoing research on The Natural History of Cities. He is author of *The Gardens of Suzhou* (University of Pennsylvania Press, 2012), *30 Trees* (Birkhauser, 2023), and cotranslator of *Analysis of the Classical Chinese Garden*, the seminal text by Peng Yigang. He frequently writes and lectures on trees in design, contemporary Asian landscapes and urbanism, and the urban design implications of autonomous vehicles.

Chris Grimley is the founder and creative director of SIGNALS. He has produced numerous books, exhibitions, archival surveys, and catalogs on architecture, the legacy of urban renewal, public art, and architectural photography. He is the coauthor and designer of *Heroic: Concrete Architecture and the New Boston* (Monacelli, 2015), and *Imagining the Modern: Architecture and Urbanism of the Pittsburgh Renaissance* (Monacelli, 2019), and the designer of *Henry N. Cobb: Words & Works 1948–2018: Scenes from a Life in Architecture* (Monacelli, 2018).

Credits

Every reasonable effort has been made to identify copyright holders and obtain their permission for reproduction. Any additions or corrections will be incorporated in subsequent printings or editions of this book, given timely notification to the publisher.

Serge Ambrose **131 bottom right, 257 top**

Richard Anderson **225**

Architectural Forum: The Magazine of Building **64**

Architectural Record **128 bottom right**

The Art Institute of Chicago, Ryerson & Burnham Libraries
A. James Speyer Collection, Harry Callahan photographer (199706_190304-007) **190**
Tadao Ando, Prints and Drawings (2019.873) **22 bottom right**
Edward A. Duckett Collection, 1931–1978 **9, 10, 78 top**

Arts & Architecture **84–85**

Hassan Bagheri **100 bottom left/ right, 103 bottom, 104 bottom left/right, 107 left, 108 bottom left/right, 109 bottom left/right**

Bauhaus-Archiv, Museum für Gestaltung, Berlin **105 top**

© Cecil Beaton Archive / Condé Nast **167**

Bik Van der Pol **232**

Bildarchiv Monheim GmbH **102 bottom right**

Tom Blanchard **192**

Werner Blaser, Living Archive, Blaser Architekten AG, Basel **62–63**

Marcus Bree, Little Buildings Co. **253 middle**

Sandra Burch **216**

Canadian Centre for Architecture, Montreal
Myron Goldsmith fonds **10, 108 top**
Guido Guidi **27**

Chicago History Museum, Hedrich Blessing Collection
Hedrich Blessing **50 HB-09522e, top; 89 HB-30037; 112 HB-17555a, bottom right; 122 HB-19312b; 127 HB-04781-x, top; 127 HB-04811-d, bottom; 128 HB-09789-a middle; 129 HB-05321-b, top left; 129 HB-09279-k, middle left; 129 HB-04382c, top right; 130** middle left; **130 HB-05253-d, middle right, 130 HB-15690-b bottom left; 131 HB-06703-x middle left; 131 HB-09276-f, middle right; 131 HB-05659w, bottom left; 132 HB-11508-d, middle left; 164 HB-13810m;** William (Bill) Hedrich **15 HB-14490s; 31 HB-14490n, top; 64 HB-14490H; 65 HB-14490f, top; 65 HB-14490h, bottom left; 66 HB-14490n; 67 HB-14490-u; 68 HB-14490-l, top; 68 HB-14490k, bottom; 69 HB-14490m, top; 69 HB-14490j, bottom;** George H. Steuer **16 bottom left, 65 HB-14490-q, bottom right;** Jon Miller **117, 118–119, 222–223**

Chicago Sunday Tribune
W. H. Wisner **39**

Bruno Conterato, courtesy Paul Conterato **52–53**

Arina Dähnick **230–231**

Howard Dearstyne, courtesy T. Paul Young **74**

François Dischinger **17 top right**

John and Chloe Doessel **240**

dpa Picture Alliance **102 bottom left**

Henry Dubin, courtesy Peter Dubin **129 top right**

David W. Dunlap collection **54 top**

William E. Dunlap **17 middle right, 18 middle left/right, 54 bottom, 55, 76, 77, 82**

Alan Dunn and Mary Petty Papers, Syracuse University Libraries **25**

Edith Farnsworth House and Historic Site **78 middle/bottom; 80 top, 81 top right/left; 88, 186** Tom Blanchard **210, 211 top left/ right, 251 top**

Hugo Erfurth **99 bottom right**

Elizabeth Ernst **187**

Dudley Fisher **28 bottom right, 29 top, 212–213 (except 213 bottom right)**

Joseph Frank collection **132 top right**

Geneva History Museum
Jacques Brownson **132 bottom**

Milton H. Greene **168 top left**

HABS (Historic American Buildings Survey)
Harold Allen **99**
Jack E. Boucher **194, 195, 196, 197, 198–99**

Jenna Cellini, Elizabeth Milnarik, Brad Roeder **251 bottom left/ right**
Leslie Schwartz **16 bottom right, 81 bottom left, 200 top**

R. Ogden Hannaford, courtesy Katharine Hannaford **19 middle, 60–61**

© John Teich Hill **12–13, 30**

Robin Hill **113, 244–45, 260–261**

Karen I. Hirsch **81 bottom right, 178 top, 201, 210 bottom, 211 bottom**

House Beautiful © Hearst Magazine **26, 70**

Inland Architect **249 top left**

Innen-Dekoration **100 top left/right**

Michael Johnson **228**

Kate Joyce **234–235**

Steve Kapas, Creative Photography **97**

André Kertész, *House & Garden* © Condé Nast **17 bottom left, 72, 114, 258 top, back cover**

Klassik Stiftung Weimar **103 top, middle, second from bottom**

Arthur Koester **102 top left**

E. C. Kropp Co. **37 top**

Joe Kunkel, Baird & Warner, and Jamie Zimpelmann, VHT Studios **131 bottom right**

Katie Kuykendall **241 bottom right**

Jeff Laird **17 top left**

George Lambros **204, 205, 227**

William Leftwich **110, 258 bottom left**

Dirk Lohan **181 middle left, bottom right, 200 bottom**

Iñigo Manglano-Ovalle **24 bottom**

Scott Mehaffey **31 bottom, 241 top left/right, 242–243 bottom left**

Midwest Aerial Surveys Inc. **38**

Lee F. Mindel **229**

Sara Mitchell **173, 175**

Derry Moore **17 bottom right, 168 top right**

Sarah Morris **233**

The Museum of Modern Art / Licensed by SCALA/Art Resource **18 MR4505_160_CC top right, 19 top, 86 AR684666, 101, 102 top right, 105 second from top, 105 bottom, 106, 107 right**

National Trust for Historic Preservation **219, 224 top, 250, 253 bottom left/right**
David Bahlman **218**
Jim Peters **221**
Whitney French **22 bottom left, 29 bottom, 220, 224 bottom, 226**

Dietrich Neumann **104 top right**

The Newberry Library, Chicago
Edith Farnsworth Papers **11 (Thomas Gorman), 21 bottom right (Thomas Gorman), 22 top left, 35, 40, 41, 42, 43, 78, 79, 83, 137, 142–43, 160**
Helen Balfour Morrison Papers **18 top left**

Hayat Palumbo **168 bottom right, 178 bottom, 201 top, 207, 208, 209, 213 bottom right, 214–215**

Peter Palumbo **202, 206**

Plano Historical Society **92 bottom**

Plano Record **249 bottom left**

Michael Ray **171**

Michelangelo Sabatino **249 middle right**

Charles Saxon papers, Columbia University **28 top left**

Robert Silman Associates Structural Engineers **253 top left**

Photograph Courtesy of Sotheby's, Inc. © 2003 **217**

Sasha Stone **103 second from top, third from top, 104 top left**

J. J. Stoner / Beck & Pauli, Lithographers **37 bottom**

© Hiroshi Sugimoto, courtesy the artist and Fraenkel Gallery, San Francisco **236–37**

Derek Swalwell **front and back cover, 16 top, 271**

Curt Teich & Co. **36**

John Vinci **258–59**

Mike Wade **96**

© Jeff Wall, courtesy the artist and White Cube **24 top**

Y. C. Wong **50 bottom, 56–59**

T. Paul Young **75**

Jim Zanzi **94, 185, 188, 190, 191**

William Zbaren **6, 22 middle right, 80 bottom, 169, 203, 238–239**

265

Image Credits

Select Bibliography and Resources

Achilles, Rolf, Kevin Harrington, and Charlotte Myhrum. *Mies van der Rohe, Architect as Educator*. Chicago: Mies van der Rohe Centennial Project, IIT, 1986.

"Award $14,467 to Architect of Glass House." *Chicago Daily Tribune*, June 9, 1953.

Beam, Alex. *Broken Glass: Mies van der Rohe, Edith Farnsworth, and the Fight Over a Modernist Masterpiece*. New York: Random House, 2020.

Becker, Lynn. "On the Block. Will Illinois let Mies's spectacular Farnsworth House slip through its fingers?" *Chicago Reader* 33, no. 5 (October 31, 2003): 52. https://lynnbecker.com/repeat/Farnsworth/farnsworth.htm.

Benjamin, Susan S. and Michelangelo Sabatino. *Modern in the Middle: Chicago Houses 1929-75*. New York: The Monacelli Press, 2020.

Bergdoll, Barry. *Mies van der Rohe: McCormick House*. Elmhurst, IL: Elmhurst Art Museum, 2018.

Bergdoll, Barry. "The Nature of Mies's Space." In *Mies in Berlin*, edited by Terrence Riley and Barry Bergdoll, 66-105. New York: Museum of Modern Art, 2001.

Blaser, Werner. *Mies van der Rohe Farnsworth House Weekend House*. Basel-Boston: Birkhäuser Publishers, 1999.

Bresler, Jenna Cellini. "Mitigating the Flooding Threat at Mies van der Rohe's Farnsworth House in Plano, Illinois." *APT Bulletin, The Journal of Preservation Technology* XLVIII, no. 2-3, (2017): 13-19.

Cadwell, Michael. *Strange Details*. Cambridge, MA: The MIT Press, 2007.

Cellini, Jenna, Elizabeth Milnarik, and Brad Roeder. "Edith Farnsworth House, 14520 River Road, Plano, Kendall County. IL." Historic American Buildings Survey Report [HABS IL-1105]. Washington, DC: US Department of the Interior, National Park Service, 2009. Library of Congress: https://www.loc.gov/resource/hhh.il0323.sheet?st=gallery. https://www.loc.gov/resource/hhh.il0323.sheet?st=gallery.

"Charges Famed Architect with Fraud, Deceit." *Chicago Daily Tribune*, October 30, 1951.

Clemence, Paul. *Mies van der Rohe's Farnsworth House*. Atglen, PA: Schiffer Pub., 2006.

Dreller, Sarah M. "Curtained Walls: Architectural Photography, the Farnsworth House, and the Opaque Discourse of Transparency." *ARRIS. Journal of the Southeast Chapter of the Society of Architectural Historians* 26 (2015): 22-40.

Dreller, Sarah M. "The Vanishing Porch in Perspective, An Interactive Companion for "Curtained Walls." https://curtainedwallstimeline.hcommons.org.

Dunlap, David W. "House Proud: Personal Visions; In a Glass Box, Secrets Are Hard to Keep." *The New York Times*, June 24, 1999.

Duke, Lynne. "National Trust Wins Bid for Mies Treasure." *The Washington Post*, Dec. 13, 2003.

Farnsworth, Edith, ed./trans. *Salvatore Quasimodo: To Give and To Have, and Other Poems*. Chicago: H. Regnery Co., 1969.

Farnsworth, Edith, ed./trans. *Provisional Conclusions: A Selection of the Poetry of Eugenio Montale*. Chicago: H. Regnery Co., 1970.

Finfer, June. *The Farnsworth House*. Filmedia, 1999.

Finfer, June. *The Glass House*. Madd River Productions, 2010.

Flamini, Roland. "The Farnsworth House Restored: Mies van der Rohe's Illinois Icon Survives the Flood." *Architectural Digest* 56, no. 2 (February 1999): 66-78.

Friedman, Alice T. *Women and the Making of the Modern House*. New York: Abrams, 1998.

Futagawa, Yukio, ed. *Ludwig Mies van der Rohe Farnsworth House*, Plano, Illinois, 1945-50. Tokyo: A.D.A. Edita, 1974/1983.

"'Glass House' on display," *Plano Record* 34, no. 33 (August 13, 2009): 1.

Goldberger, Paul, ed. *Modern Views: Inspired by Mies van der Rohe Farnsworth House and Philip Johnson Glass House*. New York: Assouline Publishing in conjunction with the National Trust for Historic Press, 2010.

Gordon, Elizabeth. "The Threat to the Next America." *House Beautiful*, April 1953.

Graff, Rebecca S. *Edith Farnsworth House Site Report: An Investigation into the Archaeology of the Fox River Valley*. Chicago: 2022.

"The Grand Old Men of Modern Architecture." *Harper's Bazaar*, June 1952.

Gravlin, Kristy Lawrie, Anne Sears, Jeanne Valentine, and the Plano Community Library District. *Images of America: Plano*. Charleston, SC: Arcadia Publishing, 2012.

Herzog, Jacques and Pierre de Meuron. *Treacherous Transparencies: Thoughts and Observations Triggered by a Visit to the Farnsworth House*. Chicago-New York: IITAC Press/Actar Press, 2016.

Johnson, Steve. "At Home with Lego Artist Adam Reed Tucker." *Chicago Tribune*, September 14, 2016.

Julia Bachrach Consulting with Teska Associates, Inc. *Edith Farnsworth House, Cultural Landscape Report*. Chicago: June 9, 2022).

Kornfeld, Albert. "The American Idea in Houses." *House & Garden*, February 1952.

Krueck + Sexton Architects, Wiss, Janney, Elstner Associates, and Liz Sargent, HLA. *Farnsworth House Preservation Plan and Cultural Landscape Study*. Chicago: October 2015.

Lambert, Phyllis, ed. *Mies in America*. New York: Harry N. Abrams, Inc, Publishers, 2001.

Lohan, Dirk. *Mies van der Rohe Farnsworth House, Plano 1945-1950*. Tokyo: ADA Edita, 1976/2000.

Lubell, Sam. "Preservationists rally to save Mies's Farnsworth House." *Architectural Record* 191, no. 12 (December 2003): 32.

"Ludwig Mies van der Rohe, Farnsworth House in Fox River, Ill." *Architectural Forum: The Magazine of Building* 95, no. 4 (October 1951): 156-61.

Lutterbach, Erin, author and producer, and Geoffrey Baer, perf. *Saved from the Wrecking Ball: The Farnsworth House*. Towers Productions, 2007, 30 min. Aired PSB WTTW11 2012.

McKuen, Pamela Dittmer. "Barn Again." *Chicago Architect*, July-August 2012.

Mertins, Detlef. *Mies*. London and New York: Phaidon Press, 2014.

Mies van der Rohe, Ludwig. "Tribute," *College Art Journal* 6 (Autumn 1946): 41-42. [republished: In Brooks, H. Allen, ed. *Writings on Wright: Selected Comment on Frank Lloyd Wright*. Cambridge, MA: MIT Press, 1961.]

Moffett, Nancy. "Gov urges potential buyers not to remove Farnsworth House." *Chicago Sun Times*, December 12, 2003.

Moisés, Puente, ed. *Conversations with Mies van der Rohe*. New York: Princeton Architectural Press, 2008.

Nelson, Jerome. State of Illinois County of Kendall, "Master's Report," *Ludwig Mies van der Rohe, Plantiff vs Edith B. Farnsworth, Defendant*, 1953.

Neumeyer, Fritz. *The Artless Word: Mies van der Rohe on the Building Art*. Cambridge, MA: The MIT Press, 1991.

Palumbo, Peter. "Farnsworth Impressions." *Inland Architect: The Midwestern Magazine of the Building Arts* 30 (March/April 1986): 45-46.

Peter, John. "Conversation with Mies." In J. Peter, *The Oral History of Modern Architecture: Interviews with the Greatest Architects of the Twentieth Century*, 154-73. New York: Harry N. Abrams, 1994.

Pierro, Albino. *Nu Belle Fatte. Una Bella Storia/A Beautiful Story*. Translated by Edith Farnsworth. Milan: Vanni Scheiwiller, All'insegna del pesce d'oro, 1976.

Pizzigoni, Vittorio. "Reflections on the Farnsworth House," In Orazio Carpenzano and Cherubino Gambardella, *My Farnsworth: Journey of Discovery of a House Built for Two*, 137–45. Macerata: Quodlibert, 2019.

Pizzigoni, Vittorio and Michelangelo Sabatino, eds. *Mies in His Own Words: Complete Writings, Speeches, and Interviews*. Berlin: DOM Publishers, 2024.

Preciado, Paul B. and Keith Harris. "Mi(E) S Conception: The Farnsworth House and the Mystery of the Transparent Closet," *Society + Space*, November 4, 2019.

Raynsford, Anthony. "Farnsworth House," National Historic Landmark Nomination Form. Washington, DC: U.S. Department of the Interior, National Park Service, 2004. https://npgallery.nps.gov/GetAsset/bdafd4cc-bd13-457f-92d5-24df171df7b6.

Robert Silman Associates, *Flood Mitigation Options for The Farnsworth House*, 2014. https://edithfarnsworthhouse.org/history-of-flooding/.

Sacharski, Susan. "Edith Farnsworth, MD: Beyond the Visual Spectrum of the Physician-Poet." Paper at the 9th Annual Hippocrates Poetry and Medicine Symposium, Center for Bioethics and Medical Humanities at Northwestern University Feinberg School of Medicine, Chicago, IL, May 10–11, 2018.

Schulze, Franz. *The Farnsworth House*. Chicago: Lohan Associates, 1997.

Schulze, Franz and Edward Windhorst. *Mies van der Rohe: A Critical Biography*. Chicago: The University of Chicago Press, 2012.

Singley, Paulette. "Living in a Glass Prism: The Female Figure in Mies van der Rohe's Domestic Architecture." *Critical Matrix* 6, no. 2 (1992): 47–76.

Soller, Kurt and Michael Snyder. "The 25 Most Significant Works of Postwar Architecture," T: *The New York Times Style Magazine*, Aug. 8, 2021.

Sotheby's International Realty, *The Farnsworth House, 1945–1951, Ludwig Mies van der Rohe, Sale 7957*. New York: Sotheby's, 2003.

Swanson, Stevenson (with Blair Kamin). "Farnsworth House saved. Last-minute donations rescue Mies masterpiece at auction." *Chicago Tribune*, December 13, 2003.

Swenson, Alfred and Pao-Chi Chang. *Architectural Education at IIT, 1938–1978*. Chicago: Illinois Institute of Technology, 1980.

Tegethoff, Wolf. *Mies van der Rohe: The Villas and Country Houses*. New York: Museum of Modern Art; Cambridge, MA, 1985.

Toomey, Shamus. "Farnsworth House will stay put. Preservationists pay $7.5 million for one-room Mies work." *Chicago Sun Times*, December 13, 2003.

Vandenberg, Maritz. *Farnsworth House: Ludwig Mies van der Rohe*. London and New York: Phaidon, 2003.

Vogel, Carol. "Landmark Mies House Goes to Preservationists," *The New York Times*, December 13, 2003.

Waite, Richard. "More amazing Lego: Mies' Farnsworth House released," *Architects' Journal*, 4 April 2011.

Weber, Hugo. "Mies Van der Rohe." *Arts and Architecture* 69, no. 6 (March 1952): 16–31.

Wendl, Nora. "Uncompromising Reasons for Going West: A Story of Sex and Real Estate, Reconsidered," *Thresholds* 43 (Spring 2015): 354–61.

Wendl, Nora. *Edith B. Farnsworth*. Washington, DC: National Trust for Historic Preservation, 2021.

Wendl, Nora. "Edith: An Architectural History." List Gallery, Swarthmore College, January 19–February 25, 2023.

Xiong, Xiangnan. *Mies at Home: From Am Karlsbad 24 to the Tugendhat House*. London and New York: Routledge, 2022.

Zemaitis, James. "Inside the Farnsworth House." *Sotheby's Preview*, auction catalog. December 2003.

Additional Resources

"Edith Farnsworth Papers 1900–1977," Chicago's Modern Manuscripts and Archives, The Newberry Library, Chicago.

Edith Farnsworth Professional and Personal Papers, Archives of Northwestern Memorial Hospital, Chicago.

Charles Deering McCormick Library of Special Collections & University Archives, Northwestern University Libraries, Chicago.

Ryerson and Burnham Libraries, Art Institute of Chicago (AIC), Chicago.

Myron Goldsmith fonds, Canadian Centre for Architecture (CCA), Montreal.

Mies van der Rohe Archive, MoMA, Museum of Modern Art, New York.

Oral History Transcripts

Chicago Oral History Project:

https://artic.contentdm.oclc.org/digital/collection/caohp.

Caldwell, Alfred. *Oral History of Alfred Caldwell/Interviewed by Betty J. Blum. Compiled under the Auspices of the Chicago Architects Oral History Project, the Ernest R. Graham Study Center for Architectural Drawings, Department of Architecture, the Art Institute of Chicago*, rev. ed. Chicago: Art Institute of Chicago, 2001.

Goldsmith, Myron. *Oral History of Myron Goldsmith/Interviewed by Betty J. Blum. Compiled under the Auspices of the Chicago Architects Oral History Project, the Ernest R. Graham Study Center for Architectural Drawings, Department of Architecture, the Art Institute of Chicago*, rev. ed. Chicago: Art Institute of Chicago, 2001.

Schweikher, Robert Paul. *Oral History of Robert Paul Schweikher/ Interviewed by Betty J. Blum. Compiled under the Auspices of the Chicago Architects Oral History Project, the Ernest R. Graham Study Center for Architectural Drawings, Department of Architecture, the Art Institute of Chicago*, rev. ed. Chicago: Art Institute of Chicago, 2009.

Summers, Gene. *Oral History of Gene Summers/Interviewed by Pauline A. Saliga. Compiled under the Auspices of the Chicago Architects Oral History Project, the Ernest R. Graham Study Center for Architectural Drawings, Department of Architecture, the Art Institute of Chicago*. Chicago: Art Institute of Chicago, 1993.

Wong, Yau Chun. *Interview with Yau Chun Wong/Interviewed by Betty J. Blum. Compiled under the Auspices of the Chicago Architects Oral History Project, the Ernest R. Graham Study Center for Architectural Drawings, Department of Architecture, the Art Institute of Chicago*. Chicago: Art Institute of Chicago, 1995.

Select Bibliography and Resources

Index

ILLINOIS INSTITUTE OF TECHNOLOGY
College of Architecture

Library of Congress Control Number: 2024930260

ISBN 978-1-58093-619-4

10 9 8 7 6 5 4 3 2 1

Printed in China

Design by Chris Grimley, SIGNALS

Monacelli
A Phaidon Company
111 Broadway
New York, New York 10006

www.monacellipress.com